Social Media, Politics and the State

This book is the essential guide for understanding how state power and politics are contested and exercised on social media. It brings together contributions by social media scholars who explore the connection of social media with revolutions, uprising, protests, power and counter-power, hacktivism, the state, policing and surveillance. It shows how collective action and state power are related and conflict as two dialectical sides of social media power, and how power and counter-power are distributed in this dialectic. Theoretically focused and empirically rigorous research considers the two-sided contradictory nature of power in relation to social media and politics. Chapters cover social media in the context of phenomena such as contemporary revolutions in Egypt and other countries; populism 2.0, antiausterity protests, the fascist movement in Greece's crisis, Anonymous and police surveillance.

Daniel Trottier is a postdoctoral fellow in social and digital media at the Communication and Media Research Institute (CAMRI) at the University of Westminster.

Christian Fuchs is a professor of social media at the University of Westminster.

Routledge Research in Information Technology and Society

Social Media, Politics and the State

Protests, Revolutions, Riots, Crime and Policing in the Age of Facebook, Twitter and YouTube

Edited by Daniel Trottier and Christian Fuchs

NEW YORK AND LONDON

First published 2015
by Routledge
711 Third Avenue, New York, NY 10017

and by Routledge
2 Park Square, Milton Park, Abingdon, Oxon OX14 4RN

*Routledge is an imprint of the Taylor & Francis Group,
an informa business*

Library of Congress Cataloging-in-Publication Data
Social media, politics and the state : protests, revolutions, riots, crime and
  policing in the age of Facebook, Twitter and YouTube / edited by Daniel
  Trottier and Christian Fuchs.
    pages cm. — (Routledge research in information technology and
  society ; 16)
  Includes bibliographical references and index.
 1. Internet—Political aspects.   2. Political participation.   3. Social
media—Political aspects.   4. Political psychology.   I. Trottier, Daniel.
II. Fuchs, Christian, 1976–
HM851.S645 2014
  302.23′1—dc23
  2014008525

ISBN: 978-0-415-74909-1 (hbk)
ISBN: 978-1-138-79824-3 (pbk)
ISBN: 978-1-315-76483-2 (ebk)

Typeset in Sabon
by Apex CoVantage, LLC

Contents

SECTION FOUR
Contested and Toppled State Power

SECTION FIVE
State Power as Policing and Intelligence

Figures

Tables

Section One

Introductions

1 Theorising Social Media, Politics and the State

An Introduction

Daniel Trottier and Christian Fuchs

1. INTRODUCTION

The purpose of this chapter is to provide a basic framework for the analysis of social media, politics and the state. This topic—which the authors in this collected volume study—can be situated in the broader field of Internet and social media studies (see Dutton 2013, as well as the contributions in Ess and Dutton 2013 for an overview). Internet and social media research can be conducted in different ways. More administrative approaches analyse how digital media are used by whom, for what purpose, addressed to which audience, bearing which content, and having which effects. In contrast, critical Internet studies go beyond the digital version of the Lasswell formula. They do not exclude studying empirically the cornerstones of digital media use, but always situate such analyses in theorising and analysing larger contexts, such as power structures, the state, capitalism, gender relations, social struggles, and ideologies, which shape and are shaped by the digital media landscape in dialectical processes (Fuchs 2008, 2014d). This collected volume, in studying social media in the context of politics and the state, suggests the approach of critical Internet and social media studies. (See also Fuchs and Dyer-Witheford 2013; Fuchs and Sandoval 2014.)

This chapter is structured the following way: section two considers what is social media, with a specific emphasis on what makes social media 'social.' Section three considers a theoretical framework to understand modern society. Following this, section four considers the nature of social media activity in relation to modern society. Section five proposes a theoretically grounded understanding of the state, while section six considers the various branches that make up the state. Section seven focuses on politics, as well as the relation between the state and politics. Section eight addresses power, specifically state power and corporate power. Section nine considers crime and policing, with an emphasis on the relation of police to the state. Section ten considers the distinctions between protests, revolutions and riots. Finally, section eleven offers some concluding remarks.

2.   WHAT IS SOCIAL MEDIA?

It is possible to trace the emergence of social media to when Tim O'Reilly (2005) introduced the term 'Web 2.0' in 2005. While O'Reilly claims that 'Web 2.0' denotes actual changes whereby users' collective intelligence co-create the value of platforms like Google, Amazon, Wikipedia or Craigslist in a "community of connected users," (O'Reilly and Battelle 2009, 1) he admits that the term was mainly created for identifying the need of new economic strategies of Internet companies after the 'dot-com' crisis, in which the bursting of financial bubbles caused the collapse of many Internet companies. So he states in a paper published five years after the creation of the invention of the term 'Web 2.0' that this category was "a statement about the second coming of the web after the dotcom bust" at a conference that was "designed to restore confidence in an industry that had lost its way after the dotcom bust" (ibid.).

Michael Mandiberg argues that the notion of 'social media' has been associated with multiple concepts: "the corporate media favourite 'user-generated content,' Henry Jenkins' media-industries-focused 'convergence culture,' Jay Rosen's 'the people formerly known as the audience,' the politically infused 'participatory media,' Yochai Benkler's process-oriented 'peer-production,' and Tim O'Reilly's computer-programming-oriented 'Web 2.0'" (Mandiberg 2012, 2). The question of if and how social the web is or has become depends on a profoundly social theoretical question: what does it mean to be social? Are human beings always social or only if they interact with others? In sociological theory, there are different concepts of the social, such as Émile Durkheim's social facts, Max Weber's social action, Karl Marx's notion of collaborative work (also employed in the concept of computer-supported collaborative work—CSCW) or Ferdinand Tönnies' notion of community (for a detailed discussion, see Fuchs 2014d). Depending on which concept of sociality one employs, one gets different answers to the questions of whether the web is social and whether sociality is a new quality of the web. Community aspects of the web have certainly not started with Facebook, which was founded in 2004 but was already described as characteristic of 1980s bulletin board systems, like The WELL, that he characterises as virtual communities (Rheingold 2000). Collaborative work, as, for example, the cooperative editing of articles performed on Wikipedia, is rather new as a dominant phenomenon on the WWW, but not new in computing. The concept of CSCW (computer supported cooperative work) was subject of a conference series that started in December 1986 with the 1st ACM Conference on CSCW in Austin, Texas. A theoretical approach is needed that identifies multiple dimensions of sociality (such as cognition, communication, and cooperation), based on which the continuities and discontinuities of the development of the Internet can be empirically studied. Neither is the wiki-concept new itself: the WikiWikiWeb was introduced by Ward Cunningham in 1984.

All computing systems, and therefore all web applications, and also all forms of media can be considered as social because they store and transmit human knowledge that originates in social relations in society. They are objectifications of society and human social relations. Whenever a human uses a computing system or a medium (also if she or he is alone in a room), then she or he cognises based on objectified knowledge that is the outcome of social relations. But not all computing systems and web applications support direct communication between humans, in which at least two humans mutually exchange symbols that are interpreted as being meaningful. Amazon mainly provides information about books and other goods one can buy; it is not primarily a tool of communication, but rather a tool of information, whereas Facebook has in-built communication features that are frequently used (mail system, walls for comments, forums, etc.).

The discussion shows that it is not a simple question to decide if and how social the WWW actually is. Therefore a social theory approach of clarifying the notion of 'social media' can be advanced by identifying three social information processes that constitute three forms of sociality:

- Cognition
- Communication
- Cooperation

According to this view, individuals have certain cognitive features that they use to interact with others so that shared spaces of interaction are created. In some cases, these spaces are used not just for communication but also for the co-production of novel qualities of overall social systems and for community building. The three notions relate to different forms of sociality: the notion of cognition is related to Emile Durkheim's concept of social facts, the communication concept to Max Weber's notions of social actions and social relations, the cooperation concept to the notions of communities and collaborative work. According to this model, media and online platforms that primarily support cognition (such as the websites of newspapers) are social media (1), those that primarily support communication (such as e-mail) are social media (2), and those that primarily support community building and collaborative work (such as Wikipedia, Facebook) are social media (3). This means that social media is a complex term and that there are different types of social media. Empirical studies show that the most recent development is that there is a certain increase of the importance of social media (3) on the Internet, which is especially due to the rise of social networking sites such as Facebook, wikis like Wikipedia, and microblogs such as Twitter and Weibo.

boyd and Ellison (2008, 211) define social network sites as "web-based services that allow individuals to (1) construct a public or semi-public profile within a bounded system, (2) articulate a list of other users with whom they share a connection, and (3) view and traverse their list of connections and those made by others within the system." In network analysis, a network is defined as a system of interconnected nodes (Wasserman and Faust 1997; Barabási 2003). Therefore, based on a strict theoretical understanding, all networked tools that allow establishing connections between at least two humans have to be understood as social network platforms. This includes not only the platforms that boyd and Ellison have in mind but also chats, discussion boards, mailing lists, e-mail, etc.—all Web 2.0 and 3.0 technologies. 'Social network site' is therefore an imprecise term. David Beer argues that this definition is too broad and does not distinguish different types of sites such as wikis, folksonomies, mash-ups and social networking sites: "My argument here is simply that we should be moving toward more differentiated classifications of the new online cultures not away from them" (Beer 2008, 519.). He suggests using Web 2.0, not SNS, as an umbrella term.

What makes sites like Facebook distinct is that they are integrated platforms that combine many media and information and communication technologies, such as webpage, webmail, digital image, digital video, discussion group, guest book, connection list or search engine. Many of these technologies are social network tools themselves. It surely is feasible, as boyd and Ellison argue, that profiles, connection lists and tools for establishing connections are the central elements, but missing is the insight that these technologies are meta-communication technologies, technologies of communication technologies. It is therefore more appropriate to speak of social networking sites (SNS) that function as integrated tools of cognition, communication and cooperation. SNS are web-based platforms that integrate different media, information and communication technologies and that allow at least the generation of profiles that display information that describes the users, the display of connections (connection list), the establishment of connections between users that are displayed on their connection lists and the communication between users. SNS are just like all computer technologies cognitive systems because they reflect and display dominant collective values of society that become objectified and confront users. They are communication technologies because they are used for communication and establishing connections in the form of connection lists. SNS are cooperative technologies because they allow the establishment of new friendships and communities and the maintenance of existing friendships. By friendship we mean a continuous social relationship between humans that is based on empathy and sympathy. Therefore SNS provide means for establishing virtual communities understood as "social aggregations that emerge from the Net when enough people carry on those public discussions long enough, with sufficient human feeling, to form webs of personal relationship in cyberspace" (Rheingold 2000). For Rheingold a virtual community is not the same as computer-mediated communication (CMC), but continuous CMC that results in feelings of affiliation.

Not all social relations established or maintained on SNS are forms of community. There might be superficial relations that just exist by a display of connection in the connection list. This can be the case, for example, if one adds friends of friends whom one has never met and with whom one does not continuously interact, if one adds people arbitrarily in order to increase one's friends list, or if one adds people who share one's interests, but with whom one also does not communicate. In this case, the usage of SNS remains on the communication level. Cooperation technologies in the sense of a virtual community are then a mere unrealized potential. It is likely that any concrete SNS will consist of many loose connections and many virtual communities that exist in parallel. SNS on the technological level provide potentials for communication and cooperation. Only the communicative level is automatically realized by establishing connections; the emergence of communities on SNS requires more sustained communicative work so that social bonds emerge. Feelings of community can either emerge on SNS or be imported from the outside world. If individuals make use of SNS for staying in touch with already established friends and contacts more easily and over distance, then existing communities or parts of them are transformed into virtual communities that crystallise on SNS. If individuals make new social bonds with people whom they did not know in advance and whom they have met on SNS, then community emerges inherently from SNS. One can speak of a virtual community in both cases. Cooperation technologies are (besides collaborative online labour, which can be found in the case of wikis, but is not a necessary condition) about the production of social bonds and feelings of belonging and togetherness.

'Social media' such as Facebook support cognition, communication/ networking and cooperation (communities, collaborative work, sharing of user-generated and other content). Therefore a lot of personal and social data about users is generated. The question of broader social phenomena on social media, such as politics, protest, crime and revolutions, rests on an understanding of these concepts, as well as an understanding of their relation to modern society. These are considered ahead.

3.   WHAT IS MODERN SOCIETY?

Modern society is based on the differentiation of social roles. In modern society, human beings act in different capacities in different social roles. Consider the example of a modern middle-class office worker, who also has roles as a husband, father, lover, friend, voter, citizen, child, fan and neighbour, to say nothing of the various associations to which he may belong. In these different roles, humans are expected to behave according to specific rules that govern the various social systems of which modern society is composed (such as the company, the schools, the family, the church, fan clubs, political parties, etc.).

Jürgen Habermas (1987, 1989) describes how modern society is grounded in different spheres, in which humans act in different roles. He says that modernity resulted in:

1. The separation of the economy from the family and the household so that the modern economy (based on wage labour and capital) emerged.
2. The rise of a political public sphere, in which humans act as citizens, vote, hold a political opinion, etc., in contrast to the earlier monarchic system, in which political power was controlled by the monarch, aristocracy and the church. This includes the shift of the economy towards a capitalist economy grounded in private ownership of the means of production and in the logic of capital accumulation. The economy started to no longer be part of private households, but became organized with the help of large commodity markets that go beyond single households. The modern economy has become "a private sphere of society that [. . .] [is] publicly relevant" (Habermas 1989, 19). The family started to no longer be primarily an economic sphere, but the sphere of intimacy and the household economy based on reproductive labour. Connected to this was the separation of the private and the public sphere that is based on humans acting in different roles (ibid., 152, 154; see also Arendt 1958, 47, 68).

Habermas (1987) argues that in modern society the economy and politics are systems that make use of the steering media of money and power to influence and colonise society. The modern economy is the capitalistic way of organizing production, distribution and consumption—that is, it is a system that is based on the accumulation of money capital by the sale of commodities that are produced by workers who are compelled to sell their labour power as a commodity to owners of capital and means of production, who thereby gain the right to exploit labour for a specific time period. The modern political system is a bureaucratic state system, in which liberal parliamentary democracy (including political parties, elections, parliamentary procedures), legal guarantees of liberal freedoms (freedoms of speech, assembly, association, the press, movement, ownership, belief and thought, opinion and expression) and the monopolisation of the means of violence by coercive state apparatuses guarantee the reproduction of the existing social order.

Besides the capitalist economy and the state, modern society also consists of the cultural sphere that can be divided into a private and a public culture. Hannah Arendt stresses that the private sphere is a realm of modern society that functions as "a sphere of intimacy" (Arendt 1958, 38) and includes family life as well as emotional and sexual relationships. Habermas adds to this analysis that consumption plays a central role in the private sphere: "On the other hand, the family now evolved even more into a consumer of income and leisure time, into the recipient of publicly guaranteed compensations and support services. Private autonomy was maintained not so much in functions of control as in functions of consumption" (Habermas 1989, 156). He furthermore points out that the private sphere is the realm of leisure activities: "Leisure behavior supplies the key to the floodlit privacy of the new sphere, to the externalization of what is declared to be the inner life" (ibid., 159). In other words, one can say that the role of the private sphere in capitalism as sphere of individual leisure and consumption that Habermas identifies is that it guarantees the reproduction of labour power so that the latter remains vital, productive and exploitable.

But there are also social forms of organizing leisure and consumption, such as fan communities, amateur sports clubs, churches, etc. This means that there are both individual and social forms of organizing everyday life. Together they form the sphere of culture understood as the sphere in which mundane everyday life is organized, and meaning is given to the world. The basic role of culture in society is that it guarantees the reproduction of the human body and mind, which includes on the one hand activities like sports, sexuality, health, social and beauty care, and on the other hand activities like education, knowledge production (such as in universities), art, literature, etc. If these activities are organized on an individual basis, then they take place in the private sphere; if they are organized on a social basis outside of the home and the family, then they take place in the sociocultural sphere.

The private and the sociocultural sphere together form the cultural sphere or what Habermas (1987) terms the lifeworld: it is a realm of society where communicative action takes place that allows definitions of a situation and participants to obtain an understanding of the subjective, social and objective world. It enables the "continual process of definition and redefinition" (ibid., 121–122). "Language and culture are constitutive of the lifeworld itself" (ibid., 125). Culture can be constituted only through the speech-acts of communication. It has a social character. The lifeworld also contains "culturally transmitted background knowledge" (ibid., 134). "The structures of the lifeworld lay down the forms of the intersubjectivity of possible understanding. [. . .] The lifeworld is, so to speak, the transcendental site where speaker and hearer meet, where they can reciprocally raise claims that their utterances fit the world (objective, social, or subjective), and where they can criticize and confirm those validity claims, settle their disagreements, and arrive at agreements" (ibid., 134). The lifeworld is the cultural realm of meaning making, definitions of situations and the gaining of understandings of the world.

According to Habermas (1989), the realms of the systems of the economy and the state on the one hand and the lifeworld (culture in our model) on the other hand are mediated by what he terms the public sphere or civil society. Hegel, who is considered one of the most influential writers on civil society (Anheier, Toepfler and List, 2010, 338), described civil society as political and as a sphere that is separate from the state and from the private life of the family (Hegel 1821, §§157, 261). Habermas' (1989) seminal work describes how eighteenth-century France and Germany were characterised by a separation of spheres. Civil society was the private "realm of commodity exchange and social labor" (Habermas, 1989, 30) that was distinct from the public sphere and the sphere of public authority. This understanding was reflected in liberal market-driven civil society conceptions of thinkers like Locke and Smith that positioned economic man at the heart of civil society (Ehrenberg and Trosman 1999). The structural transformation of the public sphere has in the nineteenth and twentieth century, according to Habermas, resulted in an increasing collapse of boundaries between spheres so that "private economic units" attained "quasi-political character" and from "the midst of the publicly relevant sphere of civil society was formed a repoliticized social sphere" that formed a "functional complex that could no longer be differentiated according to criteria of public and private" (Habermas 1989, 148). One can say that the structural transformation Habermas describes meant the emergence of the modern economy as a separate powerful sphere of modern society and the separation of the economy from civil society. This notion of civil society could be found in the works of Montesquieu, Rousseau and Tocqueville and has today become the common understanding (Ehrenberg and Trosman 1999). In later works, Habermas (1987, 320) as a result describes contemporary modern society as consisting of systems (economic system, administrative system) and the lifeworld (private sphere, public sphere). Civil society as part of the lifeworld now consists of "associational networks" that "articulate political interests and confront the state with demands arising from the life worlds of various groups" (Habermas 2006, 417). Civil society's "voluntary associations, interest groups, and social movements always strive to maintain a measure of autonomy from the public affairs of politics and the private concerns of economics" (Ehrenberg and Trosman 1999, 235). Habermas (2006) mentions these examples for civil society actors: social movements, general interest groups, advocates for certain interests, experts and intellectuals. Qualities and concepts of civil society mentioned in the literature include: voluntariness, nongovernmental associations, healthy democracy, public sphere, exchange of opinions, political debate, self-organization, self-reflexion, non-violence and struggle for egalitarian diversity (Keane 2010; Kenny 2007; Salzman 2011; Sheldon 2001, 62–63).

Salzman (2011, 199) mentions "environmental groups, bowling leagues, churches, political parties, neighbourhood associations, social networking Internet sites" as examples for civil society organizations. Keane (2010) adds charities, independent churches and publishing houses as examples. In civil society theory, the concept of hegemony in particular has been used for stressing civil society's aspects of contradiction, power, counter-power, ideology and its dialectical relation to the state and the economy (Anheier et al. 2010, 408ff.).

Habermas (1987, 320) mentions the following social roles that are constitutive for modern society: employee, consumer, client and citizen. Other roles, such as wife, husband, houseworker, immigrant, convicts, etc., can certainly be added. So what is constitutive for modern society is not just the separation of spheres and roles but also the creation of power structures, in which roles are constituted by power relations (such as employer/employee, state bureaucracy/citizen, citizen of a nation state/immigrant, manager/ assistant, dominant gender roles/marginalised gender roles). Power means in this context the disposition of actors over means that allow them to control structures and influence processes and decisions in their own interest at the expense of other individuals or groups.

Modern society is based on political and economic exchange relations. Based on different roles that humans have in the lifeworld, they exchange products of their social actions with goods and services provided by the systems of the state and the economy. Table 1.1 gives an overview of these exchanges and specifies the two sides of the exchanges. The systems of the state and the lifeworld stand in modern society in exchange relations. Lifeworld communication is according to Habermas (1987) based mainly on communicative action and is not mediated by money and power. The lifeworld is more a realm of altruistic and voluntary behaviour.

Systemic logic and exchange logic is not an automatic feature of these realms; it can, however, shape them. The political public sphere, civic cultures and private life are not independent from the political and the economic systems: they create legitimacy and hegemony (political, public, civic cultures) in relation to the political system, as well as consumption needs and the reproduction of labour power in relation to the economy (private life, family).

Claus Offe (1985) distinguishes between sociopolitical movements, which want to establish binding goals for a wider community and are recognised as legitimate, and sociocultural movements, which want to establish goals,

Table 1.1 A typology of different forms of non-institutional action (adapted from Offe 1985)

	Civil society	
Goals	Recognised as legitimate	Illegitimate
Binding for a wider community	Sociopolitical and socio-economic movements (=Political public sphere) 1) NGOs: more hierarchical, formal, lobbying 2) Social movements: grassroots, informal, protest	Terrorism
Non-binding for a wider community	Sociocultural movements (=Civic cultures) Consensus, shared interests and values, affinity Examples: friendship networks, neighbourhoods, work networks, churches, sects, sports team, fan communities, professional organizations/associations	Crime

which are not binding for a wider community (retreat) and are considered legitimate. Further forms of non-institutional action would be private crime (non-binding goals, illegitimate) and terrorism (binding goals, illegitimate). Offe's distinction between sociopolitical and sociocultural movements has been reflected in Touraine's (1985) distinction between social movements and cultural movements. Table 1.1 summarises the discussion. We add to this distinction one between sociopolitical and socio-economic movements.

The struggles of socio-economic movements are oriented on the production and distribution of material resources that are created and distributed in the economic system. They are focused on questions of the production, distribution and redistribution of material resources. One modern socio-economic movement is the working class movement, which struggles for the betterment of living conditions as they are affected by working conditions and thereby opposes the economic interests of those who own capital and the means of production. In the history of the working class movement, there have been fierce debates about the role of reforms and revolution. A more recent debate concerns the role and importance of non-wage workers in the working class movement (Cleaver 2000). Another socio-economic movement is the environmental movement, which struggles for the preservation and sustainable treatment of the external nature of humans (the environment). Whereas the working class movement is oriented on relationships between organized groups of human beings (classes) with definite interests, the ecological movement is oriented on the relationship between human beings and their natural environment. Both relations (human-human, human-nature) are at the heart of the economy and interact with each other.

Sociopolitical movements are movements that struggle for the recognition of collective identities of certain groups in society via demands on the state. They are oriented on struggles that relate to gender, sexual orientation, ethnicity and origin, age, neighbourhood, peace or disability. Examples are the feminist movement, the gay rights movement, the anti-racist movement, the youth movement, the peace movement, the anti-penitentiary movement, the anti-psychiatry movement, etc. The common characteristic of these movements is that their struggles are oriented on recognising specific groups of people as having specific rights, ways of life or identities. So, for example, the peace and human rights movement struggles for the recognition of the basic right of all humans to exist free from the threat of being killed or coerced by violence. As another example, racist movements struggle for recognising specific groups (like white people) as either superior and other groups as inferior or so culturally or biologically different that they need to be separated.

Sociocultural movements are groups of people that have shared interests and practices relating to ways of organizing one's private life. Examples include friendship networks, neighbourhood networks, churches, sports groups, fan communities, etc.

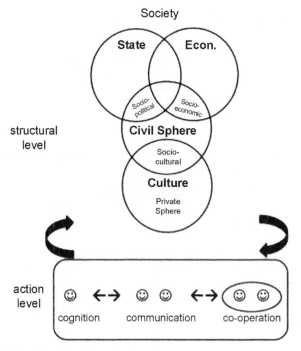

Figure 1.1   A visualisation of modern society

Figure 1.1 visualises the model of modern society introduced in this section. The model is grounded in the social theory insight that the relationship between structures and actors is dialectical and that both levels continuously create each other (for dialectical solutions of the structure-agency problem in social theory, see Archer 1995; Bhaskar 1993; Bourdieu 1986; Fuchs 2003a, 2003b; Giddens 1984).

Given that the focus of this chapter is social media, the question arises of how to locate the media more generally within a model of society. Media can be defined as structures that enable and constrain human information processes of cognition, communication and cooperation, which are practices that produce and reproduce informational structures. In modern society, media can be organized in different forms. Murdock (2011, 18) argues that the media can be organized within the capitalist economy, the state or civil society, which results in three different political economies of the media that are respectively based on commodities, public goods or gifts. In our model of society, civil society is made up of the sociopolitical, the socio-economic and the sociocultural spheres, which corresponds to the three organizational forms of the media that Murdock identifies. Therefore we identify sociopolitical (organized by the state as public service media), socio-economic (organized by private companies as commercial media) and sociocultural (organized by

Table 1.2   A typology of roles in modern society

Political roles	Sociopolitical roles
Citizen, politician, bureaucrat, political party member	Privacy advocate, electoral reform advocate, feminist activist, gay-rights activists, anti-racist advocate, youth movement advocate, peace movement activist, anti-penitentiary advocate, anti-psychiatry activist, non-governmental organization member/activist, non-parliamentary political activist (student groups, non-parliamentary fascist groups, non-parliamentary leftist groups, etc.)
Economic roles	**Socio-economic roles**
Capital owner, entrepreneur, manager, employee, prosumer, self-employee	Labour activist, union member, consumer protectionist, environmental activist
Private roles	**Sociocultural roles**
Lover, family member, friend, consumer, audience member, user	Sports group member, fan community member, parishioner, member of a sect or cult, professional organizations and associations, self-help groups, neighbourhood association, etc.

citizens and public interest groups as civil and alternative media) forms of the media. Although there are three organizational forms of the media, there is a specific political economy of the media realm that allocates resources to different media types to a different degree, generally putting civil-society media at a disadvantage, and favouring capitalist media organizations.

Based on the distinction of different spheres of modern society, we can discern various social roles that are part of the subsystems of modern society (see Table 1.2).

Based on the theoretical models of the information process and modern society, we can next characterise social media communication.

4.   WHAT IS SOCIAL MEDIA ACTIVITY IN MODERN SOCIETY?

The study of social media activity is due to the novelty of blogs and social networks like Facebook and Twitter, a relatively young endeavour (see Fuchs et al. 2012; Trottier 2012). Based on the theoretical assumptions about the information process (the tripleC model introduced in section two) and society (the model of modern society in section three), we can describe social media surveillance (see Trottier 2012; Fuchs and Trottier 2013; Trottier and Lyon 2012) based on social theory. Thus far, social theory foundations of social media activity have been underrepresented in scholarly literature.

Some constitutive features of social media like Facebook are the following:

Integrated sociality: Social media enable the convergence of the three modes of sociality (cognition, communication, cooperation) in an integrated sociality. This means, for example, on Facebook, an individual creates multi-media content like a video on the cognitive level, publishes it so that others can comment (the communicative level) and allows others to manipulate and remix the content, so that new content with multiple authorship can emerge. One step does not necessarily result in the next, but the technology has the potential to enable the combination of all three activities in one space. Facebook, by default, encourages the transition from one stage of sociality to the next, within the same social space.

Integrated roles: Social media like Facebook are based on the creation of personal profiles that describe the various roles of a human being's life. In contemporary modern society, different social roles tend to converge in various social spaces. The boundaries between public life and private life as well as the workplace and the home have become porous. As we have seen, Habermas identified systems (the economy, the state) and the lifeworld as central realms of modern society. The lifeworld can be further divided into culture and civil society. We act in different social roles in these spheres: for example, as employees and consumers in the economic systems, as clients and citizens in the state system, as activists in the sociopolitical sphere and as lovers and consumers in socio-economic sphere. We also act as family members in the private sphere, or as fan community members, parishioners, professional association members, etc. in the sociocultural sphere. A new form of liquid and porous sociality has emerged, in which we partly act in different social roles in the same social space. On social media like Facebook, we act in various roles, but all of these roles become mapped onto single profiles that are observed by different people who are associated with our different social roles. This means that social media like Facebook are social spaces, in which social roles tend to converge and become integrated in single profiles.

Integrated and converging communication on social media: On social media like Facebook, various social activities (cognition, communication, cooperation) in different social roles that belong to our behaviour in systems (economy, state) and the lifeworld (the private sphere, the socio-economic sphere, the sociopolitical sphere, the sociocultural sphere) are mapped to single profiles. In this mapping process, data about (a) social activities within (b) social roles are generated. This means that a Facebook profile holds (a1) personal data, (a2) communicative data, (a3) social network data/community data in relation to (b1) private roles (friend, lover, relative, father, mother, child, etc.), (b2) civic roles (sociocultural roles as fan community members, neighbourhood association members, etc.), (b3) public roles (socio-economic and sociopolitical roles as activists and advocates) and (b4) systemic roles (in politics: voter, citizen, client, politician, bureaucrat, etc.; in the economy: worker, manager, owner, purchaser/

consumer, etc.). The different social roles and activities tend to converge, as, for example, in the situation where the workplace is also a playground, where friendships and intimate relations are formed and dissolved and where spare time activities are conducted. This means that social media surveillance is an integrated form of surveillance, in which one finds surveillance of different (partly converging) activities in different partly converging social roles with the help of profiles that hold a complex networked multitude of data about humans.

Figure 1.2 visualises the communication process on one single social media system (such as Facebook, etc.). The total social media communication process is a combination and network of a multitude of such processes. The integration of different forms of sociality and social roles on social media means that there is a myriad of possible social functions that any single platform can serve. Individual citizens may use it to communicate with other citizens in the context of any number of social roles, as well as for purposes that may transcend roles. They may also communicate with organizations and institutions for the same purposes. They may also simply monitor the communication in which any of these social actors are engaged. Institutions, including branches of the state, may do all of the foregoing as well. For this reason, the following section considers a theoretical understanding of the state, and of related concepts, in order to underscore the relevance of social media for modern society and phenomena such as politics, protest, crime and revolutions.

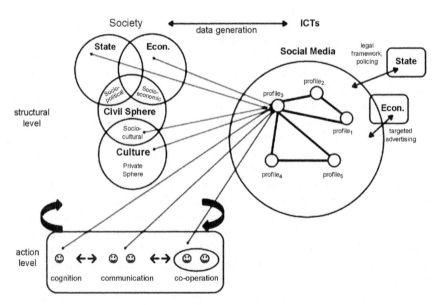

Figure 1.2   The process of social media communication

5.   WHAT IS THE STATE?

Thinkers of the modern age from Hegel to Habermas and beyond have described the emergence of modern society as a disembedding of social spheres, such that state power was separated from economic power. Whereas in feudal societies the emperors and the aristocracy controlled both political and economic power that formed a unity, modern society is based on a differentiation of the social structure. The question that arises for any political theory that wants to conceptualise the state is where to draw the boundary between what is the state and what is situated outside of it. There is a clear demarcation of the state from the economy, although the modern economy and the state are not only separate but at the same time interdependent and so form a dialectical unity in diversity. The question that arises is, however, how broad the concept of the state shall be constructed and where to draw its boundaries.

Louis Althusser (1971) distinguishes between repressive and ideological state apparatuses. The first are "a force of repressive execution and intervention 'in the interests of the ruling classes' in the class struggle conducted by the bourgeoisie and its allies against the proletariat" (ibid., 137) and include the police, prisons, the army, courts, the government, political administration and the head of state. Ideological state apparatuses include religions, the education system, the family, the legal system, the political system including parties, trade-unions, the media and communications, and culture (ibid., 143).

Althusser has the broadest possible concept of the state in so far as one theoretically presupposes a differentiation of the state from the economy. He includes in the notion of the state everything that classical Marxist theory has termed the 'superstructure.' Althusser explicitly acknowledges Gramsci's influence on his notion of the state:

> To my knowledge, Gramsci is the only one who went any distance in the road I am taking. He had the 'remarkable' idea that the State could not be reduced to the (Repressive) State Apparatus, but included, as he put it, a certain number of institutions from 'civil society': the Church, the Schools, the trade unions, etc. Unfortunately, Gramsci did not systematize his institutions, which remained in the state of acute but fragmentary notes. (1971, 142)

Although the agency and class struggle–oriented Gramsci and the structuralist and functionalist Althusser are strikingly different social theorists, their approaches converge in a comparable concept of the state.

The state is "the entire complex of practical and theoretical activities with which the ruling class not only justifies and maintains its dominance, but manages to win the active consent of those over whom it rules" (Gramsci 1971, 244). Hegemony means "an active and voluntary (free) consent" (ibid., 271). The law, military, police system, secret services and prison system are the repressive elements of the state system that aim at guaranteeing internal and external defence of the system. The state school system is for Gramsci (ibid., 258) the most important element of state hegemony that aims at creating active consent. Both "force and consent" (ibid., 271) are exercised for constituting, maintaining and reproducing the state system. But there are also elements of "cultural hegemony" (ibid., 258) outside direct state control, such as religions/churches, associations, newspapers, theatre, films, radio, other media, public meetings, language and dialects, folklore and traditions, conversations and morals (ibid., 1988, esp. 356).

The disadvantages of Althusser and Gramsci's state-concept are at least threefold:

1. It implies that ideologies are not a form of repression and violence and that repression does not also work outside of physical violence via ideological manipulation. Theories of violence, such as the one by Johan Galtung (1990), in contrast distinguish between physical, structural and ideological violence.
2. Althusser overstretches the notion of the state to such an extent that culture as the sphere of the production and reproduction of the human mind and body and communication become mere attributes of the state, which does not allow for any relative autonomy of these realms from the concept of the state.
3. As Althusser assumes that "the State [. . .] is the State of the ruling class," which as a logical consequence of his broad conception implies that ideology is the "ideology of 'the ruling class'" (1971, 146), his approach does not leave any space for a culture that is both critical of capitalist and state power—that is, a critical pedagogy, critical science, critical philosophy and theory, etc. Althusser's totalising concept of the state squashes potentials of critique and struggle that are situated in the realm of communication and information.

Another important theoretical question that arises is whether civil society and culture stand outside the state or are part of it. Gramsci says that "civil society and the state are one and the same" (1988, 210), so for him the "State = political society + civil society" (1971, 263) and "hegemony protected by the armour of coercion" (ibid., 263). A concept of the state that conceives it as the unity of coercive and ideological state apparatuses inflates the state concept to a maximum and does not leave any conceptual space for conceiving culture and civil society as neither controlled by the state nor capitalism, but as the people's common culture.

We favour a delimitation of the state in modern society that sees the latter constituted as a complex whole of interdependent spheres so that there is a distinction between the relative autonomy of the economy, culture and politics that is mediated by interlacing elements and spheres. The relevance of culture is evidenced not just by the rise of what is today termed cultural industries, knowledge production or the information society but also by the fact that state theorists such as Bob Jessop no longer find the long-standing preoccupation with the difference of the economy and the state—as also practised by French regulation theory—sufficient, but stress in addition the need of a "cultural political economy" (Sum and Jessop 2013). As media and communication scholars we are on the one hand sceptical towards the introduction of this 'discovery' as a novelty because the approach of the political economy of media and culture goes at least back to Dallas Smythe's works in the 1940s—a tradition that was followed up by Herbert Schiller, Graham Murdock, Peter Golding, Nicholas Garnham and many others and has for a long time been continued as the political economy of communication approach (for overviews, see Golding and Murdock 1997; Wasko, Murdock and Sousa 2011). On the other hand the concept implies a differentiation and important development of state theory away from Gramsci and Althusser's conflationism.

The state, like many similar concepts, is characterised by the following tension: it has an intangible quality, but can be identified in terms of some key components and functions that it performs. These components are considered in the following section. As Ralph Miliband notes, "'The state' is not a thing, that it does not, as such, exist. What 'the state' stands for is a number of particular institutions which, together, constitute its reality, and which interact as parts of what may be called the state system" (1969, 46). More concretely, he references Weber to note that the state is a "monopoly of legitimate use of physical force within a given territory" (ibid., 47). Stuart Hall et al., drawing upon Gramsci, take an abstract approach to the state, referring to it as "a particular site or level of the social formation" that is "irreplaceably by any other structure" (1978, 205). They later claim that the state takes an organizational role in society, notably in the domain of financial capital.

In order to arrive at an understanding of the state, it will help to consider its conceptual boundaries vis-à-vis closely related concepts. The state overlaps with politics, but these are two distinct social systems. Likewise, the state is not synonymous with the nation, as a state can embody several nations (Poulantzas 1978). Furthermore, Nicos Poulantzas notes a tendency to recognise only state power in state activity. While there is an intrinsic interest in recognising the state as political domination of the dominant class, this "reduces *the state apparatus* to *state power*" (ibid., 12). Poulantzas acknowledges that the state constitutes relations of production—for example, through organized physical repression as well as managing ideological relations. Yet the full activities of the state exceed this, not the least because ideology involves material practices (ibid., 28). The state is also characterised by a tension of existing in isolation on the one hand and its interdependencies with other social structures on the other hand. Indeed, it can be said that the state is meaningful only in relation to a broader theoretical understanding of society.

Political economist Bob Jessop's Strategic-Relational Approach is especially helpful in considering this conceptual and functional interdependency. It views the state as not simply existing-for-others but also with a need to self-sustain. The state also has an impact on the degree of success of various political forces. The Strategic-Relational Approach considers three shaping strategies: first, the state has resources and power that "underpin its relative autonomy," but also "distinctive liabilities or vulnerabilities, and its operations depend on resources produced elsewhere in its environment" (Jessop 2007, 6). Second, states direct political elements "through their control over and/or (in)direct access to these state capacities—capacities whose effectiveness also depends on links to forces and powers that exist and operate beyond the state's formal boundaries" (ibid.) Third, state power depends "on the structural relations between the state and its encompassing political system, on the strategic ties among politicians and state officials and other political forces, and on the complex web of structural interdependencies and strategic networks that link the state system to its broader social environment" (ibid.). The state is therefore bound by a tension between "majestic isolation" and being "embedded in wider political system" (ibid.), and this tension is not easy to reconcile. This is linked to a tension between 'self-serving' and 'at the service of others,' considered ahead.

The state can be understood as an antagonist of individual interests (through its own self-preservation), but also as being at the service of individual citizens. It is said to exist not for the sake of self-preservation but rather some kind of communitarian service. As Jessop indicates, the "*core of the state apparatus* can be defined as a distinct ensemble of institutions and organisations whose socially accepted function is to define and enforce collectively binding decisions on a given population in the name of their 'common interest' or 'general will'" (2007, 9). Yet it is immediately worth noting that any attempt to define the 'general will' reflects a particular "articulation and aggregation of interest, opinions and values" (ibid., 11). We can therefore elaborate on this institutional/individual tension by considering which individuals it serves. In other words, it can be understood as a manifestation of class relations: "The (capitalist) State should not be regarded as an intrinsic entity: like 'capital,' *it is rather a relationship of forces, or more precisely the material condensation of such a relationship among classes and class fractions, such as this is expressed within the State in a necessarily specific form*" (Poulantzas 1978, 128–129).

Poulantzas and Jessop's approach allows for differentiating the concept of the state as field-of-power forces from monolithic concepts of the state that conceive it as a homogenous apparatus or machine of the ruling class for dominating the ruled class. First, there are factions of the capitalist class (such as transnational corporations, small and medium enterprises, finance capital, commercial capital, manufacturing capital, cultural capital, etc.) that compete for shares of capital and power and therefore have to a certain degree conflicting interests. Second, although there are overlaps of the capitalist class and the political elite (e.g., when managers become politicians, bureaucrats become consultants for companies or private-public-partnerships are established as part of neoliberal governance systems), their activities, personnel and interests are not coextensive. The differentiation of the state and the capitalist economy in modern society has also brought about a division of labour between capitalists and politicians.

Third, the state's class power can be challenged by left-wing political movements that want to establish a transitory state that drives back capitalist interests and advances welfare and social benefits for all. It is, of course, doubtful in this context that a socialist state can exist in a capitalist society and that state power is necessary in all forms of society; at the same time progressive movements' goal to conquer state power is not necessarily a social democratic-reformist strategy, but can be based on politics of radical reformism that are politically immanent and transcendental at the same time. The state is, however, challenged and reproduced not just by political parties but also by social movements organized in civil society.

Given these complexities and contradictions of the state, it can be conceived only as a contradictory force field with temporal unity—a power bloc—between conflicting interests that form political alliances. The state is an "institutional crystallization," "the material condensation of a relationship of forces," "a strategic field and process of intersecting power networks, which both articulate and exhibit mutual contradictions and displacements" (Poulantzas 1980, 136). The state does not directly map or mirror the interests of the capitalist class, but rather crystallises the complexities of the class structure in contradictory ways. It is precisely through the articulation of complex factions and oppositions that dominant interests are transposed from economic power into state power and in a dialectical reversal back from state power to economic power. The "state crystallizes the relations of production and class relations. The modern political state does not translate the 'interests' of the dominant classes at the political level, but the relationship between those interests and the interests of the dominated classes— which means that it precisely constitutes the 'political' expression of the interests of the dominant classes" (Poulantzas 2008, 80).

Based on the tensions crystallising in the state, we may reflect on the nature of a state presence on social media. Insofar as the state is meant to serve its citizens, there is the possibility that a state presence on social media can be an extension of that service. Indeed, scholars have made appeals to the idea of public service social media (Brevini 2013; Fuchs 2014c) that could resemble the BBC model of public service broadcast media. On the other hand, the state may also rely on social media to maintain and enforce a particular social order by resorting to its monopoly of violence or ideological power. Indeed, there are more tangible examples of governments seeking to restrict flows of communication online, monitoring social media content that is framed as a threat to social order[1] and using these platforms as a means to promote a particular social order.[2] Yet a theoretically grounded understanding of state activity on social media will make more sense when considering the constitutive elements of the state. Public service media as well as state-owned industries show that the state is distinct from the economy to a varying degree. A public economy is based on the state's specific ownership-control of parts of the economy so that the distance between the state and the economy is smaller than in the private property economy. In public service media, the state organizes both the economy and culture of specific modes of public information and communication.

6.   WHAT ARE THE BRANCHES OF THE STATE?

We should next consider the organizations and other elements that constitute the state. Jessop notes that the state is composed of institutions above, below and around its core, and that the relations to and among these are not obvious (2007, 10). Furthermore, these institutions, articulation, and the relation to state and society depend on the "nature of social formation of past history" (ibid.). The state has components, but there is limited purpose in speaking of it in this way, as it is also conceived of as a kind of unified (albeit amorphous) entity. It is also worth noting that the state is more than the "mere assembly of detachable parts" (Poulantzas 1978, 136). Rather, Poulantzas notes that it "exhibits an *apparatus unity* which is normally designated by the term centralization or *centralism*, and which is related to the fissiparous *unity of state power*" (ibid., emphasis in original). The latter concept is explored in a section ahead.

As a first step, the state includes the government, which can briefly be described as the central, executive branch of the state. It is accompanied by the public sector, which are the industries and services that are generally infrastructural, and serve a vital role for economic life (Miliband 1969, 10). The public sector is made up of an administrative system "which now extends far beyond the traditional bureaucracy of the state, and which encompasses a large variety of bodies, often related to particular ministerial departments, or enjoying a greater or lesser degree of autonomy—public corporations, central banks, regulatory commissions, etc.—and concerned with the management of the economic, social, cultural and other activities in which the state is now directly or indirectly involved" (ibid., 47). The state is also composed of the military, which serves the dual function of the "management of violence" as well as maintaining "internal security" (ibid., 48). Another element is the judiciary, which is "constitutionally independent of the political executive and protected from it by security of tenure and other guarantees" (ibid., 49). In principle the judiciary is meant to defend citizen rights from the state, but the interpretation and execution of such a principle are not always clear. Another supplementary component of the state is the sub-central governments. These include provincial, municipal, regional and territorial branches that are approximated to be "more or less an administrative device" (ibid., 49). Although these occupy a peripheral importance for the state, their functioning often reflects local particularities, and can serve a more central role, for example, during conflicts over sovereignty. In addition to struggles between peripheral and central branches of the government, we may also consider tensions between competing governments—for example, an outgoing liberal party and an incoming conservative one. However, opposition elements are ultimately cooperative in upholding the standing and functioning of the state. As Miliband notes, "By taking part in the work of the legislature, they help the government's business" (ibid., 50).

Each of the foregoing individual state elements—and the sub-branches and individual/regional offices of which they are composed—may have their own unique kind of engagement with various social media platforms. These engagements will include a variety of ways of broadcasting their own content, communicating with other individual and institutional users and monitoring the presence of those other users. On this note, we may consider the position of the media in relation to the state. Stuart Hall et al. note that "oppositions can and frequently do arise between these institutions within the complex of power in society" (1978, 65), and in particular the media seek to broadcast information that the state would wish to contain. Here we may include state media, which may share some features with other government branches (state funding, explicitly carrying out administrative functions, such as reporting on elections), yet still have the possibility of operating at cross-purposes with the state and government.

We can also consider the possibility of social media in relation to the state. In the case of a state-operated or engineered platform, it serves as an explicit branch of the state. In the case of privately owned social media, the relation with the state becomes less obvious. The private platform might have antagonistic relationship with any single state, especially if it operates in a separate jurisdiction. Yet the more likely pattern is based on cooperation between private social media and the state. As Nick Couldry (2013) indicates, a private social media platform may directly profit from the communication activity it solicits from users, but this activity on a private platform may also simultaneously serve the interests of the state. The best example of this phenomenon is that social media companies benefit from commodifying personal data by selling targeting advertisements, and that the NSA- and GSCHQ-operated global PRISM Internet surveillance system enables the state to access the very same data collected and processed by companies such as Facebook, Google, Apple, AOL, Microsoft, Yahoo, Skype or Paltalk for the purpose of control (see Fuchs 2014c).

The state's roles in modern society include the regulation of the economy and society (by laws and taxation), control and exertion of the monopoly of the means of internal and external violence, the legitimisation of this monopoly, information gathering about citizens for the purposes of administration and policing, the legal individualisation of humans into specific roles (such as workers, voters, consumers, owners, etc.), the definition and control of membership and boundaries/closure of society, and the self-description of society in the form of imaginarily constructed narratives termed 'national identities' connected to nationalist, patriotic and racist ideologies, as well as population policies for fostering the reproduction of citizens and workforce (Fuchs 2008, 76–89).

Social media are related to all of these state roles, as these platforms contribute to an integration of social roles. We point out two examples: (1) states devise, implement and regulate laws that regulate social media companies' activities and (2) states are in charge of deriving taxes from social media companies' revenues for public purposes. Besides laws that affect all companies, states and transnational state conglomerates such as the European Union implement data protection laws that especially affect social media companies. A general problem in this respect is that nation states are spatially bound, whereas capital and information flows are global, fluid and mobile, which creates the problem of which national data protection laws shall apply for social media companies that operate globally. At the same time the different spatial mobilities of the state and global companies enable the Facebooks and Googles of our time to escape national data protection regulations by relocating their corporate headquarters.

Social media corporations are economically predominantly based on targeted advertising and the exploitation of digital labour (Fuchs 2014a, 2014d). This means that they globally derive economic revenues. Neo-liberal governance regimes have all over the world resulted in wage repression, the cutback of state expenditures for social measures and reductions of corporate taxation. Nonetheless corporation tax can be a potentially powerful source of state revenue. We live in times of global crisis, in which after decades of rising inequality and crisis-proneness due to financialisation banks and the rich have been bailed out from their own dawning collapse by a 'socialism of the rich' that uses large sums of tax-payers'—that is, predominantly employees, not companies—money. At the same time austerity measures that impact the weakest and poorest and with great likelihood increase inequality have been implemented. In this situation it has become ideologically ever more difficult to justify no or low corporate taxation.

Companies such as Google, Amazon and Starbucks had to appear before the UK Public Accounts Committee in late 2012 to discuss whether they avoided paying taxes in the UK (BBC 2012). Amazon has fifteen thousand employees in the UK, but its headquarters are in Luxembourg, where it has just five hundred employees (ibid.). In 2011, it generated revenues of £3.3 billion in the UK, but paid only £1.8 million corporation tax (0.05 per cent) (Griffiths 2012; Barford and Holt 2012). Facebook paid £238,000 corporation tax on a UK revenue of £175 million (0.1 per cent) in 2011 (Moss 2012).

Google has its headquarters in Dublin, but employs around seven hundred people in the UK (Garside 2013). Google's managing director for the

UK and Ireland, Matt Brittin, admitted that this choice of location is due to the circumstance that the corporation tax is just 12.5 per cent in Ireland, whereas in the UK it was 26 per cent in 2011 (BBC 2012). Google had a UK turnover of £395 million in 2011, but paid taxes of only £6 million (1.5 per cent) (ibid.). While large media companies pay only a very low share of taxes, governments argue that state budgets are small, implement austerity measures and as a result cut social and welfare benefits, hitting the poorest in society.

In the House of Commons' Public Accounts Committee's inquiry on tax avoidance, Google's Brittin admitted that this structure serves to pay low taxes. He said in the inquiry session conducted on 16 May 2013, that "we talked about Bermuda in the last hearing, and I confirmed that we do use Bermuda. Obviously, Bermuda is a low-tax environment."[3] Confronted with Google's low level of corporation tax paid in the UK, Eric Schmidt said that "people we [Google] employ in Britain are certainly paying British taxes" (BBC 2013). His logic here is that Google does not have to pay taxes because its employees do.

The contradiction of national and spatially bounded state power and global corporate power that manage global information flows on social media have combined with neoliberal policy regimes, resulting in the paralysis of corporate taxation and social media corporations' practices of tax avoidances. Overcoming this huge structural problem requires implementing global corporate tax laws, authorities, controls and enforcement mechanisms. It requires that the state transits from its conservative crisis politics of policing the poor and the crisis to policing corporate crimes.

7.   WHAT IS POLITICS? WHAT IS THE RELATIONSHIP OF THE STATE AND POLITICS?

We can begin with an understanding of politics as a relational activity. Mouffe refers to the political as "the potential antagonisms inherent in human relations," which "indicates the ensemble of discourses, institutions and practices which aim at establishing an order; at organising human coexistence, in a context that is always conflictual because of the presence of the political" (1993, 8). Thus, politics—at least in class societies based on contradictory interests—can be understood as a mode of social organization through conflict.

We may also extend on this definition of modern politics to note that both tangible (such as political parties, staff, events) and less tangible (such as discourses, practices) elements exist in order to raise and resolve conflicts. When we consider the full range of groups and institutions that are involved in politics, these extend beyond commonly held understandings of 'the political.' Lobbyists and pressure groups, multinational corporations, churches and other religious organizations and the mass media all have an active stake in politics. The people who head these institutions "may wield considerable power and influence, which must be integrated in the analysis of political power in advanced capitalist societies" (Miliband 1969, 51). In the most general sense abstracted from modern society, we can define politics as a system in which humans in public arrive at collectively binding decisions of how to organize society and its resources (Fuchs 2008). In dominative societies, the political system takes on a form in which one group or several groups together hold a monopoly, oligopoly or hierarchical control of decision power.

Politics are not entirely distinct from the state. State branches can perform political roles, even when this directly contradicts their mandate (Ditchburn 2013). Stuart Hall et al., drawing upon Gramsci, claim that the state "plays a critical role in shaping social and political life in such a way as to favour the continued expansion of production and the reproduction of capitalist social relations" (1978, 201). However, it bears noting that politicised components of the state (such as naturally governing parties) are directly plugged in to this role. The degree of closeness between political elements and a state can vary. For example, a ruling political party will have a more intimate relation with the state than the main opposition party, which in turn overlaps more with the state than fringe political parties. Some groups may engage in political activity that is relatively divorced from the state, such as an activist group that does not engage directly with governing political parties, state administration, state-run media, etc., and instead makes appeals to the public through non-state controlled media.

Although political procedures are typically conceived as conflictual, these conflicts can be routinised—and thus dampened—for the purpose of greater state functioning. On the topic of opposing political parties, Miliband notes "the disagreements *between those political leaders who have generally been able to gain high office* have very seldom been of the fundamental kind these leaders and other people so often suggest. What is really striking about *these* political leaders and political office-holders, in relation to each other, is not their many differences, but the extent of their agreement on truly fundamental issues" (1969, 64, emphasis in original). Thus, a highly visible and accessible conflict between a liberal and conservative political party may belie a struggle between competing visions of social organization, including alternatives to late capitalism. It is helpful to consider the discursive and communicative aspects of the political, specifically in terms of their relation to material outcomes. Jessop, drawing from Marx, notes that we ought to consider the "theatricality of politics not only as metaphor but also as a self-conscious political practice on the part of political actors as they sought to persuade and impress their audience by adopting character masks and roles from the historical past and/or from a dramatic repertoire" (2007, 89–90). Communication through staged and scripted performances is the means through which political conflicts are raised and resolved. Intangible aspects are crucial here, as "every political movement needs to find appropriate discourse and symbolism as the means of political expression to advance its interests" (ibid., 91).

Key elements of the political include the maintenance or reformulation of a particular social order through the communication of discourse and symbolism on particular stages. Politics are clearly manifest on conventional media platforms, and this is indeed the most accessible way for citizens to watch over and engage with political processes. Most citizens will be able to witness parliamentary procedure, political campaigns and political party scandal only through broadcast media. As a general observation, it would appear that the way that citizens experience politics is through media. Additionally, it is through various media formats that political branches can engage with citizens—for example, by commissioning polls to determine voting intentions. The continued engagement of social media by citizens means that political power and influence, especially insofar as citizens are concerned, will spread to platforms that feature integrated social roles, all of which can be entirely visible to political actors. If we consider the trend of political campaigns making micro-scale appeals to specific neighbourhoods (Payton 2012), campaigns and other kinds of political communication on social media can be even more minutely targeted at individual characteristics and interests. The danger that lies in this development in contemporary neo-liberal governance regimes that tend to commodify everything is that politics becomes public relations, advertising and the selling of an idea, a politician and a party as brand. Translated into the social media world, this then means that social media politics derogates into political advertising, point-and-click politics without real engagement and discussion—a form of pseudo-participation and pseudo-voice. In contrast social media, however, also have the potential to foster political communication between citizens and to support street protests that combine offline and online communication (Fuchs 2014b).

8.   WHAT IS POWER? WHAT IS STATE POWER? WHAT IS CORPORATE POWER?

As stated earlier, power refers to the ability to exert influence and control structural and procedural social elements, and is in class societies typically conceived in a zero-sum manner (as it comes at the expense of another individual or group), whereas in non-class societies power can be more equally distributed and benefit all. We can therefore consider power in abstraction as the ability to act, including both self-determined acts and the ability to act upon others. It can be diffuse and capillary (Foucault 1990), but often flows in specific directions and is unevenly concentrated. This concentration is based on the possession of resources, money, reputation, knowledge and social relations.

In its relation to the state, Poulantzas claims that all forms of power exist only insofar as materialised in certain apparatuses, including state apparatuses (1978, 44–45). Miliband endorses this understanding of state power as located in branches of the state, noting that it is in the administration, military and judiciary, among others, "in which 'state power' lies, and it is through them that this power is wielded in its different manifestations by the people who occupy the leading positions in each of these institutions" (1969, 50). We can speculate that state power is linked to the maintenance of legitimacy. Hall underscores the Gramscian notion that state power depends on a popular cohesion, which is maintained by both coercion and consent, and that it operates best when it is perceived as legitimate. Jessop notes that the way legitimacy is "institutionalised and expressed will also vary" (2007, 10) and that there are more forms of ensuring compliance than just coercion (ibid.) This assertion seems reasonable, given that each branch of the state acts upon citizens through different relations. Poulantzas echoes this by maintaining a distinction between institutions that "actualise bodily constraint and the permanent threat of mutilation" and those that operate through "a *bodily order* which both institutes and manages bodies by bending and moulding them into shape and inserting them in the various institutions and apparatuses" (1978, 29, emphasis in original).

Although one might consider the general population to be excluded from exerting state power, insofar that this power acts upon them, Poulantzas claims that the popular masses can be present in certain state apparatuses such as the military, even if these serve to otherwise exclude and coerce popular masses (1978, 152). On the topic of class-based asymmetries of power, he also notes that these "are not reducible to the State" (ibid., 37). However, the state plays a strong constitutive role, which "should be understood in the strong sense of the term" (ibid., 38). There is no such social phenomenon "as posed in a state prior to the State" (ibid., 39).

Economic power broadly refers to intervention in economic life (Miliband 1969, 10). This ability to intervene is in capitalism directly related to corporate production processes, which are "grounded on the *unity* of the labour process [. . .] the *primacy* of the relations of production over the labour process" (Poulantzas 1978, 26, emphasis in original). Corporate power involves private ownership, the labour-capital class relationship, the commodity form and structures of accumulation. Miliband notes the importance of corporate power, notably through the concentration of private economic power, and characterises late capitalism as "all but synonymous with giant enterprise" (1969, 10). Although popular discourse tends to speak about corporate power as a monolithic force, Miliband characterises corporations as "distinct groupings and interests, whose competition greatly affects the political process" (ibid., 44–45). However, such competition does not "prevent the separate elites in capitalist society from constituting a dominant economic class, possessed of a high degree of cohesion and solidarity, with common interests and common purposes which far transcend their specific differences and disagreements" (ibid.).

Corporate power and state power are intertwined. Both serve as constitutive forces in society, and the reproduction of capitalism in particular "is expressed in state economic functions, according to the precise stage and phase of capitalism; whether it is a question of repressive violence, ideological inculcation, disciplinary normalisation, the organisation of space and time or the creation of consent, the activity of the State is related as a whole to these economic functions properly so called" (Poulantzas 1978, 163). Insofar as the state serves to structure society, it stands to reason that it has a more or less tangible connection to economic power. Corporate interests can generally rely on the service and good will of governments (Miliband 1969, 85–88). Indeed, they can even flourish under fascist and other totalitarian state regimes. As Miliband indicates, corporate post-war success is not indicative of a dramatic turnaround, but rather is a testament to its functioning even during state intervention: "businesses, particularly large-scale businesses, did enjoy such an advantage *inside* the state system, by virtue of the composition and ideological inclination of the state elite" (ibid., 131, emphasis in original).

The actual relationship between corporate interests and the state is not consistent. The state may act against the economic and employment interests of civil servants and other wage-earners, but may justify this decision in the "national interest, the health of the economy, the defence of the currency, the good of the workers, and so on" (Miliband 1969, 74–75). Thus, a general perception of 'public interest' may in fact reflect a pairing of state and corporate interests, and of state and corporate power. Miliband (ibid., 51), citing Karl Kautsky (1903, 13), writes that the corporate elite "'rules but does not govern,' though he added immediately that 'it contents itself with ruling the government.'" One of the prominent ways corporate power can control state power is through regulatory capture. This is when a regulatory or otherwise administrative state branch is seized and controlled by corporate interests ("Halliburton" 2009). Miliband notes that "one of the most notable features of advanced capitalism is precisely what might be called without much exaggeration their growing colonisation of the upper reaches of the administrative part of that system [state system]" (1969, 53).

We may situate the media industries as playing an important role for corporate power: "they too are both the expression of a system of domination, and a means of reinforcing it" (Milliband 1969, 198). Here, the informational aspect of mass media is a means to render an existing state and corporate regime meaningful to its citizens (cognition), to communicate this (imaginary or non-imaginary) meaningfulness to the citizens (communication) and also to reinforce that existing social order (cooperation). Extending from Miliband's quote earlier, we may consider social media platforms in the context of intersecting state and corporate power. The most popular platforms come from Silicon Valley, which is ideologically framed in terms of an iconoclastic exceptionalism from social structures such as taxation regimes.

This suggests a kind of avoidance of regulation (taxation; data protection; broadcasting standards). Even in a context where platforms struggle to yield high profits, the founders and owners of these platforms exercise tremendous corporate power through the exploitation of their own workers,[4] as well as the exploitation of users who render platforms valuable through their own labour (see Fuchs 2014a). Low tax rates are an example where social media corporate power is at loggerheads with state power, as this is a zero-sum allocation of financial capital. However, a powerful corporate social media platform also serves state power when state actors can make use of a social media corporation's penetration into so many integrated branches of social life. In this volume, Thomas Poell provides a detailed exploration of state dependence on telecommunication and surveillance technologies, and the kind of corporate collaboration that emerges as a result. In other cases, as Sara Salem points out in her chapter in this volume, state power may be challenged by corporate power. For example, satellite media might be ideologically opposed to state-run media, or social media may constitute a kind of public sphere for activism and mobilisation. However, Salem is careful to point out that corporate interests are not aligned with citizens in these cases, and any function such interests serve for mobilisation can be fleeting (as Poell also indicates with the example of Google Reader's demise). As for the state, any attempt to disrupt or displace its power will likely result in renewed attempts to reassert such control. Elise Thorburn's chapter on live streaming technology offers a cogent account of its disruption to and reassertion of state power.

9.   WHAT IS CRIME? WHAT ARE THE POLICE? WHAT FUNCTION DOES THE POLICE HAVE AS PART OF THE STATE?

State power and hegemony may be contested through a variety of means. These affronts to state power are "moments when the whole basis of political leadership and cultural authority becomes exposed and contested" (Hall et al. 1978, 217), and are met with a shift from consent to coercion-based forms of maintaining state power. Criminal acts are made meaningful through a labelling aspect, such that seemingly identical acts may or may not be designated as criminal, depending on mitigating circumstances such as where and when the act takes place, and who is performing the act. But there is more to crime and criminal acts than simple labelling. As Hall et al. indicate, there are "historic and structural forces at work" that are often relegated to background (ibid., 185). Thus, crime, as a challenge to state power, and crime prevention (such as policing) as a reassertion of state power exist only in relation to each other (ibid.). Crime and policing are not just specific manifestations of social conflicts in contradictory societies, but at the level of culture and the state often serve as precedents for the formation of what Hall et al. (ibid.) term conservative ideologies of crime that claim that crime can be overcome only by law and order, tough prison sentences (or even the death penalty), strong presence of police and security forces, constant control of public and private spaces by surveillance technologies, and large tax expenditures for internal and external security (often at the expense of social security mechanisms).

As branches of the state, the police as well as the military are "pre-eminently repressive" (Poulantzas 1978, 127) in their efforts to maintain state power. They exist primarily to reinforce an existing social order, including private property and current wealth distribution. The parameters of criminality and state response are designated by law, which is "an integral part of the repressive order and of the organisation of violence. By issuing rules and passing laws, the State establishes an initial field of injunctions, prohibitions and censorship, and thus institutes the practical terrain and object of violence. Furthermore, law organizes the conditions for physical repression, designating its modalities and structuring the devices by means of which it is exercised. In this sense, law is *the code of organized public violence*" (ibid., 77, emphasis in original). The state can also exceed its own laws, in the higher interest of the state (ibid., 84).

The police, as a branch of the state, are able to maintain control over state and citizen perceptions of criminality through their reliance on official statements in news media. Christopher Schneider focuses on this tendency in his chapter in this volume, and indicates how police are able to transfer this ability to social media platforms, thus reasserting state power on new platforms otherwise framed in terms of citizen counter-power. Social media are also sites where the communicative aspects of crimes can occur. This may include the presentation of evidence. Trottier's chapter in this collection indicates how such online evidence may come from a variety of sources, including citizens attempting to make each other's criminal acts visible to police. In other instances, crimes that are primarily manifest as a communicative act (such as uttering death threats or hate speech) can be manifest on these platforms. As a result of the integrated sociality described earlier, any evidence of criminality, including criminalised communicative acts, has the potential of an amplified exposure and visibility. On the basis of this section and the previous section, we see that social media on the one hand are manifestations of state and corporate power, but that on the other hand these platforms have the potential of constituting (or hosting) a challenge to state power, corporate power and existing social orders. Yet, for these exact reasons, they can also be the site of redoubled efforts of the reassertion of the existing order by state and corporate actors—for example, through surveillance and censorship.

10. **WHAT ARE PROTESTS, REVOLUTIONS,**
     RIOTS AND SOCIAL MOVEMENTS? WHAT ARE
     THEIR COMMONALITIES AND DIFFERENCES?

As stated earlier, social movements refer to forms of collective action that can be motivated by political, economic or cultural goals. Such movements typically operate outside of grounded state branches, but often aim to act upon it. Della Porta and Mattoni's contribution to this volume demonstrates the fact that social movements are temporal and relational, insofar as they depend on networks that exceed any single organization, and include allies, adversaries, bystanders and mediators. As "processes that interface with societies at many different levels" (della Porta and Mattoni, this volume), social movements are not uniquely mapped onto states or corporations, and can be transnational in their scope.

In terms of how they are manifest, social movements rely on individual members to gather in public. These gatherings are typically in response to a grievance, and may be a means of communicating an explicit desired course of action. As forms of mass mobilisation, they may also be characterised by property damage and physical violence, especially with police and other repressive government branches. These manifestations may be framed as either riots or protests. The distinction between these two depends on several factors, including (1) an explicitly desired political, economic or cultural outcome, (2) association with an explicit social movement organization and (3) the absence or presence of property damage and physical violence. The first two are typically associated with protests, while the latter is associated with riots.

It is crucial to note that the distinction between protests and riots is not obvious, and is partly determined by how these events are labelled by state branches and the media (Lemert 1951). As an example, the mass demonstrations in Toronto in response to the G8/G20 summit in 2010 have been framed by the mass media as both protests (Slaughter 2013) and riots (O'Toole 2013). Protests and riots are both linked with non-hegemonic classes and operate within the framework of state. Poulantzas claims that as a consequence, "the dominated classes and their particular struggles have a specific presence within the structure of the State—a presence that is expressed by the State's material framework bound up with the relations of production, by its hierarchical-bureaucratic organization, and by the reproduction of the social division of labour within the State" (1978, 141). As a result, repressive state branches do not exist simply to "confront the dominated classes head on, but to maintain and reproduce the domination-subordination relationship at the heart of the State: the class enemy is always present within the state" (ibid.). These struggles are not an aberration from state configuration. Rather, these struggles "are bound up with its strategic configurations. As in the case with every power mechanism, the State is the material condensation of a *relationship*" (ibid., 145, emphasis in original).

Social movement activity, including protests and riots, may culminate into revolutions. These refer to political action above and beyond a particular state configuration, which then supplants that state configuration. As Skocpol states, state power is a basic consideration in revolutions, yet "state power cannot be understood only as an instrument of class domination, nor can changes in state structures be explained primarily in terms of class conflicts" (1979, 284). As a "reconsolidation of state power," revolutions require: "the reformation of state institutions that have typically been shattered with the fall of the old regime, especially the army and civil administration; it may also require the implementation (or at least recognition after the fact) of more or less extensive political and social changes in order to win or maintain the support (or at least neutrality) of various sectors of the population that have been mobilized during the revolution" (Foran and Goodwin 1993, 210). Social movements can also seize control of the state. Kompatsiaris and Mlyonas' chapter on Golden Dawn points to a kind of paradox where the movement is acting at a supra-governmental level, all while taking conventional measures to become elected and to govern. In this case state power is "both a partner and adversary for fascist politics" (Kompatsiaris and Mlyonas, this volume). Historically relevant strategies, such as reliance on propaganda, including social media, are troubling iterations of this fascism.

One element of all these kinds of manifestations is that they are typically thought of as occurring in an embodied location, and quite often in the streets. Social movements are not as geographically tangible, but these often depend on visibility for growth and support. Given that these are coordinated acts, they also depend on cognition and communication. Traditional media, notably corporate and state-run media, have historically not been supportive of these manifestations, and often framed them unfavourably. These movements may rely on newsletters and other kinds of alternate media to communicate, although these might have limited circulation. Cable's chapter in this volume indicates a problematic relation between protest movement's alternative media (including the use of social media) and mainstream media, given the ability for the latter to repurpose the former's content for their own ends. Social media allow for a greater communication with the public, including citizens and state. Gerbaudo's chapter in this volume indicates that these platforms are especially suited for amorphous social movements, as they provide "a horizontal system of decision making" (Gerbaudo, this volume). Thus, social media become platforms where the communicative aspect of protests, riots and social movements can occur. Using Anonymous as a case study, Fuchs' chapter in this volume shows how social movements can take on a bottom-up and amorphous organizational structure, to the extent that such movements can be considered social movements and anti-movements.

11. CONCLUSION

Politics in contemporary society is a force field of power involving the state, corporations, civil society and social movements in complex and contradictory relations. These articulations take place in the context of a global crisis of society that is simultaneously economic, financial, political and ideological. Political transformations thereby tend to become accelerated. Their occurrence and outcome are, however, the result of the complexity and indeterminateness of human agency and social struggles, not predetermined. Social media is predominantly a corporate-state-power phenomenon, a force field in itself, in which powerful corporate and state interests are present and meet, as evidenced by the existence of a surveillance-industrial complex (PRISM) that controls social media communication and is constituted by a collaboration of social media and Internet companies, secret services and private security companies (such as Booz Allen Hamilton, for which Edward Snowden worked before his revelations). Corporate and state power are actually and potentially challenged and contested in multiple forms. The situation of the recent crisis has made such challenges more likely and taken on diverse formats such as revolutions, rebellions, protests, the emergence of growth of new social movements or parties (such as Occupy, Anonymous, the 5* movement, Golden Dawn), riots, etc. Social media are neither causes of these phenomena nor are they entirely unimportant. Rather, they are spaces of complex manifestations of power, counter-power and power contradictions. They tend to dialectically interact with offline and street politics (Fuchs 2014b, 2014d). Civil society politics challenges corporate and state power in various complex and non-determined political and social forms. These challenges make use of a variety of resources, including communication resources. Social media politics is thereby inherently shaped by an asymmetry of resources such as visibility, attention, money, reputation, influence and social relations that makes the communicational dimensions of struggles, just like offline struggles, those of an unequal power field, in which the state and corporations are privileged actors in terms of the power they can command, which results in a specific political economy that does not make it impossible to challenge state and corporate power, but rather a struggle with unequal resources (Fuchs and Sandoval 2015; Fuchs 2014b).

The character and outcome of the challenges to predominant political powers are not predetermined; they are not necessarily or automatically progressive, conservative, liberal, fascist, etc. Situations of crises are bifurcation points, in which the future is contingent and depends on the complex dynamics of social struggles:

> The world of 2050 will be what we make it. This leaves full rein for our agency, for our commitment, and for our moral judgment. It also means that this period will be a time of terrible political struggle, because the stakes are much higher than in so-called normal times. (Wallerstein 1998, 64)

Our future is a matter of politics—for better or worse.

NOTES

1. The NSA Files, The Guardian. http://www.theguardian.com/world/the-nsa-files. Last updated 6 May 2014. Accessed 6 May 2014.
2. David Cameron, Twitter. https://twitter.com/David_Cameron. Last updated 6 May 2014. Accessed 6 May 2014.
3. Public Accounts—Minutes of Evidence—HC 112, Parliament.uk. http://www.publications.parliament.uk/pa/cm201314/cmselect/cmpubacc/112/130516.htm. Prepared 12 June 2013. Accessed 6 May 2014.
4. What's It Like to Intern at Google?, Quora. http://www.quora.com/Google-Internships/What-is-it-like-to-intern-at-Google. Last updated 23 April 2014. Accessed 6 May 2014.

REFERENCES

Althusser, Louis. 1971. *Lenin and Philosophy and Other Essays.* New York: Monthly Review Press.
Anheier, Helmut. K., Stefan Toepfler and Regina A. List, eds. 2010. *International Encyclopedia of Civil Society.* Heidelberg: Springer.
Archer, Margaret S. 1995. *Realist Social Theory: The Morphogenetic Approach.* Cambridge, UK: Cambridge University Press.
Arendt, Hannah. 1958. *The Human Condition.* Chicago, IL: University of Chicago.
Barabási, Albert-László. 2003. *Linked.* New York: Plume.
Barford, Vanessa, and Gerry Holt. 2012. Google, Amazon, Starbucks: The Rise of "tax sharing." BBC Online. 4 December. http://www.bbc.co.uk/news/magazine-20560359.
BBC. 2012. Starbucks, Google and Amazon Grilled over Tax Avoidance. BBC.co.uk. 12 November. http://www.bbc.co.uk/news/business-20288077.
BBC. 2013. Google Boss Defends UK Tax Record to BBC. BBC.co.uk. 22 April. http://www.bbc.co.uk/news/business-22245770.
Beer, David. 2008. Social Network(ing) Sites Revisiting the Story So Far: A Response to danah boyd & Nicole Ellison. *Journal of Computer-Mediated Communication* 13 (2): 516–529.
Bhaskar, Roy. 1993. *Dialectic: The Pulse of Freedom.* London: Verso.
Bourdieu, Pierre. 1986. *Distinction: A Social Critique of the Judgement of Taste.* New York: Routledge.
boyd, danah, and Nicole B. Ellison. 2008. Social Networking Sites: Definition, History, and Scholarship. *Journal of Computer-Mediated Communication* 13 (1): 210–230.
Brevini, Benedetta. 2013. *Public Service Broadcasting online: A Comparative European Policy Study of PSB 2.0.* Basingstoke: Palgrave Macmillan.
Cleaver, Harry. 2000. *Reading Capital Politically.* Edinburgh: AK Press.
Couldry, Nick. 2013. *A Necessary Disenchantment: Myth, Agency and Injustice in the Digital Age.* Inaugural lecture, London School of Economics, London. 21 November.
Ditchburn, Jennifer. 2013. Fantino's Office Involved in Posting Partisan Diatribes to Government Website: Documents. *Globe and Mail*, 30 May. http://www.theglobeandmail.com/news/politics/fantinos-office-involved-in-posting-partisan-diatribes-to-government-website-documents/article12258009/.
Dutton, William, ed. 2013. *The Oxford Handbook of Internet Studies.* Oxford: Oxford University Press.
Ehrenberg, John, and Harry Trosman. 1999. *Civil Society: The Critical History of an Idea.* New York: New York University Press.

Ess, Charles, and William Dutton, eds. 2013. Special issue: The Rise of Internet Studies. *New Media & Society* 15 (5): 633–796.

Foran, John, and Jeff Goodwin. 1993. Revolutionary Outcomes in Iran and Nicaragua: Coalition Fragmentation, War, and the Limits of Social Transformation. *Theory and Society* 22 (2): 209–247.

Foucault, Michel. 1990. *The History of Sexuality*. Vol. 1, *An Introduction*. New York: Vintage Books.

Fuchs, Christian. 2003a. Some Implications of Pierre Bourdieu's Works for a Theory of Social Self-Organization. *European Journal of Social Theory* 6 (4): 387–408.

———. 2003b. Structuration Theory and Self-Organization. *Systemic Practice and Action Research* 16 (4): 133–167.

———. 2008. *Internet and Society: Social Theory in the Information Age*. New York: Routledge.

———. 2014a. *Digital Labour and Karl Marx*. New York: Routledge.

———. 2014b. *OccupyMedia! The Occupy Movement and Social Media in Crisis Capitalism*. Winchester: Zero Books.

———. 2014c. Social media and the public sphere. *tripleC: Communication, Capitalism & Critique* 12 (1): 57–101.

———. 2014d. *Social Media: A Critical Introduction*. London: SAGE.

Fuchs, Christian, Kees Boersma, Anders Albrechtslund, and Marisol Sandoval, eds. 2012. Internet and surveillance. The challenges of web 2.0 and social media. New York: Routledge.

Fuchs, Christian, and Nick Dyer-Witheford. 2013. Karl Marx @ Internet Studies. *New Media & Society* 15 (5): 782–796.

Fuchs, Christian, and Marisol Sandoval, eds. 2014. *Critique, Social Media and the Information Society*. New York: Routledge.

———. Forthcoming. The Political Economy of Capitalist and Alternative Social Media. In *The Routledge Companion to Alternative and Community Media*, edited by Chris Atton. New York: Routledge.

Fuchs, Christian, and Daniel Trottier. 2013. The Internet as Surveilled Workplayplace and Factory. In *European Data Protection: Coming of Age*, edited by Serge Gutwirth, Ronald Leenes, Paul de Hert and Yves Poullet, 33–57. Dordrecht: Springer.

Galtung, Johan. 1990. Cultural Violence. *Journal of Peace Research* 27 (3): 291–305.

Garside, Juliette. 2013. Google and Auditor Recalled by MPs to Answer Tax Questions. *Guardian Online*. 1 May. http://www.guardian.co.uk/technology/2013/may/01/google-parliament-tax-questions.

Giddens, Anthony. 1984. *The Constitution of Society: Outline of the Theory of Structuration*. Cambridge, UK: Polity Press.

Golding, Peter, and Graham Murdock, eds. 1997. *The Political Economy of the Media*. 2 vols. Cheltenham: Edward Elgar.

Gramsci, Antonio. 1971. *Selections from the Prison Notebooks*. New York: International Publishers.

———. 1988. *The Antonio Gramsci Reader: Selected Writings 1916–1935*, ed. David Forgacs. London: Lawrence and Wishart.

Griffiths, Ian. 2012. Amazon: £7bn Sales, No UK Corporation Tax. *Guardian Online*, 4 April. http://www.guardian.co.uk/technology/2012/apr/04/amazon-british-operation-corporation-tax.

Habermas, Jürgen. 1987. *Theory of Communicative Action*. Vol. 2, *Lifeworld and system*. Boston, MA: Beacon Press.

———. 1989. *The Structural Transformation of the Public Sphere*. Cambridge, MA: MIT Press.

———. 2006. Political Communication in Media Society. *Communication Theory* 16 (4): 411–426.

Hall, Stuart, Chas Critcher, Tony Jefferson, John N. Clarke and Brian Roberts. 1978. *Policing the Crisis: Mugging, the State and Law and Order.* Basingstoke: Palgrave Macmillan.

"The Halliburton Loophole." 2009. Editorial. *New York Times*, 3 November. A28.

Hegel, Georg. W. F. 1821. *Grundlinien der Philosophie des Rechts oder Naturracht und Staatswissenschaft im Grundriss.* Frankfurt: Suhrkamp.

Jessop, Bob. 2007. *State Power: A Strategic-Relational Approach.* Cambridge, UK: Polity Press.

Kautsky, Karl. 1903. *The Social Revolution.* London: Twentieth Century Press.

Keane, John. 2010. Civil Society: Definitions and Approaches. In *International Encyclopedia of Civil Society*, edited by Helmut K. Anheier, Stefan Toepfler and Regina A. List, 461–464. Heidelberg: Springer.

Kenny, Michael. 2007. Civil Society. In *Encyclopaedia of Governance*, edited by Mark Bevir, 91–95. London: SAGE.

Lemert, Edwin. 1951. *Social Pathology.* New York: McGraw-Hill.

Mandiberg, Michael. 2012. Introduction. In *The Social Media Reader*, edited by Michael Mandiberg, 1–10. New York: New York University Press.

Miliband, Ralph. 1969. *The State in Capitalist Society.* New York: Basic Books.

Moss, Stephen. 2012. Should We Boycott the Tax-Avoiding Companies? *Guardian Online*, 17 October. http://www.guardian.co.uk/business/shortcuts/2012/oct/17/boycotting-tax-avoiding-companies.

Mouffe, Chantal. 1993. *Return of the Political.* London: Verso.

Murdock, Graham. 2011. Political Economies as Moral Economies: Commodities, Gifts, and Public Goods. In *The Handbook of Political Economy of Communications*, edited by Janet Wasko, 13–40. Malden, MA: Wiley-Blackwell.

Offe, Claus. 1985. New Social Movements: Challenging the Boundaries of Institutional Politics. *Social Research* 52 (4): 817–867.

O'Reilly, Tim. 2005. What Is Web 2.0? http://www.oreilly.de/artikel/web20.html.

O'Reilly, Tim, and John Battelle. 2009. *Web Squared: Web 2.0 Five Years On.* Special report. http://assets.en.oreilly.com/1/event/28/web2009_websquared-whitepaper.pdf.

O'Toole. Megan. 2013. Toronto Police "Nearing the End" of Lengthy Investigation into 2010 G20 Riots. *National Post*, 6 March. http://news.nationalpost.com/2013/03/06/two-american-men-in-toronto-court-today-to-face-g20-summit-charges/.

Payton, Laura. 2012. Ethnic Riding Targeting Key to Conservatives' 2011 Victory: More Than 30 "Very Ethnic" Target Ridings Led to Majority Government in 2011. CBC.ca. 23 October. http://www.cbc.ca/news/politics/ethnic-riding-targeting-key-to-conservatives-2011-victory-1.1142511.

Poulantzas, Nicos. 1978. *State, Power, Socialism.* London: Verso.

———. 2008. *The Poulantzas Reader.* London: Verso.

Rheingold, Howard. 2000. *The Virtual Community.* Cambridge, MA: MIT Press.

Robbins, Martin. 2013. Cameron's Internet Filter Goes Far beyond Porn—and That Was Always the Plan. *New Statesman*, 23 December. http://www.newstatesman.com/politics/2013/12/camerons-internet-filter-goes-far-beyond-porn-and-was-always-plan.

Salzman, Ryan. 2011. Civil Society. In *21st Century Political Science: A Reference Handbook*, edited by John T. Ishiyama and Marijke Breuning, 193–201. London: SAGE.

Sheldon, Garrett. W. 2001. *Encyclopedia of Political Thought.* New York: Facts on File.

Skocpol, Theda. 1979. *States and Social Revolutions: A Comparative Analysis of France, Russia and China.* Cambridge, UK: Cambridge University Press.

Slaughter, Graham. 45-Day Jail Sentence for Toronto Police Officer Who Beat G20 Protester. TheStar.com. 9 December. http://www.thestar.com/news/crime/2013/12/09/45day_jail_sentence_for_toronto_police_officer_who_beat_g20_protester.html.

Sum, Ngai-Ling, and Bob Jessop. 2013. *Towards a Cultural Political Economy: Putting Culture in Its Place in Political Economy.* Cheltenham: Edward Elgar.

Touraine, Alain. 1985. An Introduction to the Study of Social Movements. *Social Research* 52 (4): 749–787.

Trottier, Daniel. 2012. *Social Media as Surveillance.* Farnham: Ashgate.

Trottier, Daniel, and David Lyon. 2012. Key Features of Social Media Surveillance. In *Internet and Surveillance: The Challenges of Web 2.0 and Social Media,* edited by Christian Fuchs, Kees Boersma, Anders Albrechtslund and Marisol Sandoval, 89–105. New York: Routledge.

Wallerstein, Immanuel. 1998. *Utopistics, or, Historical Choices of the Twenty-First Century.* New York: New Press.

Wasko, Janet, Graham Murdock and Helena Sousa, eds. 2011. *The Handbook of the Political Economy of Communications.* Chicester: Wiley-Blackwell.

Wasserman, Stanley, and Katherine Faust. 1997. *Social Network Analysis.* Cambridge, UK. Cambridge University Press.

2 Social Networking Sites in Pro-democracy and Anti-austerity Protests

Some Thoughts from a Social Movement Perspective[1]

Donatella della Porta and Alice Mattoni

1. INTRODUCTION

In the past years, massive protests developed in several countries across the world. Already in September 2008, people in Iceland began to mobilise against the financial crisis that was hitting their country: demonstrations intensified in January 2009 when thousands of protesters took the streets in Reykjavik, the capital of the country. Although various forms of protest had already developed in Latin America as well as Africa, the uprising in Iceland was the first moment of rebellion in Europe against the way in which national governments managed the harsh consequences of the financial and economic crisis. While European mainstream media did not cover Icelandic demonstrations, and their relatively positive outcomes, the news about what was going on in the northern European country was traveling quickly through the web. About one year later, another wave of uprisings shook the Middle East and North Africa region when massive demonstrations occurred first in Tunisia, late in 2010, and then in Egypt, Libya, Yemen, Syria and Bahrain during 2011. In this case mainstream media across the world gave wide visibility to the protests. But many commentators also underlined the important role of social networking platforms, like Facebook and Twitter, in nurturing and supporting protests as well as in keeping the mass media informed about protesters' claims and actions. Activists in the Middle East and North Africa asked for accountable and democratic political systems in their countries: a demand that was also present in the protests that broke out during the spring of 2011 in many European countries, including Portugal, Spain and Greece. Frequently labelled as the Indignados movements, these protests targeted the political elites who were considered irresponsible in the way they faced the economic crisis. People in the streets were indeed against the austerity measures that followed the injunctions of the European Union, the European Central Bank and the International Monetary Fund.

And, at the same time, they asked for a deep change in the democratic practices of their respective governments: as the Spanish protesters claimed, they wanted a "real democracy now." Also in this case, the spreading of information and communication technologies seemed to be central in the development of such movements and in the diffusion of information from one European country to the other: pictures, slogans and manifestos journeyed laptops and mobiles of many activists across the globe through social media platforms. The news, of course, also reached the North American shores: looking at protest camps set up in so many squares in 2011, the editors of the Canadian *Adbusters* magazine decided to give it a try also in the U.S. They first circulated a call for action in their networks on July 13, asking if people were ready for a "Tahrir moment," echoing protests in Egypt that received wide coverage in North America. Later on they designed a poster calling for a demonstration on September 17. It was the beginning of Occupy Wall Street in New York, soon followed by a number of other encampments in many cities across the U.S., as well as in other countries such as the United Kingdom and Australia. The general assemblies that supported and organized protest activities were live-streamed and the related accounts were posted in the Occupy Wall Street websites. Tumblr, a social media platform mostly devoted to the sharing of pictures, became the place in which the protesters could voice their anger and explain why they felt part of the movement in the blog "We Are the 99%." At the same time, Facebook groups and pages gathering local networks of people flourished. They included long-term activists and newcomers in political mobilisations, who organized Occupy Wall Street protest camps in their cities. At the moment of writing this chapter, moreover, new uprisings are developing in Turkey and Brazil: as in previous mobilisations, social networking sites seem to constitute a relevant actor in the making of communication flows surrounding protests in the two countries.

The brief overview just presented shows that the use of Internet services and web platforms, and especially of social networking sites, was a common feature in mobilisations unfolding worldwide from 2008 onwards. Many observers and analysts, including journalists in the mainstream press, also recognised this characteristic and singled out Facebook and Twitter as the two determinant tools in many of the uprisings just listed. A debate developed quickly that saw critical voices (e.g., Gladwell 2010; Morozov 2012) confronting more optimistic views on the power of social networking sites in triggering protests and revolts (e.g., Bensalah 2012; Castells 2012). In this chapter we go beyond this debate and argue that social movement literature has to offer some analytical tools to foster our understanding of social networking sites with regard to pro-democracy and anti-austerity protests—in order not just to discuss their role (or not) in recent uprisings, but also to address more complex patterns of entrenchment between social movements and social media platforms. In particular, in what follows we first present some common aspects of current mobilisations across the world, discussing in particular the similarities of their "repertoire of communication" (Mattoni 2012; 2013b). Following some recent development in research on communication and social movements, we will indeed single out complex communication strategies and practices in which information develops (also) from below (della Porta 2013). We then introduce two analytical dimensions rooted in social movement studies—the temporal and the relational dimensions of social movements—that we consider relevant to foster a critical discussion about social networking sites in current mobilisations. We go a step further in our discussion, considering protests in the Middle East, in North Africa, in southern Europe and in North America to show how these two dimensions might help us to put into perspective platforms such as Facebook and Twitter. Conclusions summarise our main arguments and suggest further lines of inquiry in contemporary social movements.

2. SHARED TRAITS IN PRO-DEMOCRACY AND ANTI-AUSTERITY MOVEMENTS

The opening summary just presented shows that protest occurred in countries as diverse as Iceland and Egypt in a relatively short 5-year time frame, from 2008 to 2013. The debate is still open on whether we should consider these protests as part of the same global cycle of contention, especially if we consider the previous cycle of protest that shook the world from late in the 1990s to early in the 2000s. The so-called global justice movement (della Porta 2007) that became visible worldwide in November 1999 during the massive protests against the WTO meeting in Seattle developed in different countries across the world, but its activists always acted within a common framework by fighting against the neo-liberal globalisation supported through transnational governmental bodies. At the same time, through the organizations of social fora at the global and regional level, activists were able to create spaces to elaborate concrete alternatives and foster emerging alliances so that the slogan 'another world is possible' could become a reality. These protests and meetings were nomadic, because they followed the summits of such international organizations, and clearly transnational, because the political and economic powers against which protesters struggle were supranational governmental bodies beyond the nation states. It was to some extent easy, despite the obvious differences, to link under a common label protests and meetings in diverse cities such as Seattle, Porto Alegre, Prague, Gothenburg, Genoa and Florence, just to name a few of them. On the contrary, mobilisations breaking out in the past five years are much more oriented towards the national level: protesters in Tunisia and Egypt asked for the end of their authoritarian regimes, targeting first their national political systems; those in southern Europe were against the way in which their corrupted political elites were managing the economic crisis, as the example of Portugal shows well (Baumgarten 2013); in the U.S., finally, activists targeted one of the symbols of global finance, Wall Street, but also remained deeply anchored to some pressing domestic issues related to the economic crisis, like property foreclosures and students debts; also in more recent mobilisations in Turkey and Brazil, the demands of those who took the streets were prominently oriented towards the domestic level. However, despite claims often focused on national governments, with only a few attempts in organizing transnational protest actions (Tejerina et al. 2013), there are some elements that link in subtle ways the rage of thousands of Icelanders back in 2008 and the uprising of millions of Brazilians in 2013. This is not just a matter of temporality—all these mobilisations happened in the midst of a global financial and economic crisis. There are other connections that let these protests echoing each other go beyond the sometimes deep political, social and cultural differences that characterise them.

First, in the majority of the cases we can see at work the diffusion through adaptation of forms of protests beyond the usual demonstration in the streets. Indeed, almost all of these mobilisations put the protest camp at the centre of the repertoire of contention. Activists across the world, indeed, opted for a stable and visible place in which they carried out the daily protest activities that sustained their mobilisations. The protest camp became very much entrenched with the collective identity characterising these mobilisations, despite its organization and the meaning changing according to the social, political and cultural context in which it was embedded. Second, practices and imageries of direct democracy were central in general assemblies, group meetings and other informal gatherings among protesters. The protest camps quickly became a political laboratory where activists experimented with direct democracy combined with a strenuous critique of existing forms of political systems: whether totalitarian regimes or representative democracies, the political elites with power in the countries where mobilisations took place were always opposed to the people who mobilised from below, pushing forward a different idea of politics and societies. Third, the resonance of similar frames across different protests was consistent with the activists' acknowledgement of being part of a common global struggle for justice and dignity. This was especially clear in the framing of protesters and their protest targets. Protest participants, indeed, represented themselves through the plain language of "the people" opposing political and economic elites—often referred to as corrupted, irresponsible and ambiguous. In this sense, protesters across the world engaged in an "attribution of similarities" (Tilly and Tarrow 2007, 95) to otherwise different contexts. Finally, protesters all over the world also shared a similar "repertoire of communication" (Mattoni 2012; 2013b). Social networking platforms—like Facebook, Twitter and YouTube—often used in combination with smartphone and other portable devices, seem to hold a central position.

The use of information and communication technologies in social movements is certainly not a novelty. Activists in the global justice movement organized across space through the use of Internet tools like IRC chats and mailing lists, and online forums (Juris 2005). In 1999, moreover, they gave life to the famous alternative informational website Indymedia, which was first set up on the occasion of protests in Seattle against the WTO summit and quickly replicated all over the world (Kidd 2003; Morris 2004; Pickard 2006). Indymedia became a point of reference for activists in many countries who had their own space to provide grassroots coverage of their own protests, inspired by the slogan, 'Don't hate the media. Become the media.' In the same vein, a number of national and international websites flourished that supported social movement groups and organizations all over the world. Activists created their own spaces of communication, used to share information, coordinate actions and organize protests (della Porta and Mosca 2005). Although differing in quality (especially in terms of interactivity), organizational websites allowed for more internal transparency, the spreading of alternative information and mobilisation instruments (ibid.). Notwithstanding the many challenges new technologies posed, the appropriation of and experimentation with information and communication technologies expanded the repertoire of communication, adding yet another important tool of (self-)mediation to the hands of activists. It does not come as a surprise, therefore, that mobilisations occurring from 2008 onwards made use of social networking platforms that began to emerge late in 2004: the repertoire of communication, which had quickly included the previous generation of Internet tools and web platforms, expanded again when activists began to employ Facebook, Twitter, YouTube and other social networking sites during their mobilisations. This development implied something more than an increase in the number of tools available for communication in the hands of protesters. More specifically, we argue that "activist media practices" (Mattoni 2012; 2013b) in current protests showed some continuities but also some crucial differences along three dimensions that are useful to understand the cultures of participation and communication in social movements: collectiveness, openness and possession (della Porta and Mattoni 2012).

The degree of collectiveness in the creation of media contents is the first axis. In the global justice movement many alternative informational websites and outlets were based on the collective production of contents to be published and spread through activists networks. With this regard, Indymedia was an exception—and to some extent a prefiguration of what came with social networking sites—in that individual activists across the world could upload their own media content, whether written accounts or pictures/videos of protests. However, they did this within a shared activist culture, signalled, for instance, by the fact that in almost all the cases the faces of those involved in protest actions reported through pictures were rendered unrecognisable to protect their privacy. Social networking sites, on the contrary, went beyond activist culture because they included a large amount of newcomers with regard to political participation. Therefore, they not only produced and uploaded media content at the individual level but also did so independently from a shared activist culture. This had some consequences on the spread of different organizational frames among protesters. As Juris noted, "Whereas the use of listservs and websites in the movements for global justice during the late 1990s and 2000s helped to generate and diffuse distributed network-ing logics, in the #Occupying movements social media have contributed to powerful logics of aggregation" (Juris 2012, 260–261). While the logic of networking aims at connecting diverse collective actors, the logic of aggrega-tion involves the assembling of diverse individuals in physical spaces. Rather than networks of networks, social media facilitate a mass aggregation of indi-viduals (ibid., 267). In fact, the very characteristics of the technology used by the activists have been said to play an important role in the creation of a participatory ethics that stresses individual involvement over organizational involvement (ibid.). Cheaper and easier to use than the previous Internet instruments of communication, social media allow for more subjective inter-vention that extends beyond traditional activist communities, but also a more submerged and fragmented form of communication.

The second axis is the degree of openness of participation in the making of media content. Indeed, some media platforms and technologies are more open than others with regard to who can produce and diffuse texts, pictures and videos. In the global justice movement there were many examples of alterna-tive media outlets that were open towards participation. Again, Indymedia is a good example here, because it was based on an open publishing system that granted the anonymity of those who wished to publish articles, comments and other contributions. Pictures and other materials published in Indymedia about counter-summit demonstrations provided broader visibility to the social movement actions, and mainstream media journalists used these websites as grassroots news sources to cover protests. But beyond activist circles, alter-native informational websites like Indymedia were much less known and used. In comparison, social media platforms were incredibly more open to the contribution of a diverse range of users, many of whom did not have any previous activist engagement. Long before the first protests in Iceland and Tunisia erupted, millions of people around the world were already employing Facebook and other social networking sites as a mundane and routine plat-form to interact with friends, colleagues and acquaintances beyond the sphere of activism. Activists, of course, might have used them before, but alongside millions of other users who were not actively engaged in politics. In this sense, social networking sites presented themselves as much more accessible, and therefore open, web platforms than the alternative informational websites created in the context of the global justice movement.

Finally, the third axis is the degree of possession of the media outlet and/or technological infrastructure. It indicates the extent to which individual activists or activist groups that use media outlets also exert some form of control and/or ownership on the media outlet and/or technological infra-structure that they are using. In the global justice movement, activists who organized and supported mobilisations were to some extent early (creative) adopters of the latest available communication technology. Moreover, they created spaces for alternative communication that remained, in the majority of the cases, in their hands and worked within a non-profit logic: the Indymedia servers, for instance, were directly managed by activists. It is certainly true that commercial and corporate interests were at play also in the late 1990s with regard to the Internet, and that commercial Internet providers controlled some services, like private e-mails, that were broadly used within activists communities. Overall, however, the attention for the construction of independent Internet infrastructures and services was generally high within the global justice movement. In current protests, on the contrary, the widely used social networking sites were created independently from activist circles. Unlike alternative media entirely produced and controlled by social movement actors, social media platforms are commercial and corporate environments where activists spread alternative messages.

3. SOCIAL NETWORKING SITES FACING THE TEMPORAL AND RELATIONAL DIMENSIONS OF SOCIAL MOVEMENTS

Social movement scholars often mention that their own object of study is difficult to define at the empirical level. This is because social movements are neither concrete objects—like a poster calling for a demonstration— nor palpable subjects—like an association with its members and offices. Rather, social movements can be conceived as processes that interface with societies at many different levels. When conceptualising social movements as processes, two dimensions have a crucial role in the understanding of such empirical phenomena: the temporal and the relational dimensions. Social movements indeed unfold over time—sometimes they progress across weeks, and other times they take some months to develop; in some cases they even last years.

First, to take into consideration the temporality of social movements is certainly useful when considering the role of social networking sites during mobilisations. It indeed makes quite a difference to claim that Facebook had a positive role for the Egyptian uprising and, after some careful empirical analysis, to show that Facebook contributed to the first stages of the Egyptian protests, while it became less central once millions of protesters were in the streets at the end of January 2011. In other words, to address the temporality of social movements allows us to appreciate the dynamism of explanatory variables in the development of mobilisations, because their role is more often subjected to variation than confined to static interaction with protests (Koopmans 2004). We can indeed recognise, following much of current literature on the topic, that social networking sites clearly affected the spread of protests in the Middle East, in North Africa, southern Europe and North America. But in doing so it is necessary to think that, despite some stable features, their role changed according to the stage of mobilisation, the activities sustaining protests as well as the social actors who were using them.

Second, the debate on the use of social media platforms must be embedded within the complex nets of relations constructed within and outside social movements. Indeed, social movement actors are part of complex networks that go beyond the social movement organizations and groups promoting protests and include also their allies and adversaries, as well as "bystander publics, third parties and mediators" (Rucht 2004a, 212; see also Gamson 2004). Also in this case, to adopt an "ecological perspective" (Koopmans 2004) on social movements, inserting them in their broader organizational field, would allow us to understand that social networking sites are not just tools in the hands of activists. Rather, they are available to, and actually employed by, many other social actors who have a stake in the mobilisations and who simply watch protests evolving as distant audiences. Moreover, according to this perspective, we can go even further and consider social networking sites, or better the companies owning and managing them, as yet another social actor with whom activists interact during mobilisations.

In what follows we discuss the use of social networking sites in current mobilisations through the two analytical dimensions introduced earlier. In doing this, our aim is twofold. On the one side, we aim to critically bridge social movement literature and media studies literature—for a long time and still often developing in parallel without acknowledging each other (Downing 2008; Mattoni 2012; della Porta 2013)—in reflecting on how Facebook and Twitter sustained the mobilisations in the Middle East, in North Africa, southern Europe and North America. Indeed we use some of the analytical tools available in social movement studies to move beyond the polarisation of common positions about the role of social media in mobilisations, which oscillate between overly enthusiastic estimations and overly dismissive attitudes about the role that Facebook and Twitter played in recent protests. On the other side, our objective is to advance some preliminary hypotheses on the role of social networking sites during protests and to embed them in a broader space of mobilisation and communication processes.

3.1. The Temporal Dimension

Social movements occurred in specific stretches of time and, as such, they are immersed in diverse yet interrelated temporalities varying according to their duration over time. From a long-term perspective, social movements intertwine with "cultural epochs of contention" in which specific templates of contention are available to protesters (McAdam and Sewell 2001, 112). In fact, this concept echoes the idea of "repertoires of contentions" (Tilly 1978; 1995) that changes slowly over time and, as such, is characterised by a *longue durée*. There is then a medium-term temporality often referred to through two metaphors that have been also applied to current pro-democracy and anti-austerity mobilisations: "cycle of contention" (Tarrow

1989, 1994), "waves of protest" (Koopmans 2004) or "tides" (Beissinger 2002). Despite some conceptual difference, those terms convey the idea that social movement activities change over time. Even when cycles, waves or tides of contention go beyond their peaks, and visible protests become more rare, social movement actors are still there, if only in a state of latency (Melucci 1989). A third, more short-term temporality comes into play when social movements are in their mobilisation stage: a punctuated event that has a transformative power on the very unfolding of protests actions while they are occurring (McAdam and Sewell 2001).

Considering these three temporalities with regard to recent mobilisations can be particularly useful when analysing the role of social networking sites, in that instead of asking general questions like "Did Facebook sustain the Indignados movements?" we can focus on narrower inquiries about the overlapping of social networking sites from the long-, medium- and short-term perspective in social movements. Other authors already claimed that information and communication technologies, and not just social networking sites, altered considerably the "repertoire of contention" social movement actors use when they arise, to the point that we can speak today about a "digital repertoire of contention" (Earl and Kimport 2011). Following the work of Bennett and Segerberg (2013) we can see changes even at the level of the "cultural epoch of contention" because we live in times in which the usual logic of collective action did not disappear, but is now accompanied by a novel 'logic of connective action' based on technologies for personal communication. Either coordinated by social movement organizations or moved by more spontaneous crowds, the logic of connective action contributes to the diffusion of "personal action frames" (ibid.). Focusing on the Middle East and North Africa, Howard (2010, 201) also pointed out the influence of information and communication technologies on democratic change from 1994 to 2010 in seventy-five countries with large Muslim communities. He stressed, in fact, the role of the Muslim diaspora in the West in generating a transnational collective identity through a "significant amount of politically critical content via mass media such as radio, television, film, and newspapers" that is more and more accessible in Arab countries. So, "the internet has a causal and supportive role in the formation of democratic discourse in the Muslim communities of the developing world" (ibid., 40).

At the other extreme of the temporality spectrum stand short-term events that inform the unfolding of mobilisations when they are at their peak, when social movements articulate and re-articulate their activities and protests on a daily basis. For instance, like in a virtuous circle, the use of social media increased when mobilisations were at their peak in Egypt: "Facebook became something one had to have. Egypt gained more than 600,000 new Facebook users between January and February 2011 alone. On the day the Internet switched back on (February 2), 100,000 users joined this social networking space and it became the most accessed website in the country (followed by YouTube and Google), and aljazeera.net saw an incredible increase in page views and search attempts" (Aouragh and Alexander 2011, 1348). However, social media platforms were inserted in a media environment that revealed its multilayered composition, especially when protests accelerated. The quick tactical moves and changes that characterise mobilisations during their peak stages also intertwine with a composite media ecology in which social media platforms are just one of the means of communication that activists employ. Some evidence about Occupy Boston, one of the main protest camps during Occupy campaigns, proves, however, that the combined use of smartphones and social media platforms was relevant during the occupations. In the Occupy movement, "the combination of Twitter and smartphone, in particular, allows individuals to continually post and receive updates as well as to circulate images, and texts, constituting real-time, user-generated news feeds" (Juris 2012, 267). In Egypt, activists in the Tahrir Square also used other Internet services and platforms to spread information about protests: from e-mails to flyers, and from mobile text messages to pamphlets (Lim 2012). A recent study on mobile phones in the Spanish Indignados, moreover, pointed out that *"mobile ensembles, that is, the unique set of mobile (and other) technologies"* (Monterde and Postill 2014) changed according to the micro-phases of protest that punctuated the daily development of mobilisations. In other words, activists rapidly selected and combined different media practices from those available in their repertoire of communication when engaged in the most visible stages of contention. Of course, face-to-face interactions among activists also were important to support the passage of information, especially when the mobilisations entered in the stage of protest camps, in which general assemblies and working group meetings were mostly based on the physical co-presence of protest participants. Also, in southern European and Arab countries, where the connective tissue is based on stronger and denser social networks than in North America, face-to-face interactions were particularly important to spread news about demonstrations, especially at the beginning of the uprising (Lim 2012), as well as when the Egyptian government made it almost impossible to use Internet connections and mobile telephones, as we will also show in the next section. However, activists in Tahrir Square collected the videos and pictures that protest participants shot when the Internet was down in Egypt (Aouragh and Alexander 2011). They did so, once again, through the recombination of various media technologies, as an activist recalled:

> We built a media camp in Tahrir Square. It was two tents, and we were around five or six technical friends with their laptops, memory-readers, hard disks. We had all physical means with us and we hung a sign in Arabic and English on the tent itself saying, 'Focal point to gather videos and pictures from people in the street.' And we received a huge amount of videos and pictures and then we go back online and keep posting them online. In the first few hours, I gathered 75 gigabytes of pictures and videos from people in the streets. (ibid., 1352)

Finally, the medium-term temporality seems particularly relevant for contextualising the use of social networking sites in current protests. As we already pointed out, cycles, waves or tides include peaks in mobilisations, preceded and followed by stages of less visible grassroots politics in which activists do not organize contentious collective action. During these stages of latency, social and political actors that participated in protest engage in daily practices of resistance, focused on the continuation of interactions among activists and the circulation of information about contentious issues, which will then render possible the emergence and diffusion of other stages of mobilisation (Melucci 1982). Research on the role of social networking sites after the uprisings is still ongoing, but many scholars already argued that in stages of latency before mobilisations social networking sites prepared the ground for many of the current protests. In the recent protests, digital media also had a role during the "preparation stage" of protests, in which a number of web platforms contributed to the development of "shared grievances [. . .] and collective political goals" (Howard and Hussain 2013). The initial presence of a critical blogosphere and the increased use of Facebook groups and pages played an important role before mobilisations (Lim 2012). Bloggers were particularly important in denouncing police brutality in the years before the revolution took place in Egypt. The practice of blogging, however, went beyond the diffusion of counter-information since bloggers in the Arab world began to meet face-to-face in conferences devoted to the Internet, and this fostered the creation of social networks of like-minded bloggers, which then formed an important basis for protests (Tufekci and Wilson 2012). In other words, the presence of social media platforms can foster the creation of communities of practices—for instance, bloggers who begin to meet outside the blogosphere and construct social networks of like-minded individuals who trust one another.

Different digital media were used, however, in different ways. Facebook allowed for spreading information from (virtual) friend to (virtual) friend, as it is a social network enabling one to send messages to thousands of people, "with the added benefit that those receiving the messages were already interested and trusted the source" (Nunns and Idle 2011, 20). Facebook became a place where people could express their anger against the police, especially after the killing of Khaled Said, an Egyptian blogger who had denounced the involvement of police forces in drug trafficking, in June 2010. The Facebook page "We Are All Khaled Said," founded by Google executive Wael Ghonim and named after the young blogger killed by the police, already had over 350,000 members before January 14, 2011. Within Facebook, the pages of activist groups like the April 6 Youth Movement, founded in 2008, and the profiles of high-profile individuals such as Mohamed al-Baradei, Aida Seif-al-Dawla or Hossam el-Hamalawy not only were meeting points particularly instrumental in mobilising youth but also contributed to the circulation of many SMS, e-mails, tweets and Facebook posts (Aouragh and Alexander 2011, 1348). Social media, often paired with other Internet tools and web platforms, allowed the expression and sharing of emotions that triggered a sense of collective belonging based on opposition to police brutality. When Wael Ghonim invited "We Are All Khaled Said" Facebook members to protest on January 25, within three days more than fifty thousand people responded that they would attend. In this sense, social net-working sites acted as a tool of "hyper coordination" (Ling and Yttri 2002), similar to what happened with mobile telephones in many Middle Eastern and North African countries before the uprisings (Ibahrine 2008). Indeed, a recent study proves that "a spike in online revolutionary conversations often preceded major events on the ground" (Howard and Hussain 2013, 65).

Influenced by mobilisations in Tunisia, Egypt and other countries in the Middle East and North Africa, the protest of the Spanish Indignados was also highly mediated. Not by chance, at its origin was the campaign No Les Votes (Don't Vote for Them), asking people not to vote for any of the three major parties responsible for a hotly contested bill accused of attack-ing digital freedom in favour of media lobbies (as documents published by Wikileaks confirmed). Network organizations emerged during this cam-paign, among them Youth without a Future (Juventud Sin Futuro) and Real Democracy Now! (Democracia Real Ya! DRY). Following its roots in cam-paigns on media rights, the Spanish movement of the Indignados showed great skill in the use of new technologies. As Postill (2012) rightly described, "The key role played in the inception and coordination of the movement by hackers, bloggers, micro-bloggers, technopreneurs and online activists is hard to overestimate." In fact, "what is striking about 15-M nanostories is how successfully leading activists used Twitter in the build-up towards the 15 May protests across Spain. By means of Twitter hashtags such as #15M or #15mani (#15mdemo), DRY [Democracia Real Ya] supporters were able not only to rally protesters at short notice but also to set the changing political and emotional tone of the campaign" (ibid.). In the words of two activists, "The direction (el sentit) is created mostly on Twitter. Hashtags serve not only to organise the debate but also to set the collective mood: #wearenot-going, #wearenotafraid, #fearlessbcn, #awakenedbarrios, #puigresignation, #15mmarcheson #closetheparliament" (ibid.). In fact, "the nanostories being shared about specific protests or power abuses may be short-lived, but over time they add up to a powerful sense of common purpose amongst hundreds of thousands of people. Together, they form a grand narrative of popular struggle against a corrupt political and economic order" (ibid.).

To consider the temporal dimension of social movements from the perspective of their medium-term temporality also casts lights on the connec-tions with previous protests only apparently not related to the current ones. And this, in turn, might enrich the understanding of social networking sites—and the media practices around them. Frequently mobilisations have some kind of linkage with social movement actors that originated from protests that preceded them. This was also true in the case of protests in the Middle East and North Africa (Gelvin 2013; Alexander 2010; El-Mahdi and Marfleet

2009), but also in the case of Occupy Wall Street protests (Bang 2011; Graeber 2012) and the Indignados movement (Romanos 2013). The latter is a particularly good example in this vein. The 15m protests can indeed be interpreted as the last act of a flow of civil disobedience in Spain, whose most immediate precedent is the unstable and intermittent *online crowd* (Sampedro 2005) that took to the streets in Spain on March 13, 2004, in response to the electoral manipulation of the terrorist attacks of March 11. Previous mobilisations contributed to the sedimentation of a diverse range of media practices that then converged in the Indignados movement, in which social media were inserted in a broad repertoire of communication. In this regard, Postill's partial lists of media use that made the M5 movement shows that a wide range of media technologies beyond Facebook and Twitter were used during the mobilisation: "web forums [. . .], blogs [. . .], collaborative documents such as manifestos, press releases and directories; pedagogical materials [. . .]; analogic versions of digital media forms, e.g. post-it tweets on square kiosks; cartoons published online as well as in print form; mainstream and alternative radio phone-ins; citizen photography, including Flickr group Spanish Revolution; videoclips [. . .]; live streaming by small alternative media; aggregators and link recommendation sites" (Postill 2012). Occupy Wall Street also deployed a diverse range of mediation tools that went beyond Internet services and web platforms: journals and publishing venues were created (Gitlin 2012) beyond websites. Bennet and Segerberg (2013, 180; see also 182) list new technologies used within a crowd-enhancing logic: "SMS networks, email lists, Facebook, Livestream, you Tube and Twitter." The Tumblr site was used to invite individuals to present their personal stories, through a full photo and a (short or long) statement (ibid., 181). In many cities, activists engaged in the creation of self-produced radical magazines about the camps and the protests in order to reach people who did not have an Internet connection. In doing this, they reconnected with the long-standing tradition of radical zines related to underground cultures, sometimes linked with subterranean politics of resistance (Duncombe 1997).

3.2. The Relational Dimension

Another dimension of social movements is their relational character, according to which they are embedded in a network of relations that goes beyond activist circles. Indeed, they are situated in organizational fields where a number of social actors also interact with and respond to protesters. Keeping this in mind is particularly relevant when thinking about the ubiquity of social networking sites: as we pointed out earlier, unlike other kinds of movement media used in past mobilisations, social networking sites were used well before the protests spread all over the world. And they were used for many other reasons than political engagement. When looking at the uprising in Egypt and Tunisia, for instance, research on Twitter communication flow reveals that a variety of social actors employed these tools to produce meaning around the two uprisings (Lotan et al. 2011). While some of them were individual activists and activist groups, others were not related to protests in a direct manner. Rather, they were positioned outside the social movement milieu: they were mainstream press—both offline and online—and journalists; non-media organizations; Internet celebrities and researchers; and even, although in a small percentage according to the study, political actors linked to the regime targeted by protests (ibid.). Beyond the data gathered, this research clearly shows that social networking sites were embedded in the broader networks of relations in which social movements develop. For this reason it makes sense to consider the relation between social media platforms and social movements from different angles, taking into consideration how they intertwined with regard to the multiple relations that occur within and beyond the social movement milieu.

The relational side of social movement is first of all related to the interactions among activists who participate in the same protest. Within the social movement milieu, indeed, not everyone is equal: different degrees and modes of participation usually characterise activists involved in the same protests. Not all act as leaders and, even in more horizontal social movements, not all have the same degree of engagement in protest activities. The very use of social media platforms can also have an impact on the informal hierarchies of relations within social movements. At the beginning of the protests in Egypt and Spain, for instance, Facebook groups that eventually became intrinsically linked to protests—such as the 'We Are All Khaled Said' group in Egypt and the 'Democracia Real' group in Spain—were set up by tech-savvy individuals who became relevant figures within the movement (Gerbaudo 2012). During the Egyptian revolution, moreover, the flow of tweets revealed the presence of celebrities among Twitter users, based on the frequency of their tweets, which also imparted the idea that information about the revolution was not based on a horizontal network of interactions (Papacharissi and Oliveira 2012). In the Occupy Wall Street protests the intense use of Facebook groups frequently furthered the development of harsh discussions among protesters concerning issues related to Occupy Wall Street at the general level, the daily life at the camp and the management of the Facebook group itself (Mattoni 2013a). While the first two issues were also able to play a role in the emergence of a shared understanding of protests, recombining the presence of different activist political cultures, the third issue introduced the question of power within social media, a topic that could also have an impact at the level of offline general assemblies (ibid.).

A second important aspect when considering the network of relations on which social movements rest is those activists who might be engaged—or willing to engage—in similar protests in other parts of the world. Similar to what happened with alternative informational websites during the global justice movement, social media were also able to bridge movements cross-nationally. This was also due to the relatively low cross-country variation in platforms' appearance and affordances that provided a homogeneous global infrastructure for communication to the people in countries as diverse as Tunisia, Spain and the U.S. While the use of the Internet during the global justice movement also depended on the Internet culture of different activist groups and organizations (Kavada 2013), the largely diffuse and often individual use of social networking sites tended to create a transnational communication culture (Cottle 2011) in which the very practice of uploading and sharing a video denouncing police brutality, as happened in Egypt some months before the mobilisation began, could quickly create "visual injustice symbols" (Olesen 2013), gaining regional and global resonance in diverse audiences across the world. Of course, examples of cross-national bridging between movements also occurred at the regional level. In protests across the Middle East and North Africa, thanks to the combination of old and new communication techniques, information overcame borders—as "Egyptian activists were supported by the flow of information coming to them from abroad, while simultaneously influencing international public opinion abroad, through their own coverage of the Egyptian uprising and the information they provided on it" (Khamis and Vaughn 2011). When the mobilisation began, messages from Tunisian protesters spread on the Egyptian blogs: they "advised their Egyptian counterparts to protest at nighttime for safety, to avoid suicide operations, to use media to convey their message for outside pressure, to spray-paint security forces' armored vehicles black to cover the windshield, and to wash their faces with Coca-Cola to reduce the impact of tear gas" (Eltantawy and Wiest 2011, 1215). Activists from different countries also used Facebook to exchange advice: "Tunisian activists on Facebook posted 'Advice to the youth of Egypt: Put vinegar or onion under your scarf for tear gas' and brainstormed with their Egyptian counterparts on how to evade state surveillance, resist rubber bullets, and construct barricades" (Khamis and Vaughn 2011).

Supporters of protests, when not directly involved in street protest activities, contributed to raise the visibility of mobilisations on social networking sites. Facebook and probably even more so Twitter continued to be important for those living outside Egypt, who expressed their support for the uprising and exchanged information about the revolution on social media platforms. The blogging service Twitter (with 175 million registered users in 2010) allowed participants to post their comments, and 'tweet' about specific subject, including hashtags that (such as #Jan25 for Egypt or #sidibouzid for Tunisia) permitted people to launch as well as to follow protest events. In the very first week of the protest as many as 1.5 million Egypt-related tweets were counted (Aouragh and Alexander 2011), in many cases allowing for contact between activists and foreign journalists (Lotan et al. 2011). The #Jan25 hash tag produced up to twenty-five tweets per minute during the day of the protest (ibid.). However, similar to what has been observed during the Iranian uprising in 2009 (Morozov 2012), the majority of tweets about protests in the Middle East and North Africa were produced outside the region and the majority of them were produced by major mainstream news organizations (Aday et al. 2013).

Another relevant social actor in the network of relations in which social movements are embedded is mainstream media (Gamson 2004; Gamson and Wolfsfeld 1993). Literature on the topic points out the existence of an "asymmetric relationship" (Rucht 2004b) between mainstream media and activists: the latter, indeed, need the former to be visible to broader publics, while mainstream media can continue to function and exist without protests in the streets. As we also pointed out, already with the first generation of Internet services and web platforms, activists found new channels through which their own coverage of protest events spread, bypassing journalists. Media activism indeed grew considerably during the global justice movement, to the point that alternative informational websites like Indymedia also became a news source for mainstream media during counter-summit and social fora. But it was through social networking sites coupled with the spread of smartphones that virtually everyone participating in protests could become an individual broadcaster. Similar to what happened in many other countries around the world, in the Middle East and North Africa social networking sites supported "citizen journalism" (Allan and Thorsen 2009) that went beyond the self-censoring, state-controlled flows of information by first denouncing police repression and then documenting protest activities. As an activist declared, "To have a space, an online space, to write and talk [to] people, to give them messages which will increase their anger, this is my favorite way of online activism. This is the way online activism contributed to the revolution. When you asked people to go and demonstrate against the police, they were ready because you had already provided them with materials which made them angry" (Aouragh and Alexander 2011, 1348). In other words, social media platforms were relevant in "promoting a new form of citizen journalism, which provides a platform for ordinary citizens to express themselves and document their own versions of reality" (Khamis and Vaughn 2011).

Moreover, social networking sites allow for an easy and cheap transfer of content from one platform to another. This affordance in social media rendered the passage of information from specialised to general audiences more fluid and also quick. A good example is the video of twenty-six-year-old activist Asmaa Mahfouz that stated, "If you stay home, you deserve all that's being done to you, and you will be guilty before your nation and your people. Go down to the street, send SMSes, post it on the 'Net, make people aware" (Wall and El Zahed 2011, 1333). The video was first uploaded on Facebook on January 18, and it quickly went viral on YouTube after a few hours, reaching people beyond the personal ties of the activist. Eventually it was translated and published on the websites of mainstream western news organizations, like the *New York Times* (ibid.). Social networking sites not only became a relevant source of information for western mass media but also supported the ability of activists to quickly transcend the boundaries of the social movement milieu and, although in a mediated manner, to gain contact with dispersed and fragmented audiences across the world. In this sense, social networking sites went beyond the blurring of the usual cleavage between media producers and media consumers. They also added a further level of complexity to the usual differentiation in the network of relations in which social movement actors are embedded. At the same time, the use of social media, interacting with other means of communication, could contribute to the creation of some foundational events (della Porta 2014). Protests, such as the ones in Tahrir or in Sol, were filmed and tweeted, increasing their emotional impact over a much broader constituency than the ones who were actually present. Images circulated through social media increased the spread of the emotional intensity of the protests. In this vein, the use of Twitter during the revolution proved to be a tool for sharing information, but also for expressing solidarity and emotions related to the uprising, leading to the emergence of hybrid journalistic practices revolving around "affective news" (Papacharissi and Oliveira 2012).

While it is certainly true that social media partially reversed the asymmetry between activists and journalists, it is also true that mainstream channels of communication remained central in amplifying the messages of protesters in the Middle East, North Africa, in southern Europe and in North America. As Postill (2012) noted,

> The combination of a politicised pan-Arab TV network (Al Jazeera), widely available mobile phones with photo and video capabilities, and the rapid growth of social media such as Facebook and YouTube since 2009, has created a 'new media ecology' that authoritarian regimes are finding very difficult to control.

The information cascade generated through the social media was impossible to stop for the authorities, since it spread simultaneously through a diverse range of media channels and platforms.

Finally, social movements interact with public authorities that are often hostile. The control of media technologies, and the activists' content that is spread through them, has been always at stake during waves of protests, especially when public authorities have perceived massive mobilisations as a direct threat to their power. States in both democratic and authoritarian countries often use a very basic, but also to some extent effective, way to control digital media. During mobilisations they attempt to interrupt online communication through four different forms of repression: forcing Internet service providers to deny access to their online services; arresting and/or intimidating individual activists who are central in the production of movements' information; shutting down specific websites and/or portals; and shutting down the entire Internet network in the country (Howard, Agarwal and Hussain 2011). In the case of mobilisations in the Middle East and North Africa, indeed, the best evidence that digital media were an important causal factor in the Arab Spring is that dictators treated them as such. The months during which the Arab Spring took place had the most national blackouts, network shutdowns, and tool blockage to date. But just as activists had a long history of using digital media, authoritarian regimes had a history of responding to political communication occurring over digital networks. (Howard and Hussain 2013, 69)

In the case of the Egyptian uprising, for instance, the authoritarian regime decided to shut down Internet access when mobilisations in the streets gained participants. Moreover, similar to the case of mobilisation, there is also in the case of counter-mobilisation a process of double diffusion, implying adaptation by learning but also innovation (della Porta and Tarrow 2011). Again, in the uprisings that happened in the Middle East and North Africa, security services in countries such as Bahrain, Saudi Arabia and Syria learned from the mistakes of their counterparts in Egypt and Tunisia, not only censoring the information on the web but also using new technologies to control the emerging opposition. Indeed, the use of Internet technologies in the hands of states can be much more sophisticated in the prevention and repression of mobilisations, as other chapters in this volume also suggest. With regard to prevention, state actors might engage in subtle counter-information campaigns on social media platforms, as happened in 2009 in Azerbaijan when two bloggers confronted police brutality and were then arrested. In the months following these events, political participation dramatically decreased in the country, as well as the number of engaged political bloggers, as a result of networked authoritarianism tactics on the side of state actors (Pearce and Kendzior 2012). With regard to repression, state actors might buy and use corporate Internet technologies to increase their intelligence capabilities against activists of the political opposition. So-called deep packet inspection software that is able to perform high-level data mining of activists' online activities has been used as one of the repressive tools in Iran, Lybia, Barhain and Syria, where it was also used to monitor and repress the activities of the regime opponents (Fuchs 2013). During Occupy Wall Street protests, instead, police forces used facial recognition software coupled with Facebook visual data in order to profile activists who participated in the mobilisations (Hodai 2013).

However, the use of Internet technologies in the context of political mobilisations always developed according to "a pendulum swing from activist advantage to government revanche to dense tactical contention between the two" (Joyce 2011). Indeed, as it is frequently the case when activism is a highly risky activity, information and communication technologies were also used during protests in the Middle East and North Africa to reduce the risks of repression (e.g., through the use of tools such as Hotspot Shield and Tor, which protect the anonymity of the user), spread information about how to improve security and call for attention when in danger (Eltantawy and Wiest

2011, 1215). Creative responses were given to the regime's ban on Internet and mobile phone access (from January 28, 2011, and for about five days): tweeting the websites of proxy servers; setting up FTP (file transfer protocol) accounts to transmit videos to international media; "using landlines to connect to internet services in neighbouring countries by calling international numbers with older dial-up modems"; even resorting "to using Morse code, fax machines, and ham radio to get the word out about events on the ground" (Khamis and Vaughn 2011). The website of the group We Rebuild transcribed transmissions from Egyptian amateur radio stations; resources for circumventing the blackout were published; there was the smuggling of "satellite phones and satellite modems into Egypt, which did not depend on Egypt's infrastructure to function" (ibid.). Blogs gave advice about how to use dial-up on mobile phones and laptops, and suggested connecting to the Internet service provider Noor, which was left operational as it was used by the Egyptian stock exchange and western companies. To facilitate communication by protesters some of its subscribers even removed their passwords for Wi-Fi access. When the Al Jazeera television channel in Cairo was taken down, people started watching Al Jazeera via Hotbird and Arabsat. Citizens also continued to tweet by calling friends abroad and asking them to tweet their messages or using the 'speak to tweet' tool, provided by engineers from Twitter, Google and SayNow, which transformed voice messages into Twitter messages (Eltantawy and Wiest 2011). Social networking sites like Facebook and Twitter, moreover, were ubiquitous with regard to the category of users who engage with them: if it is true that they were massively employed by protesters, it is equally true that during recent mobilisations, countermovements, governmental actors and surveillance forces attempted to control them through actions against the physical infrastructure of information and communication technologies, in order to employ them against protesters during different stages of mobilisations (Howard and Hussain 2013). Facebook, Twitter and other social networking sites can also be transformed into oppressive tools by authoritarian governments that may use them as powerful means of digital surveillance to track down the accounts of protesters or, in addition, to fuel crowd practices of repression by asking users of social media platforms to recognise and denounce activists involved in protests.

In short, social networking sites might be used by activists as well as by their opponents in a dynamic relationship of power and counter-power based on actions and reactions that become more intense during the peak of mobilisations. It is also true, though, that social media platforms constitute a corporate power in themselves that also challenge activists during latency stages. Social networking sites such as Facebook, indeed, have a commercial and corporate nature that can function as a constraint for social movement actors in at least two manners: through the platform design and the company policies (Youmans and York 2012). At the same time, data produced through and circulated across social networking sites are owned and controlled by private corporate companies: this renders activists using them more vulnerable with regard to their privacy and contents, especially when private corporate interests align with the desire of state repression in times of mobilisation. It has to be said, though, that social movement actors attempted to counterbalance the power of commercial and corporate social networking sites by engaging with the development of independent infrastructures for communication. Even before recent protests, and during stages of latency in which they do not engage in protests, activist groups have begun to experiment with the creation of social media platforms positioned outside market logic in recent years. Although targeting individuals who also act outside the social movement milieu, these social media platforms are intrinsically linked to activism. They support the creation of independent infrastructures for communication, often designed with activists' needs in mind—for instance, in terms of data protection. The creation of such independent infrastructures for communication can be seen as a form of activism in itself. Well before the diffusion of social media platforms, collectives of radical techies, such as Riseup and Autistici/Inventati, provided activists with e-mails, discussion lists, forums and blog services that allowed high levels of data protection (Barassi and Treré 2012). Recently, moreover, social movement actors have begun to experiment with Internet services and platforms that offer similar functionalities to corporate media platforms paired with strong data protection and platforms designed with activists' needs in mind, including Crabgrass, Briar and Thimbl.

4.   CONCLUSIONS

In this chapter we discussed three different aspects related to social networking sites in protests that recently occurred in the Middle East, North Africa, southern Europe and North America. We first considered the similarities between this diverse group of protests, considering in particular their repertoire of communication and contrasting it with the Internet use during the global justice movement that occurred between the late 1990s and the early 2000s. We then introduced two relevant dimensions for the study of mobilisation—the temporal and the relational dimensions—and employed them to inform some reflections on how social media platforms were embedded with the pro-democracy and anti-austerity protests. Based on secondary sources and existing studies on the topic, our chapter shows that at least two lines of inquiry seem particularly fruitful to understand the role of social media platforms in contemporary mobilisations. Apart from inserting social networking sites in the broader repertoire of communication that social movements deploy, research would benefit from more explicit comparative frameworks. On the one side, cross-time comparison that takes into account the diverse temporalities of social movements is required to grasp the differences that social networking sites have: from a long-term perspective, thus comparing communication flows and media practices in current and past social movements; from a medium-term perspective, hence comparing the use of social media platforms in the different stages of mobilisations and, in particular, contrasting their role in latency and visibility phased of contention; and finally form a short-term perspective, therefore looking at how social networking sites are used during different social movement activities in the daily unfolding of events at the peak of mobilisations. On the other side, taking into consideration the relational dimension of social movements paves the road to a cross-actor comparison in the use of social networking sites during mobilisations. This approach would be particularly interesting to cast light on the power dynamics that occur within and beyond the social movement milieu when social networking sites come into play. It would be also useful to understand, to what extent supporters, mass media and opponents employ social media platforms during mobilisations and with what objectives.

NOTE

1. The two authors discussed and wrote collaboratively and equally the present chapter. However, Donatella della Porta is the principal author of the sections "Introduction," "Shared Traits in Pro-democracy and Anti-austerity Movements" and "Conclusions"; Alice Mattoni is the principal author of the section "Social Networking Sites Facing the Temporal and Relational Dimensions of Social Movements."

REFERENCES

Aday, Sean, Henry Farrell, Deen Freelon, Marc Lynch, John Sides and Michael Dewar. 2013. Watching from Afar: Media Consumption Patterns around the Arab Spring. *American Behavioral Scientist* 57 (7): 899–919.

Alexander, Anne. 2010. Leadership and Collective Action in the Egyptian Trade Unions. *Work, Employment & Society* 24 (2): 241–259.

Allan, Stuart, and Einar Thorsen. 2009. *Citizen Journalism: Global Perspectives.* New York: Peter Lang.

Aouragh, Miryam, and Anne Alexander. 2011. The Egyptian Experience: Sense and Nonsense of the Internet Revolution. *International Journal of Communication* 5: 1344–1358.

Bang, Aragorn. 2011. *Occupy Everything: Anarchists in the Occupation Movement 2009–2011.* Berkley, CA: Little Black Cart.

Barassi, Veronica, and Emiliano Treré. 2012. Does Web 3.0 come after Web 2.0? Deconstructing theoretical assumptions through practice. *New Media & Society* 14 (8): 1269–1285.

Baumgarten, Britta. 2013. Geração à Rasca and Beyond: Mobilizations in Portugal after 12 March 2011. *Current Sociology* 61 (4): 457–473.

Bennett, W. Lance, and Alexandra Segerberg. 2013. *The Logic of Connective Action: Digital Media and the Personalization of Contentious Politics.* Cambridge, UK: Cambridge University Press.

Bensalah, Mounir. 2012. *Reseaux Sociaux et Revolutions Arabes?* Paris: Michalon Editeur.

Beissinger, Mark R. 2002. *Nationalist Mobilization and the Collapse of the Soviet State.* Cambridge, UK: Cambridge University Press.

Castells, Manuel. 2012. *Networks of Outrage and Hope: Social Movements in the Internet Age.* Malden, MA: Polity Press.

Cottle, Simon. 2011. Media and the Arab Uprisings of 2011: Research Notes. *Journalism* 12 (5): 647–659.

Della Porta, Donatella. 2007. *The Global Justice Movement: Cross National and Transnational Perspectives.* London: Paradigm.

———. 2013. *Can Democracy Be Saved: Participation, Deliberation and Social Movements.* Oxford: Polity Press.

———. 2014. *Mobilizing for Democracy.* Oxford: Oxford University Press.

Della Porta, Donatella, and Alice Mattoni. 2012. Cultures of Participation in Social Movements. In *The Participatory Cultures Handbook*, edited by Aaron Delwiche and Jennifer Jacobs Henderson, 170–181. London: Routledge.

Della Porta, Donatella, and Lorenzo Mosca. 2005. Global-Net for Global Movements? A Network of Networks for a Movement of Movements. *Journal of Public Policy* 25 (1): 165–190.

Della Porta, Donatella, and Sidney Tarrow. 2011. Interactive Diffusion: The Coevolution of Police and Protest Behavior with an Application to Transnational Contention. *Comparative Political Studies* 45 (1): 119–152.

Downing, John. 2008. Social Movement Theories and Alternative Media. *Communication, Culture & Critique* 1 (1): 40–50.

Duncombe, Stephen. 1997. *Notes from Underground: Zines and the Politics of Alternative Culture.* London: Verso.

Earl, Jennifer, and Katrina Kimport. 2011. *Digitally Enabled Social Change: Activism in the Internet Age.* Boston, MA: MIT Press.

El-Mahdi, Rabab, and Philip Marfleet. 2009. *Egypt: The Moment of Change.* London: Zed Books.

Eltantawy, Nahed, and Julie B. Wiest. 2011. Social Media in the Egyptian Revolution: Reconsidering Resource Mobilization Theory. *International Journal of Communication* 5: 1207–1224.

Fuchs, Christian. 2013. Societal and Ideological Impacts of Deep Packet Inspection Internet Surveillance. *Information, Communication & Society* 16 (8): 1328–1359.

Gamson, William A. 2004. Bystanders, Public Opinion and the Media. In *The Blackwell Companion to Social Movements*, edited by David A. Snow, Sarah A. Soule and Hanspeter Kriesi, 242–261. Oxford: Blackwell.

Gamson, William A., and Gadi Wolfsfeld. 1993. Movements and Media as Interacting Systems. *Annals of the American Academy of Political and Social Science* 528: 114–125.

Gelvin, Jame L. 2013. Conclusion: The Arab World at the Intersection of the National and the Transnational. In *The Arab Spring: Change and Resistance in the Middle East*, edited by Mark L. Haas and David W. Lesch, 238–255. Boulder, CO: Westview Press.

Gerbaudo, Paolo. 2012. *Tweets and the Streets: Social Media and Contemporary Activism.* London: Pluto Press.

Gitlin, Todd. 2012. *Occupy Nation: The Roots, the Spirit, and the Promise of Occupy Wall Street.* New York: It Books.

Gladwell, Malcolm. 2010. Small Change. *New Yorker*, October 4. http://www.newyorker.com/reporting/2010/10/04/101004fa_fact_gladwell.

Graeber, David. 2012. *The Democracy Project: A History, a Crisis, a Movement.* London: Allen Lane.

Hodai, Beau. 2013. *Dissent or Terror: How the Nation's Counter Terrorism Apparatus, in Partnership with Corporate America, Turned on Occupy Wall Street.* Center for Media and Democracy. http://www.prwatch.org/files/Dissent%20or%20Terror%20 FINAL_0.pdf.

Howard, Philip N. 2010. *The Digital Origins of Dictatorship and Democracy: Information Technology and Political Islam.* Oxford: Oxford University Press.

Howard, Philip N., Sheetal D. Agarwal and Muzammil M. Hussain. 2011. When Do States Disconnect Their Digital Networks? Regime Responses to the Political Uses of Social Media. *Communication Review* 14 (3): 216–232.

Howard, Philip N., and Muzzamil M. Hussain. 2013. *Democracy's Fourth Wave?: Digital Media and the Arab Spring.* Malden, MA: Oxford University Press.

Ibahrine, Mohammad. 2008. Mobile Communication and Sociopolitical Change in the Arab World. In *Handbook of Mobile Communication Studies*, edited by James E. Katz, 257–272. Cambridge, MA: MIT Press.

Joyce, Mary. 2011. The Proof Is in the Pendulum: A History of Digital Activism and Repression. *Meta-Activism Blog.* http://wp.me/p12vbQ-DB.

Juris, Jeffrey S. 2005. The New Digital Media and Activist Networking within Anti-corporate Globalization Movements. *ANNALS of the American Academy of Political and Social Science* 597 (1): 189–208.

———. 2012. Reflections on #Occupy Everywhere: Social Media, Public Space, and Emerging Logics of Aggregation. *American Ethnologist* 39 (2): 259–279.

Kavada, Anastasia. 2013. Internet Cultures and Protest Movements: The Cultural Links between Strategy, Organizing and Online Communication. In *Mediation and Protest Movements*, edited by Bart Cammaerts, Alice Mattoni and Patrick McCurdy, 75–94. Bristol: Intellect.

Khamis, Sahar, and Katherine Vaughn. 2011. Cyberactivism in the Egyptian Revolution: How Civic Engagement and Citizen Journalism Tilted the Balance. *Arab Media and Society* 13 (3). http://www.arabmediasociety.com/?article=769.

Kidd, Dorothy. 2003. Indymedia.org: A New Communications Commons. In *Cyberactivism: Critical Theories and Practices of On-line Activism*, edited by Martha McCaughey and Michael D. Ayers, 47–69. New York: Routledge.

Koopmans, Ruud. 2004. Protest in Time and Space: The Evolution of Waves of Contention. In *The Blackwell Companion to Social Movements*, edited by David A. Snow, Sarah Anne Soule and Hanspeter Kriesi, 19–46. Oxford: Wiley-Blackwell.

Lim, Merlyna. 2012. Clicks, Cabs, and Coffee Houses: Social Media and Oppositional Movements in Egypt, 2004–2011. *Journal of Communication* 62 (2): 231–248.

Ling, Richard, and Birgitte Yttri. 2002. Hyper-Coordination via Mobile Phones in Norway. In *Perpetual Contact Mobile Communication, Private Talk, Public Performance*, edited by James E. Katz and Mark Aakhus, 139–169. Cambridge, UK: Cambridge University Press.

Lotan, Gilad, Erhardt Graeff, Mike Ananny, Devin Gaffney, Ian Pearce and danah boyd. 2011. The Revolutions Were Tweeted: Information Flows during the 2011 Tunisian and Egyptian Revolutions. *International Journal of Communication* 5: 1375–1405.

Mattoni, Alice. 2012. *Media Practices and Protest Politics: How Precarious Workers Mobilise.* Burlington, VT: Ashgate.

———. 2013a, February 14. Beyond Celebration: Toward a More Nuanced Assessment of Facebook's Role in Occupy Wall Street. Fieldsights—Hot Spots, *Cultural Anthropology* Online. http://www.culanth.org/fieldsights/84-beyond-celebration-toward-a-more-nuanced-assessment-of-facebook-s-role-in-occupy-wall-street.

———. 2013b. Repertoires of Communication in Social Movement Processes. In *Mediation and Protest Movements*, edited by Bart Cammaerts, Alice Mattoni and Patrick McCurdy, 39–56. Bristol: Intellect.

McAdam, Doug, and William H. Sewell Jr. 2001. It's about Time: Temporality in the Study of Contentious Politics. In *Silence and Voice in the Study of Contentious Politics*, edited by Ronald Aminzade, 89–125. Cambridge, UK: Cambridge University Press.

Melucci, Alberto. 1982. *L'invenzione Del Presente?: Movimenti, Identità, Bisogni Individuali*. Bologna: Il Mulino.

———. 1989. *Nomads of the Present?: Social Movements and Individual Needs in Contemporary Society*. Philadelphia, PA: Temple University Press.

Monterde, A., and John Postill. 2014. Mobile Ensembles: The Uses of Mobile Phones for Social Protest by Spain's Indignados. In *The Routledge Companion to Mobile Media*, edited by Gerard Goggin and Larissa Hjorth. London: Routledge.

Morozov, Evgeny. 2012. *The Net Delusion: The Dark Side of Internet Freedom*. New York: PublicAffairs.

Morris, Douglas. 2004. Globalization and Media Democracy: The Case of Indymedia. In *Shaping the Network Society: The New Role of Civil Society in Cyberspace*, edited by Douglas Schuler and Peter Day, 325–352. Cambridge, MA: MIT Press.

Nunns, Alex, and Nadia Idle. 2011. *Tweets from Tahrir: Egypt's Revolution as It Unfolded, in the Words of the People Who Made It*. New York: OR Books.

Olesen, Thomas. 2013. "We Are All Khaled Said": Visual Injustice Symbols in the Egyptian Revolution, 2010–2011. *Research in Social Movements, Conflicts and Change* 35 (March): 3–25.

Papacharissi, Zizi, and Maria de Fatima Oliveira. 2012. Affective News and Networked Publics: The Rhythms of News Storytelling on #Egypt. *Journal of Communication* 62 (2): 266–282.

Pearce, Katy E., and Sarah Kendzior. 2012. Networked Authoritarianism and Social Media in Azerbaijan. *Journal of Communication* 62 (2): 283–298.

Pickard, Victor W. 2006. United Yet Autonomous: Indymedia and the Struggle to Sustain a Radical Democratic Network. *Media Culture and Society* 28 (3): 315–336.

Postill, John. 2012. New Protest Movements and Viral Media. *Media/anthropology*. http://johnpostill.com/2012/03/26/new-protest-movements-and-viral-media/.

Romanos, Eduardo. 2013. Collective Learning Processes within Social Movements: Some Insights into the Spanish 15M/Indignados Movement. In *Understanding European Movements: New Social Movements, Global Justice Struggles, Anti-austerity Protest*, edited by Cristina Flesher Fominaya and Laurence Cox, 203–219. Abingdon: Routledge.

Rucht, Dieter. 2004a. Movements Allies, Adversaries and Third Parties. In *The Blackwell Companion to Social Movements*, edited by David A. Snow, Sarah Anne Soule and Hanspeter Kriesi, 197–216. Oxford: Wiley-Blackwell.

———. 2004b. The Quadruple "A": Media Strategies of Protest Movements since 1960s. In *Cyberprotest: New Media, Citizens and Social Movements*, edited by Wim B. Van de Donk, 25–48. London: Routledge.

Sampedro, Victor Blanco. 2005. *13-M: Multitudes on Line*. Madrid: Los Libros de la Catarata.

Tarrow, Sydney. 1989. *Democracy and Disorder: Social Conflict, Political Protest and Democracy in Italy, 1965–1975*. New York: Oxford University Press.

———. 1994. *Power in Movement*. Cambridge, UK: Cambridge University Press.

Tejerina, Benjamín, Ignacia Perugorría, Tova Benski and Lauren Langman. 2013. From Indignation to Occupation: A New Wave of Global Mobilization. *Current Sociology* 61 (4): 377–392.

Tilly, Charles. 1978. *From Mobilization to Revolution*. Reading, MA: Addison-Wesley.

———. 1995. Contentious Repertoires in Great Britain, 1758–1834. In *Repertoires & Cycles of Collective Action*, edited by Mark Traugott, 15–42. Durham, NC: Duke University Press.

Tilly, Charles, and Sidney G. Tarrow. 2007. *Contentious Politics*. Boulder, CO: Paradigm.

Tufekci, Zeynep, and Cristopher Wilson. 2012. Social Media and the Decision to Participate in Political Protest: Observations from Tahrir Square. *Journal of Communication* 62 (2): 363–379.

Wall, Melissa, and Sahar El Zahed. 2011. "I'll Be Waiting for You Guys": A YouTube Call to Action in the Egyptian Revolution. *International Journal of Communication* 5: 1333–1343.

Youmans, William Lafi, and Jillian C. York. 2012. Social Media and the Activist Toolkit: User Agreements, Corporate Interests, and the Information Infrastructure of Modern Social Movements. *Journal of Communication* 62 (2): 315–329.

Section Two

Global and Civil Counter-Power

3 Populism 2.0

Social media activism, the generic Internet user and interactive direct democracy

Paolo Gerbaudo

1. INTRODUCTION

The much celebrated adoption of social media as Facebook and Twitter in the popular protest wave, or in short 'popular wave,' of anti-austerity and anti-establishment politics of 2011–2013—exemplified by protest movements such as Occupy Wall Street and the Indignados, and by the rise of new digital parties such as the 5 Star Movement in Italy and the Partido X in Spain—should not be seen much as a new step in the linear evolution of Internet activism. Rather, the use of social network sites such as Facebook and Twitter—as platforms of organization, recruitment and mobilisation—constitutes in many respects a veritable rupture in this trajectory. The shift towards the use of commercial platforms of communication not only belies practical motives of efficiency—such as the aim of reaching more people—but also reflects a different world view than the one pervading radical politics in previous decades. Specifically it manifests a break with the approach that underscored the anti-globalisation movement, which put much emphasis on the need to construct autonomous and self-managed platforms, epitomised by the development of alternative news sites as Indymedia and alternative Internet service providers (ISPs).

For anti-globalisation activists the Internet was to a great extent a continuation of their small-group politics of affinity groups, collectives and social centres, all networked together in unstable federations (see, e.g., Juris 2008). For the activists of the popular wave instead, corporate social media have been appropriated and turned into an expansive medium of mass mobilisation (Gerbaudo 2012). Social network sites come to constitute the tools for an emerging anti-establishment digital mass politics that in this chapter I explore through the notion of 'populism 2.0.'[1] Populism 2.0, not to be intended in a pejorative sense, designates an ideology[2] or more precisely an ideological orientation that sees social media as means to address 'the people,' in the sense of the totality or near-totality of the political community, as perfectly captured by the famous Occupy slogan 'we are the 99 per cent.' Traditional populism, starting with People's Party in the U.S., used the mass media of the press and later broadcasting as the key channel through which to address that nebulous entity that goes under the name of the 'people'

(Postel 2007; Kazin 1998). Contemporary activists are using the Web 2.0 of social network sites to fulfil very much the same purpose. They strive to make use of the massive reach social media facilitate, as well as of their interactive features, such as liking, sharing, commenting and re-tweeting, to construct a new form of mass politics fitting a society pervaded by the diffusion of social network sites and faced with the social consequences of the financial crisis of 2007–2008.

Trying to capture the spirit of populism 2.0, in this chapter I analyse different forms of 'social media activism' to be understood in the basic descriptive sense as activism supported by social media platforms. I look at the development of social media activism across different social and political movements that have emerged during the 'popular wave,' paying attention to the emerging discourses, practices and imaginaries that accompany the use of social media. Specifically, I focus on a selected number of social movements and political parties that have been at the forefront of this political wave. I utilise two sets of case studies, with two cases each: (1) the use of social media in the popular movements of 2011–2013, with particular reference to the Indignados in Spain and Occupy Wall Street in the U.S.; (2) the use of social media within emerging digital parties connected with the popular wave, focusing on the cases of the anti-establishment and anti-corruption 5 Star Movement party in Italy and the Partido X in Spain. Admittedly, these case studies display some important differences that will be discussed in some detail. Nevertheless they can be analysed together, as part of the same 'population,' because they have looked at each other as part of a common political wave, and have shared a number of practices and visions, including the use of social media as political tools.

Having sketched out the general purpose and scope of this chapter, its argument can be now summarised as follows. Contemporary social media activism comes to reflect some rhetorical features traditionally associated with populism, but updated in a way that fits the dynamics proper to the communicative architecture of Web 2.0, with its valuing of interactivity and participation. In this context, traditional features of populism (appeal to unity, anti-establishment and anti-institutional rhetoric, strive for direct democracy, suspicion of intermediaries) come to be matched with a set of tropes that make up what we could call the 'ideology of social media' (interactivity, openness, directness). Emerging movements and parties in the popular wave utilise these social media features as means to appeal to a highly diversified yet homogeneous mass of Internet users and to address the ideal subject of the 'generic Internet user' to be mobilised against economic and political elites. The product of this adaptation is the rise of an interactive and participatory populism: a populism 2.0.

The adaptation of populist logics to the communication ecology of social media will be understood in detail by focusing on two axes (see Table 3.1), at which we can appreciate the matching of universal populist features with the particular material affordances of Web 2.0: (1) the *ideal subject* that is the addressee of mobilising efforts; (2) the *unifying demand* that underlies

Table 3.1: Equivalence between traditional populist logics and populism 2.0

	Traditional populism	Populism 2.0
Ideal subject	The common man	The generic Internet user
Unifying demand	Direct democracy	Democracy 2.0

mobilising discourses. At the level of the ideal social subject, we see an adaptation of the traditional imaginary of the 'common man' that in its various adaptations punctuates the history of populism, into the figure of the generic Internet user. At the level of the unifying demand we witness the adaptation of the demand for direct democracy that constitutes a typical feature of populist movements since the time of the People's Party in the U.S. (Mény and Surel 2002) into the project of an interactive democracy, or a democracy 2.0. We can now look at these two levels in more detail.

1. Within movements of the popular wave, communications come to be addressed to the 'generic Internet user' (GIU), as a Web 2.0 adaptation of the populist *ideal subject* of the 'common man.' The generic Internet user is an imaginary 'average' Web 2.0 user. This is a subject whose subscription to a number of services, such as Facebook, Twitter, Google+ or YouTube, is seen as automatically qualifying him/her as a target for mobilising appeals. The GIU is addressed regardless of his or her political, cultural or social affiliations. He or she is targeted simply based on the techno-utopian assumption that by being an Internet user he/she will most likely share with other Internet users a common suspicion towards established bureaucracies, as well as direct access to uncensored information, likely to make him/her a conscious political subject (see, e.g., Mason 2012).

2. The traditional populist demand for direct democracy is translated into the project of an interactive democracy or a democracy 2.0. Democracy 2.0 designates a democratic project that makes use of the interactive features of Web 2.0, such as liking, commenting and sharing. These features are adopted as the means of a permanent consultation, of a plebiscitary cyber-democracy, based on the principle of 'one like, one vote.' Movements and parties of the popular wave continuously measure their support and assess the viability of their claim to represent the totality of the citizenry through these tools. In certain cases they also ask for these practices to be integrated into existing institutions as is evident with the case of emerging 'Internet parties,' such as 5 Star Movement and Partido X. Democracy 2.0, besides being a crucial demand, also acquires the role of a source of identification for these formations. This idea and its multifarious avatars becomes for these movements the "empty signifier" (Laclau 2005), that element that allows for their identity to hold together regardless of their internal differences.

The main body of this chapter is structured around an analysis of these two levels, which will be looked at in depth in dedicated sections. Before entering this empirical discussion, I will spend some time developing a theoretical framework to make sense of the relevance of populist logics for an understanding of social media activism. Furthermore I will provide some background information about the different movements considered in this chapter. Then, after conducting the empirical analysis of the two levels of populism 2.0, I will turn to its political implications. Specifically, I will scrutinise its emancipatory promise and look at two fundamental threats lying in the road of populism 2.0: (1) *techno-plebiscitarianism*, as seen in the tendency to upset the principle of pluralism, and (2) *techno-proceduralism*, as seen in the obsession with methods and the comparative neglect of substantive demands beyond the very demand of democracy 2.0.

2.   POPULISM IN THE 'MASS SOCIAL WEB'

At first talking of 'populism 2.0' or social media populism appears incongruous, given that the connotations associated with these two terms seem to be at odds with one another. Social media and the Internet more generally are associated with the imaginary of the network, of a one to one structure, in which every node maintains its autonomy, as popularised in the scholarship of Manuel Castells (see, e.g., 1996, 2000). The term 'populism,' instead, immediately conjures up ideas of mass politics, homogeneity and strong collective solidarity. So how is it possible that these apparently opposite poles come together? In which way do current forms of activism developed on social media resemble populist logics? As I will demonstrate in this theoretical section, there are surprising resonances between the features of Web 2.0 and typical characteristics of populist politics. Populism's traditional emphasis on unity of otherwise atomised individuals chimes well with social media's combination of an individualistic framing of the user and the increasing massification of the platforms sustaining his or her interactions (Gerbaudo 2013a). This resonance between populist politics and Web 2.0 proves particularly fecund at a time of widespread political discontent and in the aftermath of the global economic crisis of 2007–2008, which has affected a wide and diversified array of social demographics.

The first obstacle to be overcome in developing a discussion of populism 2.0 is the fact that in public debates the very term 'populism' is mostly used in a pejorative sense. In Europe in particular this term has been used to refer to right-wing xenophobic politics, as exemplified by phenomena as the Lega Nord in Italy, the English Defence League and Jobbik in Hungary. This pejorative use of the term, however, overlooks the long history of progressive populism, from the Russian *narodniki* to the American People's Party, to end with the socialist neo-populism of Hugo Chavez and Evo Morales. Furthermore, it is possible to see behind some stigmatisations of populism, regardless of its progressive or regressive nature, a certain elitist attitude with the tendency and to look with fear at those occasions in which people mobilise outside of pre-established structures (Mény and Surel 2002). This negative understanding of populism has also dominated the debate about the transformation of populist politics in a digital era, as seen in the work using notions as "network populism" (Bratich 2011) or "digital populism" (Bartlett, Birdwell, and Littler 2012).

My own discussion of populism treats this term as a neutral, rather than pejorative, notion that can in each specific occasion assume regressive or progressive qualities. My understanding of this concept is informed by the work of Gramsci on the notion of 'people' and of the 'national-popular' (1973) as well as by the neo-Gramscian theorist Ernesto Laclau's analysis of populism as a political logic, present to varying degrees in most forms of politics (2005). In Gramsci's work the 'people' constitutes a category that transcends notions of class. The 'people' is an "amorphous" mass (Gramsci 1973, 72) that has often been reduced to passivity throughout history, and whose activation and mobilisation constitute a fundamental challenge for emancipatory politics. It is on this vision of 'the people' as an expansive, almost all-encompassing category that Ernesto Laclau has built his influential analysis of populism (see, in particular, 2005). For Laclau, contrarily to well-established theorists of populism as Margaret Canovan (1981, 2005) and Paul Taggart (2000), populism is not a specific ideology. To the contrary populism is a transversal political logic, which revolves around the anti-sectional appeal to the 'people' as the totality of the political community, and which can be utilised by both the Right and the Left.

Central to populism as a political logic is fundamentally an allergy for divisions among 'the people' and a connected emphasis on unity, or more specifically popular unity. According to Laclau this condition is enforced when a "chain of equivalence" is built across an array of demands. In this context, one of the many demands comes to act as "empty signifier," a demand that by having lost its specific meaning is capable of condensing all other demands (2005, 73–77). When this happens the political space is split into two neatly separated camps, with possible nefarious consequences for power-holders that have to confront broad-based movements. This part of Laclau's account, and its emphasis on the unifying logics of populism resonates well with Daniele Albertazzi and Duncan McDonnell's argument that populism is an ideology that "pits a virtuous and *homogeneous* people against a set of elites and dangerous 'others' who were together depicted as depriving (or attempting to deprive) the sovereign people of their rights, values, prosperity, identity, and voice" (2008, 3). What matters greatly from a political perspective at this level is that the regressive or progressive character of populism depends to a large extent on the 'others' against whom 'the people' are pitted and united, regardless of whether they are migrants and ethnic minorities (as in the case of right-wing populism) or economic elites and corrupt politicians (as in the case of progressive populism).

But how does this emphasis on popular unity typical of populism sit with the individualised user experience characteristic of social network sites as Facebook and Twitter? The key logical step to solve this brain-teaser is that while populism is constantly animated by the desire to recompose 'the people', this ambition stems from a diagnosis of society as ridden with individualisation. Populist movements appeal to an ideal subject that is seen as highly atomised, and thus in need of a process of reintegration in the social body. Fundamental in the populist narrative is the figure of the 'common man' in all its multiple avatars: the hard-working man, the 'average man,' the working poor, the unwilling unemployed, the unrepresented citizen. Populist movements appeal to individuals rather than to classes or to other pre-established collective aggregations. They appeal to them on the basis of a sense of common victimisation in front of large-scale organizations, be they corporations or the state, that act against their interests. This social imaginary undergoes a powerful re-adaptation in social media activism, with the ideal subject of the common man now updated to the figure of the 'generic Internet user' as the imaginary addressee of populist appeals.

Appeals to popular unity and the role played by the common man as an ideal subject are not sufficient to grasp the nature of populism. Another important feature is the role played by direct democracy as the central demand of populist movements. Yves Mény and Yves Surel have interestingly argued that populism should be understood in opposition to constitutionalism (2002). Constitutionalism is a legalistic vision of politics concerned with the defence of institutions and law and order seen as the only bulwark of true democracy. Populism instead puts stress on popular sovereignty, and advocates for forms of direct intervention of the citizenry in the decisions affecting them. It is significant at this level that populist movements, starting with the People's Party in the U.S., have been the main proponents of institutions of direct democracy, including referenda and popular initiatives. At this level, we find a peculiar resonance between populism and anarchist politics, which similarly to populism has criticised representative democracy and argued for forms of grassroots democracy as practised in assemblies or workers' councils. Naturally there are important differences between these traditions. Yet, at the same time, there are also interesting parallels that are highly relevant to get to grips with the specificity of contemporary protest culture, and the rise of anarcho-populism, as a marriage of anarchism and populism at its centre (Gerbaudo 2013b).

So far we have excavated the meaning of populism beyond the pejorative meaning often associated with it. But what about populism 2.0? This notion—that has sometimes been utilised in journalistic descriptions of emerging movements and parties—identifies, in my own use of the term, the connection between some typical populist traits and some of the specific affordances of Web 2.0. This connection needs to be appreciated at two levels: (1) the individualisation of user experience, which is conducive to a re-adaptation of the discourse of the common man as an atomised agent, who needs to be recomposed in the collective body of 'the people'; (2) the mass character of the contemporary web, which chimes well with mass appeals of the popular type. These two contradictory trends should be seen as a contemporary manifestation of the complementarity between the imaginary of the common man and the imaginary of the mass that, as we have seen, lie at the root of populism.

Individualisation is a process that is highly relevant to understanding the nature of Web 2.0. Web 2.0 is a term that has often been used to describe the contemporary web dominated by social network sites such as Facebook and Twitter, and are characterised by the centrality of so-called user-generated content. Danah boyd and Nicole Ellison have described social network sites as

> web-based services that allow *individuals* to (1) construct a public or semi-public profile within a bounded system, (2) articulate a list of other users with whom they share a connection, and (3) view and traverse their list of connections and those made by others within the system. (2007, 210)

Typical of social network sites is thus the framing of individual users (rather than groups or activities) as basic nodes or units in the network. Social network sites and the type of user experience available in them can thus be seen as the most extreme reflection of the contemporary individualised society (Bauman 2001; Beck and Beck-Gernsheim 2002), and in particular of that situation that Barry Wellman has captured with the notion "networked individualism": a condition whereby people rather than places "become the portal" of social relationships (see Wellman and Haythornwaite 2002, 17).

The contemporary Web 2.0 is, however, not just a 'social web' based on one-to-one social connections. It is also increasingly a mass web, shaped by mass and broadcasting logics of communication. With the momentous expansion in the user base, Web 2.0 has rapidly become a sort of new mass medium, very different from the pioneering and highly elitist medium that was web 1.0. Total Internet users in 2012 stood at 2.7 billion people, around 40 per cent of the world population (ITU 2013). For comparison, in 2001, at the peak of the anti-globalisation movement only 8 per cent of the world population and 30 per cent in developed countries had access to the Internet (ITU 2013). Facebook's surpassing of the one billion users' mark in October 2012 represents a truly historical moment, marking the point at which social network sites are capable of reaching user bases previously associated only with TV mega-events such as the Football World Cup final or the Super Bowl.

This process of massification of the web forces us to rethink the models through which we have tried to understand its working. The understanding of Internet communications can no longer be exclusively reduced to 'molecular' processes of networking and narrow-casting that dominated the analysis of web 1.0. Rather what we are witnessing here is the return in new forms of those mass logics of broadcasting that were traditionally associated with mass media, of radio, television and the press. This return of mass logics can be seen in the operations of popular political Facebook fan pages and Twitter accounts, followed by tens and hundreds of thousands of users. Castells, the theorist of the network society, has himself begun acknowledging this shift, when talking of a "mass self-communication" logic (Castells 2009) in the contemporary web. Yet he and other theorists working within the framework of network theory have struggled to fit the empirical trend towards massification in their pre-established theoretical models that propose a tendency towards increasing autonomy and diversity. The study of social media activism can provide some very interesting insights to make sense of this contradictory host of processes. Specifically in the continuation of the chapter I will focus on two main questions: (1) what are the ways in which the movements and parties of the popular wave tap into the potentials of this massified Web 2.0?; (2) how do they rejuvenate populist rhetorics to fit the dynamics of social network sites?

3.   SQUARES' MOVEMENTS AND NET PARTIES

The phenomenon of populism 2.0 analysed in this chapter needs to be understood in the context of the politics of the 'popular wave.' The term "popular wave" designates a "cycle of contention" (Tarrow 1998, 24) against austerity politics and a corrupt political class sparked by the economic crisis of 2007–2008 and the widespread discontent the crisis caused, with rising levels of unemployment and cuts to public services. This political wave has seen its initiation in the so-called squares' movements, 'take-the-square' or occupation movements of 2011, such as the Indignados and Occupy Wall Street, which have taken inspiration from the Arab Spring to construct a new popular protest politics. These movements have been characterised by an effort to reclaim public space as a space for radical politics, as seen in the tactic of all-out protest camps. Furthermore, they have made use of social media such as Twitter and Facebook to construct new arenas of participation and decision making. Besides these movements, we have also seen the rise and development of new 'digital' or 'net' parties that share much in their vision and methods with Occupy and the Indignados. The most prominent of these is undoubtedly the 5 Star Movement, led by comedian Beppe Grillo in Italy, an anti-establishment party that has won a sizeable number of MPs in the 2013 parliamentary elections. Another example of this wave of net parties is the case of Partido X (X Party), a political formation emerging out of the Indignados movement in Spain, and appealing to common citizens to overthrow the corrupt political class. Let us now look at these different emerging movements and parties.

The Indignados movement emerged in Spain with the 15 May 2011 protests against the economic crisis and political corruption. Protesters occupied Puerta del Sol in Central Madrid, taking inspiration from the occupation of

Tahrir square during the Egyptian revolution. For around a month they created general assemblies to discuss solutions to the crisis, and occupations spread to tens of other cities and towns in Spain, and abroad. After the main protest camps were lifted in June, the movement developed into a series of 'indignant marches' across the country, with a number of subsequent protests against the Spanish government and the situation of increasing social distress. Crucial in the movement culture was the use of social network sites, including Democracia Real Ya's Facebook page, which was one of the key platforms in the mobilisation, as well as Twitter accounts, blogs, websites and other web-based media.

The Occupy Wall Street movement followed in the footsteps of the Indignados. It launched an occupation of Zuccotti Park, on the 17 September 2011, nearby the site of the New York Stock Exchange. The movement campaigned against the consequences of the economic crisis on unemployment and social welfare, and attempted to create new spaces of democracy and self-help. It developed into hundreds of protest camps all over the U.S., mobilising diverse sectors of American society united in their anger against the economic system and against the political class. The movement, which was originally named with a Twitter hashtag as #occupywallstreet, made use of the micro-blogging site, as well as of Facebook and Tumblr to build public support and mobilise participants. After an upsurge in support and visibility Occupy progressively faded away from public view. A wave of evictions in mid-November 2011 proved a death blow for the movement and sparked a debate about organizational and political alternatives.

The MoVimento 5 Stelle (5 Star Movement) is an Italian political party campaigning against corruption and social injustice. The party (although activists maintain it is not a party but a movement) was founded by the maverick comedian Beppe Grillo, in collaboration with his Internet guru Gianroberto Casaleggio. Its origins hark back to the 'Amici di Beppe Grillo' (Beppe Grillo's friends) local electoral lists launched in 2005, and to the V Day of 2007, from which the party takes its middle V in the word 'movimento' (V for the Italian insult "vaffanculo"—fuck off, directed at the political class). Progressively the movement has fielded candidates in the local and regional elections, until the national elections of 2013, where it won 25.55 per cent of the seats in the Chamber of Deputies, and secured a strategic position in the Senate. The movement has made ample use of the blog of Beppe Grillo,[3] one of the most popular blogs in the world, of MeetUp groups, Facebook pages and Twitter channels, and has experimented with online voting systems to decide on various issues and select candidates.

The Partido X, also known by the alternate name Partido del Futuro (Future Party), is a political formation that appeared publicly in Spain in January 2013. Its founders are connected to the Indignados movement and the free software movement. The party struggles for what it calls 'democracy 4.0,' which is a direct democracy facilitated by electronic technologies of communication. Its slogan 'democracia y punto,' translated as 'democracy full stop,' condenses well the programme of the party, whose four demands all have to do with democratic rights. Specifically the party asks for: (1) transparency in public administration; (2) wiki-government and wiki-legislation—that is, a system of online consultation for governmental decisions; (3) right to a real and permanent vote—that is, the possibility to vote online on issues of concern when they are debated in parliament; (4) institution of referenda and popular initiatives.

These various groups are admittedly highly different from one another. First, Occupy and Indignados are protest movements, while the 5 Star Movement and Partido X are parties, although very peculiar ones, given that they come close to the typology of so-called 'protest parties.' Secondly, there is an important debate to be had as to the political orientation of these groups, and their location on the left and right spectrum. Indignados and Occupy have been widely considered as progressive movements (see, e.g., Gitlin 2012), because of their raising the issue of class and inequality and because of how much some participants in these movements have declared themselves neither Left nor Right. While the Partido X's call for transparency and direct democracy might fit with a radical liberal platform, it can be considered left wing because its initiators stem from the autonomous movement in Barcelona and Madrid and because of its rhetorical opposition to neoliberalism and austerity politics.

Regardless of their differences, these various cases share some important similarities that justify analysing them *en bloc*. First and foremost, they share a common oppositional culture that is visible in their use of common icons, including the famous Guy Fawkes mask from the V for Vendetta movie, in their anti-establishment position and in their faith in the Internet and social media as providing a new space for democracy, or a 'democracy 2.0.' Secondly, participants in these parties and movements have often seen one another as part of a common popular wave of protest and radical politics (Gerbaudo 2012), fighting against the financial system and the old party politics, and striving for new forms of democracy. This sense of commonality is indicated, for example, by the meeting between *Adbusters* editor and Occupy initiator Micah White and Beppe Grillo in October 2013, and the declarations of sympathy on behalf of the Occupy movement made by White.[4]

Given the controversy that has surrounded it, it is worth saying a few additional words about the ideology of 5 Star as an odd case within the popular wave, yet one that stands to represent much of the complexity of this political cycle. The 5 Star Movement is difficult to pigeonhole in familiar categories, and to locate in the left-right spectrum. Indicative is the policy platform presented by the party at the 2013 general elections in Italy. The twenty main demands[5] were topped by the demand for a citizen's income. This has been a typical demand of the radical Left in Italy, one promoted by many Marxist autonomists, including Antonio Negri. The party programme also included policies on renewable energy and public transport, which have been traditionally associated with Green parties. The party has, however, been sometimes characterised as right-wing because of its position on a number of other issues. The most important question in this context is the issue of migration. Grillo has often declared himself against birthright citizenship. In one occasion he overturned a decision taken by some of his MPs to reform the law on migration and abolish the crime of clandestinity. The party has also often been accused of totalitarian tendencies, because of its scathing attacks against journalists and politicians opposing it, and of its ambition to represent 100 per cent of the population. Another issue of contention has been the role played by the non-official leaders of the movement, Grillo and Casaleggio, and their resistance to debates about the organizational structure of the party. Since the elections Grillo has often assembled the party MPs in away-days where he has dictated the political line, and he has expelled a number of representatives of the party who had publicly raised criticisms about the party's conduct and the role of Grillo.

All in all, it is apparent that the 5 Star Movement is a reflection of the ambiguity of the new wave of dissent in the popular movements that have emerged since the beginning of the crisis. These movements are characterised by composite popular fronts that cut across traditional political divisions and class allegiances. This also means that possible authoritarian deviations of this movement constitute a serious risk, as it is highlighted by the contradictions between proclamations of absolute democracy and a reality of top-down decisions taken by Grillo and his clique. However, these fallacies by no means allow terming the movement 'fascist' as some critics have proposed. It is important to continue scrutinising the actions of the 5 Star Movement and to keep an eye out for possible authoritarian involutions. Yet, at the same time, as many in the Italian Left have understood, it is important not to demonise this party, and to acknowledge the importance of the political innovations it has put forward.

Before moving to the empirical analysis of the various case studies, it is imperative to make a brief methodological note. These different case studies are analysed by making use of: (1) the dataset of interviews, observations and social media messages collected for my book *Tweets and the streets* (Gerbaudo 2012); (2) archival documents collected for my new research project about digital parties, including party's programmes, manifestos, declarations and selected social media messages. While empirically informed, the aim of this chapter is theoretical, in that it aims to construct a theory of populism 2.0, and of its different traits. For this reason, I will refer to specific cases, documents and quotes with parsimony, and only for the purpose of exemplification.

4.   THE GENERIC INTERNET USER AS THE NEW COMMON MAN

An Internet connection and a Facebook account: that is everything you need to be part of the 'people' at the time of Web 2.0, one could jokingly say to capture the gist of the communication of the movements and parties of the popular protest wave. For contemporary popular movements, social network sites such as Twitter and Facebook have become the means through which to address Internet users as the new prototypes of the 'common man' of populism: the ordinary hard-working citizens, victimised by an unfair political and economic establishment (see, for example, Kazin 1998). In the discourse of movements and parties of the popular wave of radical politics, the common man is translated into a figure that I name the 'generic Internet user' (GIU). The generic Internet user, as an imaginary average Internet user, becomes the ideal addressee of the all-encompassing appeals made by social media activists, which in the anti-sectional spirit proper to populism intend to reach everybody regardless of her political, cultural or religious inclinations.

If one looks at the manifestoes and self-descriptions of movements like the Indignados and Occupy, one immediately encounters actualisations of the traditional figure of the 'common man' as the tiny individual which together with other tiny individuals makes up that great collective body that goes under the name of the 'people.' In the manifesto of Democracia Real Ya, the organization that launched the 15-M movement in Spain, activists described themselves as "normal, ordinary people" and went on to declare, "we are *like you:* people who get up every morning to study, work or find a job, people who have family and friends. People who *work hard* every day to provide a better future for those around us." In the "We Are the 99 Percent" Tumblr blog, where supporters of Occupy Wall Street could post their pictures and stories, one would find the following description:

> We are the 99 percent. We are getting kicked out of our homes. We are forced to choose between groceries and rent. We are denied quality medical care. We are suffering from environmental pollution. We are working long hours for little pay and no rights, if we're working at all. We are getting nothing while the other 1 percent is getting everything. We are the 99 percent.

What we find here appear as contemporary re-adaptations of the classic hero of populism: the common man, as the hard-working person, victimised in many different ways by the system, and in urgent need to unite against the "1 per cent [who] is getting everything."[6] A somehow similar logic is reflected in the discourse of the citizen and citizenship, that has often appeared in the indignados, as well as in the Partido X that has called itself a "citizens network" (Red Ciudadana), and has used the motto "only the citizenry can stop them" (solo la ciudania puede pararlos). These expressions have lead to talking, within the Spanish debate, of the rise of an ideology of "citizenism," opposing entire citizenry to corrupt institutions in way that strongly resonates with populist logics.

If we stopped here, we could just say that the Indignados and Occupy simply propose a re-edition of traditional populist rhetoric, with no substantial change. Yet, what is more interesting is how these appeals of a populist flavour are actualised to fit the condition of society at the time of social networks. In this context, the very experience of online connectivity becomes itself an element of "commonality" to be invoked when searching for the "common" of the contemporary common man. This situation leads to a transfiguration of the populist "common man," into the imaginary figure of the "generic Internet user." People, or better citizens, are not appealed to only based on their grievances, but also on the assumption that their possession of online connectivity and the experience of everyday interactivity afforded by it predisposes them to active political participation. For example, in the case of the "We are the 99%" Tumblr blog, website users were asked to take a "selfie" of themselves while holding a message stating their specific conditions. In this context, a practice of digital popular culture as ubiquitous as the selfie is turned into a means of collective political identification, allowing an highly diverse public of users to express their shared sense of belonging to the 99%. These all-encompassing appeals to the "generic Internet user" are often accompanied by motivational assertions, calling people to break out of their individualised condition and to use their connectivity as a springboard to join a collective mobilisation. This is exemplified by expressions such as the one found on Occupy Together's website stating that "the #occupy movement is driven by individuals like you coming together to create real change from the bottom up." In these messages, the "generic Internet user" is ambivalently framed as, on the one hand, someone who is atomised and isolated, alone in front on the screen, and, on the other hand, as someone who in her possession of online connectivity can be easily turned into an active participant.

This adaptation of the imaginary of the common man into the imaginary of the generic Internet user is often found in connection with expressions as 'Internet people' or 'people of the web' that have become prominent in activist discourse, as a sort of designation of the broader constituency of contemporary movements. Slogans such as 'power to the Internet people' or 'we the Internet people' have appeared on many websites connected with the Occupy and Indignados mobilisation. Many of my Occupy interviewees referred to the 'web people' or alternatively the 'Internet people' as a sort of backdrop of the movement. They were those who were following the events from home, because they could not make it to protest camps. But it was also more generally a term for all 'the people' who had joined the movement after being informed about it on the web. The similar expression 'people of the web' is a figure that has been explicitly referred to by Beppe Grillo and other members of his party, the 5 Star Movement, as the designation of the social base supporting the anti-establishment political formation. These expressions manifest an adaptation of a long-standing populist tradition, in which often 'the people' have been identified with one medium. A relatively recent example is the phenomenon of the so-called "fax people," a term for those citizens supporting anti-corruption judges in Italy in the early 1990s, by sending them solidarity fax messages (Tarchi 2003).

To sum up, what matters in the notion of 'generic Internet user,' as an ideal addressee for social media messaging, is that Internet users are seen as possible participants, regardless of their social and economic status, and social and political affiliations, the possession of internet connectivity being seen as a sufficient condition for their participation in protest movements and net parties. The GIU is framed as one grain in the heap of sand that goes by the name of 'the people,' or better 'the Internet people': an individual whose small contribution is invisible, yet instrumental to the success of the collective. The availability of an Internet connection and a social media subscription becomes a condition to be an active part of the 99 per cent. This framing is based on the assumption that an Internet connection automatically predisposes people for active political participation. Populism 2.0 thus incorporates much of the techno-utopianism that dominates current debates about the Internet (see, e.g., Shirky 2008; Mason 2012). It operates with the idea that the Net automatically provides a horizontal infrastructure where democracy can flourish. This aspect leads us straight to the second axis of populism 2.0: the level of political demands, where we see the updating of the ideal of direct democracy in the idea of an interactive democracy or a democracy 2.0.

5.   DEMOCRACY 2.0 AS DIRECT DEMOCRACY

At the heart of the popular wave lies a recurrent stress on the need for a 'real democracy' and more specifically a direct democracy to supersede what activists see as the inauthentic representative democracy manifested in parliamentary and party politics. This orientation is clearly visible in a number of practices and slogans: from the general assemblies that have become such a powerful icon for the Indignados and Occupy Wall Street to the slogan 'they don't represent me,' often heard in the Indignados protest camps of Madrid and Barcelona, to end with the name of Democracia Real Ya (Real Democracy Now), the leading organization in the Indignados protest wave. Of course, this demand for new and alternative forms of democracy is anything but new. In fact, it constitutes a new instance in a long array of democratic struggles that have been intensifying since the 1968 student protests, and were manifested in movements such as ecologism, feminism and the anti-globalisation movement. What is specific about contemporary movements is the fact that demands for democracy are increasingly tied to an idea of the 'digital' as constituting a new terrain for expanding democracy. More specifically, activists in the movements and parties of the popular wave see social media as creating the opportunity for a 'democracy 2.0.' This adaptation involves the utilisation of the Web 2.0 logic of interactivity, and features such as likes, comments, re-tweets and similar form of interactions and connected metrics as the means of a sort of informal digital mass democracy, following the principle of 'one like, one vote.'

The notion of democracy 2.0 builds on the strong resonance between the values of contemporary activists and the deep valuing of participation embedded in social media and connected discourses. The term participation, often mentioned by activists in connection with their discussion of new forms of democracy, was precisely the term used by the Internet guru Tim O'Reilly to spell out the specificity of Web 2.0 vis-à-vis Web 1.0, based on a logic of publishing (O'Reilly, quoted in Mandiberg 2012). In marketing circles this valuing of participation has been seen in discussions around the term 'prosumer' as a consumer who at the same time is also a producer. Authors such as Jay Rosen have argued that the contemporary media ecology completely departs from the logic of mass media, whereby the idea of a passive audience or public becomes untenable (Rosen quoted in Mandiberg 2012). Furthermore, social media gurus such as Clay Shirky (2008, 2010) have contributed in turning the 'amateur' (Keen 2007) into the new hero of Web 2.0. All in all the narrative of Web 2.0 resonates with typical populist discourses in casting the generic Internet user into a new avatar of the common man of populism: the atomised individual fighting against big power structures, as discussed in the foregoing section.

Crucial to the political deployment of such a participatory imaginary of Web 2.0 is an emphasis on the emancipatory character of disintermediation and directness. Activist discourse in the 'popular wave' is accompanied by a profound critique of all intermediary structures, be they corporate or governmental, seen as alienating individuals from their right to participate directly in public affairs. Activists attack parties, trade unions, politicians and institutions as parasites which prevent the 'directness' of a genuine democracy. A clear example of this discourse comes from Beppe Grillo, who has drawn inspiration from socially minded IT entrepreneur Adriano Olivetti's idea of "democracy without parties" (1951), whereby the representative system is substituted by a network of self-governed communities, and from Simone Weil's manifesto *On the Abolition of All Political Parties* (2013). Similar is the gist of the discourse of Partido X. In one of his campaign videos, Partido X has declared its intention to "do away with the political class, and all intermediaries."[7] Besides net parties, the protest movements of 2011 were also imbued with a deep valuing of directness and disintermediation. This can be seen in the discourse of people such as Fabio Gandara, one of the founders of DRY (*Democracia Real Ya,* Real Democracy Now), who explained that the main contribution of social network sites was the fact that "they gave people the impression that they could participate directly in public affairs" (Gerbaudo 2012, 88).

Concretely, what these movements often propose in combination with this critique of existing democracy is a form of digital democracy or e-democracy (see, e.g., Wilhelm 2000): the use of electronic platforms as means for decision making and voting. In order to analyse the nature and implications of this emerging democratic process it is necessary to take into account the different notions that have emerged in the field of digital democracy. Christian Fuchs has summed up this debate as revolving around three different visions: (1) representative digital democracy, (2) plebiscitary digital democracy, and (3) grassroots digital democracy (2008, 234–237). Of specific interest for comprehending what is meant by democracy 2.0 are the latter two. Plebiscitary digital democracy is an electronic adaptation of plebiscitary democracy manifested in referenda and popular initiatives, in countries such as France, Switzerland and Italy. It is enacted in practices such as online surveys, online polls and online voting, where much emphasis is laid on the numbers as quantitive measures of the general will of the public (ibid., 235). Grassroots digital democracy puts instead an emphasis on the qualitative and community-based character of participation, and it is connected with ideas of self-management (ibid., 237).

While arguably digital grassroots democracy was the model dominant among anti-globalisation activists who pioneered the use of the Internet as a political means, the notion of democracy 2.0 utilised by activists in the popular wave possibly approximates more to what Fuchs names "digital plebiscitary democracy" (ibid., 234). This change in the model of digital democracy has largely to do with the shift in scale brought about in the transition to Web 2.0. The anti-globalisation movement utilised its own autonomous platforms as spaces for small group politics, often involving a few hundred individuals. By using social media platforms instead contemporary activists scale up to the level of mass politics, and become concerned once again with claiming mass support for their proposed lines of actions. In this context, the utilisation of social media platforms appears as a contemporary adaptation of the traditional populist striving for 'direct democracy' or plebiscitary democracy that, as Mény and Surel have observed (2002), has constituted a traditional cause for populist movements.

This striving for a digital direct democracy is visible in the development of a number of activist online voting platforms. This includes the Pirate Party's Liquid Feedback project and e-vote initiatives such as GeneralWill.org and OpenAssembly.org. In the case of Spain the most famous example has been the Democracia 4.0[8] project, launched by some information freedom activists connected to the Indignados movement in Madrid, which was approved by the assembly of Puerta del Sol. In Italy, the 5 Star Movement has launched its own online consultation to decide the candidates to run in the 2013 parliamentary elections, in which 20,252 people participated; it used an online polling system to poll supporters about which candidate for the presidency of the Republic to vote for in parliament. These are undoubtedly all interesting experiments. But they are still small scale phenomena that involve only a core of activists. Much more important in terms of overall reach is the way in which the groups of the popular wave have been using their social media platforms as means of mass direct democracy.

Social media platforms such as Twitter and Facebook have acquired the role of an informal voting system, operating on the principle of 'one like, one vote,' in which liking, sharing or re-tweeting assumes the nature of a vote of confidence on a certain message or proposal. Activists I interviewed in Spain, Egypt and the U.S. agreed that the response of Internet users constituted for them an indicator of their support for a certain course of action or a certain message. Some of them used features such as polls available on

Facebook fan pages to ask page users to express their opinion on different issues. But more generally they considered the number of likes, tweets and shares they received as an indication of approval/disapproval for a certain proposal, on the basis of which they could decide whether to go ahead or to change plans. Within social media activism the number of likes/shares/ re-tweets comes to constitute a crucial source of legitimacy. These metrics, of which Web 2.0 abounds, come to indicate the extent to which a certain message or proposal is really backed up by bottom-up enthusiasm, a decisive factor in order to secure its ultimate success. They become the means for a permanent consultation, a sort of ongoing 'temperature check' by which to gauge the mood among the social base of parties and social movements.

6. TECHNO-PLEBISCITARIANISM AND TECHNO-PROCEDURALISM

The experimentation developed by parties and movements in the popular wave opens up important opportunities for a new emancipatory politics matching the affordances of the ecology of social media. At the same time, however, it also raises important risks that need to be carefully scrutinised. Many activists, such as the Spanish Javier Toret, have with good reason celebrated the power of the emerging 'techno-politics' that we see across the parties and movements of the popular wave. However, it is also important for sympathetic academics to be able to identify the risks involved in this venture and the possible distortions that can arise. Such critical assessment is what I intend to perform in this discussion section, focusing on two crucial dangers faced by the groups subscribing to the ideological orientation of populism 2.0: (1) techno-plebiscitarianism and (2) techno-proceduralism.

The emergence of a digital plebiscitary democracy entails a risk of techno-plebiscitarianism, to be intended negatively as an authoritarian exacerbation of the centralising tendencies inherent in digital plebiscitary democracy. Plebiscitary democracy has often been criticised for the risk of impinging on the rights of minorities and the principle of political pluralism (Mouffe 2005). In the case of Occupy the claim to be the 99 per cent has been criticised by people of colour and gender-based groups, who felt that this naming ran the risk of diminishing their own specific identity. In the Italian case, furthermore, Beppe Grillo's claim about his wish to win 100 per cent of the votes, and thus eliminate all party factionalisms, has sparked parallels with fascism. Some of these criticisms are no doubt exaggerated, and sometimes they reflect a stubborn attachment to political minoritarianism that leaves little room for constructing a truly emancipatory politics. Furthermore, some groups such as the Partido X have put much emphasis on the need to defend difference and have devised complex internal decision-making mechanisms precisely to allow for different views to be taken into account. But it is evident that unless popular movements accept that they are not really the totality of the political citizenry but only a "partiality that wants to be a totality" (Laclau 2005, 87), they might run the risk of being turned towards authoritarian ends.

Another problem connected with techno-plebiscitarianism is the continuing presence of invisible forms of leadership, despite claims to horizontality (see, e.g., Mason 2012). Fuchs has rightly noticed how one of the problems with plebiscitary democracy is that the selection of the issues on which 'the people' are asked to vote is almost invariably in the hands of few charismatic leaders (2008, 226). The risk is that participants can end up only approving or rejecting a plan that has already been devised by someone else. Social media activism reflects some of these problematic aspects of plebiscitary democracy. In fact, as I have argued in my previous work (Gerbaudo 2012), there continue to be forms of leadership in social movements of the popular wave, and the same applies to emerging parties, as the role of Beppe Grillo in the 5 Star Movement blatantly demonstrates. In this context, we see the presence of clear asymmetries between organizers and common participants, even though the border between these two categories is porous and the way in which leaders are selected is often meritocratic. Common participants have indeed some room for intervening on decisions and influencing the debate that takes place on social media platforms. However, the interaction that is hereby offered is, in all earnestness, often more a form of reaction than a symmetrical two-way interaction. It is true that the 'generic Internet user' can have his or her say heard, more than it would have been the case in a traditional bureaucratic party or movement. But often this say takes the form of a reaction to something that has already largely been 'pre-packaged,' so to speak, something which he/she can like or not like, re-tweet or not re-tweet, or comment upon positively or negatively. In other words the influence of participants is often rather limited in qualitative terms and often is reducible to quantitative actions approximating a 'yes' or 'no' vote, adding to the tallies.

The almost obsessive focus on the issue of direct democracy that has been documented in the foregoing section raises a second risk: the danger of techno-proceduralism. Contemporary popular movements put much stress on the need to construct a new political process, and they see in social media promising means to fulfil this task. Yet, at the same time, they sometimes reflect a certain degree of political vacuousness in their tendency not to put forward substantive economic and social demands, beyond the very demand of direct democracy. While I don't think that there is a predetermined solution to this riddle, or that this solution goes under the evergreen name of 'communism' (see Badiou 2012), I share with Alain Badiou a suspicion towards the over-emphasis on democracy that has characterised movements and parties of the popular wave. This is because democracy as such is a procedure (Schumpeter 1947), and struggling for a procedure alone, irrespective of its ends, seems self-serving, especially at a time of economic and social emergency such as the one we are currently living in. Unless parties and movements subscribing to populism 2.0 dissociate themselves from this obsession with methods and begin working on a more coherent and substantive political programme, they will run the risk of fizzling out and further exacerbating that very political cynicism from which they have drawn so much energy.

7. CONCLUSION

In the current situation of anti-political cynicism that dominates a sizeable number of western countries in the aftermath of the 2007–2008 financial crisis, social media, and the valuing of participation attached to them, have come to offer protest movements and emerging parties a powerful channel through which to construct new forms of engagement with that "amorphous" (Gramsci 1973) social base that goes under the name of the 'people.' The means of communication of Web 2.0 have come to be utilised as a platform of interpellation of the common people, now identified with the generic Internet user of Web 2.0. This user is invited to participate in these movements and parties of the popular wave, with the promise of a democracy 2.0, an interactive direct democracy, in which the affordances of social network sites are seen as providing a horizontal system of decision making, capable of superseding the discredited institutions of parliamentary democracy and party politics.

In the social media activism practised by movements such as the Indignados and Occupy Wall Street, or in Internet parties such as the 5 Star Movement and the Partido X, we find valuable attempts to reinvent democracy, and in so doing to deal with the crisis of representation and the crisis of legitimacy of traditional democratic institutions. These practices testify to a renewed desire to participate in political decisions and in collective action that can be read as a positive reaction to the situation of economic and political despair affecting many western countries in the aftermath of the crisis of 2007–2008. Yet it is evident that populism 2.0 also raises a series of contradictions and risks that need to be carefully scrutinised. The major risk faced by this orientation is no doubt techno-plebiscitarianism. The practice of a digital plebiscitary democracy, through both formal and informal modalities of online voting, can bring about a disregard for the right of minorities and lead to new authoritarian involutions, as seen, among others, in the case of the role of Beppe Grillo in the 5 Star Movement. Furthermore there is a risk of techno-proceduralism. In their obsession with web procedures and tools, often emerging movements and parties do not appear sufficiently concerned with political content and run the risk of not devoting enough attention to developing a coherent political programme.

In conclusion, the emergence of populism 2.0 constitutes a powerful manifestation of the possibilities and threats that characterise the current era of global economic crisis, political innovation and fast diffusion of social network technologies. Social media activism represents a terrain for constructing new forms of mass politics, and thus supersedes the minoritarianism that characterised the communications of the anti-globalisation movement and other forms of radical politics in previous decades. Furthermore, activists have found in the promise of a digital direct democracy a powerful unifying demand to pull together very different constituencies, and to construct a sense of civilisational mission. It remains to be seen to what extent populism 2.0 will sidestep the dangers of techno-plebiscitarianism and techno-proceduralism and deliver on its promise of democratic renewal. Yet this vision has already influenced a profound reshaping of activist understanding of communication technologies and favoured the development of a digital mass politics whose potentials are enormous.

NOTES

1. The term 'populism' is not used in the usual derogatory sense but in the sense of politics of the 'people,' as discussed, among others, by Ernesto Laclau (2005).
2. My use of the term 'ideology' is not in the Marxian sense of 'false consciousness' but in the sense used within the Gramscian current of analysis that sees ideology as an action-oriented system of values and beliefs that allows different groups to make sense of the world (Gramsci 1973).
3. Beppe Grillo's official blog http://www.beppegrillo.it.
4. Andrea Giambartolomei, Occupy Wall Street, Micah White: "Dobbiamo fare come M5S" [Micah White: We need to do like the 5 Star Movement], *Il Fatto Quotidiano*, October 6, 2013, http://www.ilfattoquotidiano.it/2013/10/06/occupy-wall-street-micah-white-dobbiamo-fare-come-m5s/734775.
5. Grillo, Beppe. 7 Feb 2013. 'Lettera agli Italiani' (Letter to italians). Beppe Grillo's official blog, http://www.beppegrillo.it/2013/02/lettera_agli_italiani.html.
6. Website description on the homepage of the "We Are the 99 Percent," Tumblr blog, http://wearethe99percent.tumblr.com.
7. Partido X: Democracia y punto. #DemocraciaYPunto. Available at http://www.youtube.com/watch?v=g5n3mkLi2qo.
8. Partido X. 9 Apr 2013. 'Partido X: Democracia y punto. #DemocraciaYPunto' (X Party: Democracy full stop). YouTube. https://www.youtube.com/watch?v=g5n3mkLi2qo

REFERENCES

Albertazzi, Daniele, and Duncan McDonnell. 2008. *Twenty-First Century Populism: The Spectre of Western European Democracy.* Houndmills, UK: Palgrave Macmillan.
Badiou, Alain, and Gregory Elliott. 2012. *The Rebirth of History.* London: Verso.
Bartlett, Jamie, Jonathan Birdwell, and Mark Littler. (2012). *The new face of digital populism.* Lodon: Demos.
Bauman, Zygmunt. 2001. *The Individualized Society.* Cambridge, UK: Polity Press.
Beck, Ulrich, and Elisabeth Beck-Gernsheim. 2002. *Individualization Institutionalized Individualism and Its Social and Political Consequences.* London: SAGE.
boyd, danah, and Nicole Ellison. 2007. Social Network Sites: Definition, History, and Scholarship. *Journal of Computer-Mediated Communication* 13 (1): 210–230.
Bratich, Jack Z. (2011). Pox Populi Network Populism, Network Sovereigns, and Experiments in People-Powers. *Cultural Studies Critical Methodologies* 11 (4): 341–345.
Canovan, Mary. 1981. *Populism.* New York: Harcourt Brace Jovanovich.
———. 2005. *The People.* Cambridge: Polity.
Castells, Manuel. 1996. *The Rise of the Network Society.* Malden, MA: Blackwell.
———. 2000. *End of Millennium.* Oxford: Blackwell.
———. 2009. *Communication Power.* Oxford: Oxford University Press.

Democracia Real Ya. 2011. Democracia Real Ya's Manifesto. http://www.demo craciarealya.es/manifiesto-comun/manifesto-english/.

Eurispes. 2013. *Rapporto Italia 2013*. Rome: Eurispes.

Fuchs, Christian. 2008. *Internet and Society: Social Theory in the Information Age.* New York: Routledge.

Gerbaudo, Paolo. 2012. *Tweets and the Streets: Social Media and Contemporary Activism.* London: Pluto Press.

———. 2013a. Online Aggregation in the "Mass Web." *Opendemocracy.* http://www.opendemocracy.net/paolo-gerbaudo/online-aggregation-in-mass-web.

———. 2013b. When Anarchism Goes Pop. *Opendemocracy.* http://www.open democracy.net/paolo-gerbaudo/when-anarchism-goes-pop.

Gitlin, Todd. 2012. *Occupy Nation: The Roots, the Spirit, and the Promise of Occupy Wall Street.* New York: It Books.

Gramsci, Antonio. 1973. *Selections from the Prison Notebooks of Antonio Gramsci.* Edited by Geoffrey Nowell-Smith and Quintin Hoare. London: Lawrence & Wishart.

International Telecommunication Union. (2013). World Telecommunication/ICT Indicators Database 2013 (17th edition) [data file]. Geneva: ITU. http://www.itu.int/en/ITU-D/Statistics/Pages/publications/wtid.aspx.

Jenkins, Henry. 2006. *Fans, Bloggers, and Gamers: Exploring Participatory Culture.* New York: New York University Press.

Johnson, Lawrence Jeffrey. 2013. Las raíces internacionales del 99% y la "política de cualquiera." *IC Revista Científica de Información y Comunicación* 10: 52–72.

Juris, Jeffrey S. 2008. *Networking Futures: The Movements against Corporate Globalization.* Durham, NC: Duke University Press.

Keen, Andrew. 2007. *The Cult of the Amateur: How Today's Internet Is Killing Our Culture.* New York: Doubleday/Currency.

Laclau, Ernesto. 2005. *On Populist Reason.* London: Verso.

Maeckelbergh, Marianne. 2009. *The Will of the Many: How the Alterglobalisation Movement Is Changing the Face of Democracy.* London: Pluto Press.

Mandiberg, Michael. 2012. *The Social Media Reader.* New York: New York University Press.

Mason, Paul. 2012. *Why It's Kicking Off Everywhere: The New Global Revolutions.* London: Verso.

Mény, Yves, and Yves Surel. 2002. *Democracies and the Populist Challenge.* Basingstoke: Palgrave.

Mouffe, Chantal. 2005. *The Return of the Political.* London: Verso.

Olivetti, Adriano. 1951. *Democracy without Political Parties.* Ivrea: Community Movement.

Schumpeter, Joseph A. 1947. *Capitalism, Socialism, and Democracy.* New York: Harper & Brothers.

Shirky, Clay. 2008. *Here Comes Everybody: The Power of Organizing without Organizations.* New York: Penguin Press.

———. 2010. *Cognitive Surplus: Creativity and Generosity in a Connected Age.* New York: Penguin Press.

Taggart, P. A. 2000. *Populism.* Buckingham: Open University Press.

Tarchi, Marco. 2003. *L'Italia Populista: Dal Qualunquismo Ai Girotondi.* Bologna: Il Mulino.

Tarrow, Sidney G. 1998. *Power in Movement: Social Movements and Contentious Politics.* Cambridge, UK: Cambridge University Press.

"We are the 99%" Tumblr blog. 2011. http://wearethe99percent.tumblr.com/.

Weil, Simone. 2013. *On the Abolition of All Political Parties.* Collingwood: Black Inc.

Wellman, Barry, and Caroline A. Haythornthwaite. 2002. *The Internet in Everyday Life.* Malden, MA: Blackwell.

Wilhelm, Anthony G. 2000. *Democracy in the Digital Age: Challenges to Political Life in Cyberspace.* New York: Routledge.

4   Anonymous
Hacktivism and Contemporary Politics

Christian Fuchs

1. INTRODUCTION

It is Friday, August 6, 2012, on the Internet. Sixty-seven years earlier, on August 6, 1945, the U.S. dropped the first atom bomb on Hiroshima. One hears a song by Trey Parker: "America. Fuck yeah. [. . .] So lick my butt and suck on my balls, America, fuck yeah! Whatcha' gonna do when we come for you now? (. . .) McDonalds, fuck yeah! Wal-Mart, fuck yeah!" Pictures of cats that look human are accompanied by the request, "I want to start a collection of my fetish catboys so post moar!" There is a link to a live cam on Times Square. One also finds an image showing a burning American flag that is accompanied by the logos of McDonald's and images of a can of Mountain Dew, the Statue of Liberty, a guitar player and a screaming bear. "You should kill yourself, fucking AMERRRICCAAA, you little faggot." A rapper writes a new song and says that the first few minutes of the discussion in his thread will become part of the song. There is a story about a brother who tries to seduce his sister, but it turns out that his sister is a large arthropod. There is a thread with images of female buttocks, accompanied by an announcement that one of the portrayed girls receives prank phone calls. One sees a picture of a couple having oral sex accompanied by the text "PORNO FUCK YEAH!" as well as a picture of a drunk sleeping man accompanied by the text "buddy passed out after 11 Coors lights and 2 bud lights" and the suggestion that a game will decide what the person who posted the picture will do to the drunk. There is a screenshot of a female teenager's profile on Facebook, suggesting "54, 72, 37 or 00 decides what I write," meaning that the fifty-fourth, seventy-second, thirty-seventh or hundredth posting determines what the person will write to the girl on Facebook. The subsequent interaction is posted online (e.g., "Hi, i liked you since high school i wanted to date you, but i was very young and very angry, perhaps that's no excuse. You're really hot and whenever i see you my wee wee goes woop, please go out with me or I'll skyrim myself"), the girl answers and each answer to her is determined in a new game. The girl temporarily closes her Facebook profile and the action ceases.

Welcome to 4chan.org.[1] Christopher Poole founded 4chan in 2003. It is the space where the movement that has become known as 'Anonymous' originated (Stryker 2011). It works as a series of forums, each oriented on a specific topic (or allowing all topics, such as the forum 'b'). Users can post text, images, links, content and answers to other threads. The postings are anonymous and therefore the word 'Anonymous' is displayed as the username in all threads and posts. As the examples show, 4chan is at the same time anarchistic, mean, rude, absurd, pornographic, political, creative, playful, sarcastic, a display of black humour, etc. Anonymous makes use of the wisdom and creativity of the crowd in its campaigns. This organized wisdom can hit randomly selected everyday people alongside powerful organizations and individuals. 4chan features "depraved images and nasty jokes," yet is "at the same time a source of extraordinary, unhindered creativity" (Olson 2012, 32).

The wider public has gained knowledge of Anonymous, especially because of the latter's support of WikiLeaks in December 2010. Distributed denial of service (DDoS) attacks were used for shutting down the websites of PayPal, PostFinance, Visa, MasterCard and the Bank of America that disabled donation possibilities to WikiLeaks. Anonops, a node in the Anonymous network that maintains an Internet Relay Chat (IRC), a blog, a Twitter account and YouTube video channel, is said to have originated Operation Payback that attacked film companies opposed to file sharing and supported WikiLeaks (Reissmann, Stöcker and Lischka 2012, 127–128):

> Anonymous' campaign will defend against any individual, organization, corporation, and/or government entity that seeks to hinder the free flow of information on the Internet and beyond. [. . .] We are using the LOIC [the Low Orbit Ion Cannon, a software tool for DDoS attacks] to conduct distributed denial of service attacks against businesses that have aided in the censorship of any person. [. . .] Our current goal is to raise awareness about WikiLeaks and the underhanded methods employed by the above companies to impair WikiLeaks' ability to function. [. . .] The continuing attacks on PayPal are already tested and preferable: while not damaging their ability to process payments, they are successful in slowing their network down just enough for people to notice and thus, we achieve our goal of raising awareness.[2]

Anonop's message titled "A Letter from Anonymous: Our Message, Intentions, and Potential Targets" was distributed as text and as multiple videos at different platforms.[3] Such videos are often made in an artistic way and are spread on multiple popular Internet platforms, which shows that Anonymous is also about creative, aesthetic and artistic expression of dissent and the use of user-generated content sites for communicating to the public and organizing distributed actions.

The task of this chapter is to reflect on what kind of movement Anonymous is. For doing so, I first give an overview of Anonymous' history (section two). I then make a theoretical analysis of its status as a social movement and of its power, as well as the state counter-power that it is facing (section three). I also analyse how Anonymous relates to political world views (section four). The analysis presented in this chapter is grounded in political theory. Anonymous reconfigures the power of social movements and at the same time is facing state power's attempt to infiltrate and monitor activists.

2.   ANONYMOUS: A BRIEF HISTORY

Anonymous is a networked movement that has its origins in 4chan (Stryker 2011). It has different nodes organized around IRCs and forums, such as Anonnet,[4] AnonOps,[5] VoxAnon,[6] AnonPlus[7] and affinity groups like the Peoples Liberation Front (PLF), LulzSec or AntiSec. Anonnet describes its task in the following way: "AnonNet, an anonymous IRC network, exists to enable the free flow of ideas and communication without fear of third party interception, monitoring, intimidation or coercion. We believe in freedom of expression, and we want to help you make your voice heard."[8]

The history of Anonymous can only be summarised briefly here (for details see Olson 2012; Reissmann, Stöcker and Lischka 2012; Stryker 2011). According to Reissmann, Stöcker and Lischka (2012, 32–33), one of Anonymous' first collective actions planned on 4chan was the blockage and disturbance of the teenager online community Habbo Hotel in 2006. Hundreds of Anonymous activists entered the community at the same time and disturbed the normal course of action. Also in 2006, a campaign against the fascist U.S. talk show host Hal Turner was started, in which his talk radio programme was disturbed, personal data about him was posted on the Internet and his Internet radio station was blocked. In 2008, a video about Scientology's practices was released on YouTube. Scientology made a legal claim to remove the video, which resulted in Anonymous' Project Chanology against Scientology. When Anonymous started engaging in such campaigns, it became common to use IRC channels as communication tools for coordinating and organizing the actions (Olson 2012, 52). In 2009, Anonymous created a website in support of the Iranian protests. In 2009 and 2010, it attacked computers and websites of Australian government institutions due to new Internet censorship laws. In 2010, Anonymous attacked the websites of organizations that defend intellectual property rights (like the Recording Industry Association of America, the Motion Picture Association of America and the British Phonographic Industry). In 2010, it started Operation Payback, which included DDoS attacks against Amazon, MasterCard, PayPal, PostFinance and Visa after they disabled payment possibilities to WikiLeaks. In 2011, Anonymous attacked Sony websites because the media company launched legal claims against George Hotz, who released instructions for how to jailbreak the Sony PlayStation 3. During the Arab Spring, a small group of AnonOps activists organizing themselves in the private IRC channel #InternetFeds attacked the websites of the governments of Tunisia, Libya, Egypt and Syria (Olson 2012, 425–426). The hackers Sabu, Tflow and Kayla, who participated in #InternetFeds, joined with Topiary, AVunit and Pwnsauce to form the group LulzSec, which in 2011 conducted various hacking activities over a fifty-day period (Olson 2012, 427ff.).

In solidarity with the protests against the plans to eliminate collective bargaining rights of public employment unions in Wisconsin, Anonymous attacked websites of Koch Industries, which supported anti-union activities in Wisconsin. Also in 2011, Anonymous attacked websites of the government of Malaysia because the latter blocked websites. It attacked private and local government websites in Orlando, Florida, because activists of Food Not Bombs were arrested for giving food to homeless people in Lake Eola Park. It blocked child porn sites and published data about the sites' users. After the maltreatment of the alleged WikiLeaks source Bradley Manning by prison personnel, it announced that it would attack the communications of the Quantico high security prison and its personnel. It called for mass protests against the U.S. Stop Online Piracy Act. Probably Anonymous' most visible activity in 2011 was the support of the Occupy Wall Street movement. It called its members to participate in the movement. After a policeman pepper sprayed non-violent student protesters at the University of California Davis campus, Anonymous released videos with the policeman's personal contact data. In December 2011, Anonymous started Nazi-Leaks, a platform that leaks the contact data of alleged neo-Nazis and their supporters.

Anonymous has made use of tactics such as DDoS attacks, anonymous phone calls, mobbing, publication of private data, death threats, sending black pages to fax addresses, ordering hundreds of pizzas to be delivered to one address simultaneously (Reissmann, Stöcker and Lischka 2012), d0xing (posting personal data about targets publicly on the Internet), signing people up for junk mail, defacing websites, hacking into servers, downloading databases from servers with the help of SQL injection attacks, publishing e-mail and address lists, rickrolling (links that pretend to lead to sexual or other content, but bring up Rick Astley's video "Never Gonna Give You Up"), releasing logins and passwords, and street protests (Norton 2011, 2012a, 2012b). Their targets are sometimes politically chosen, but in many cases more arbitrary, which, for example, also includes teenagers such as the then fifteen-year-old teenager Boxxy, against whom a harassment campaign was started on 4chan in 2007 because users thought that her YouTube videos were stupid.[9] Users, for example, posted nude pictures of themselves, writing on their breasts or other body parts messages such as "Kill Boxxy," "Fuck Boxxy" or "Boxx Sucks" (ibid.).

Anonymous users say they engage in such actions for fun, for "the lulz" (which stands for "laughing out loud"), as they say—"laughter at someone else's expense."[10] Anonymous is an unpredictable, anarchistic, disturbing, ambiguous, confusing, exaggeratory collective of the nameless, a loose network without members that has loose goals in which everyone can participate and that struggles for Internet freedom (Reissmann, Stöcker and Lischka 2012). At the same time, this openness also can be a source of contradictions: "Because everyone can call himself Anonymous, the collective is full of contradictions" (ibid., 12). When the 4chan culture turned into the Anonymous movement, actions were no longer just performed "for the lulz," but began to serve more political purposes (ibid.). The anarchistic culture with arbitrary targets never ceased to exist, but over the years a more political agenda tended to emerge in parallel and by making use of the culture of playfulness.

3.   ANONYMOUS: SOCIAL MOVEMENT POWER
AND STATE POWER

Gabriella Coleman (2012) describes Anonymous as "hackers, technologists, activists, human rights advocates and geeks" who organize collective actions online and offline that "advance political causes" but are also organized "for sheer amusement." Coleman (2011a; see also Ralph and Coleman 2011), who has conducted an in-depth ethnography of Anonymous, observed that Anonymous after its emergence on 4chan developed from the IRC and online community Anonet's focus on trolling ("the act of agitating or fooling people for fun under false pretenses") (Stryker 2011, 94) used for fun ("lulz": from "lol"—laughing out loud) and concerns for freedom of speech (as in the campaign against Scientology) into a more complex structure, focusing on hacking as collective political protest action that is signified by the emergence of the IRC and online community AnonOps in 2001, which advanced Operation Payback, the WikiLeaks solidarity campaign, and other campaigns (Olson 2012, 421ff.). Since 2008, when the campaign against Scientology started, Anonymous has become more political (Coleman 2012; Norton 2012b). According to Coleman, it has "no consistent philosophy or political program," and due to anonymity is based on fluid participation, which enables fast intensification and abandonment of actions. Coleman, drawing from Gilles Deleuze and Félix Guattari (1987), therefore describes Anonymous as rhizomatic. Coleman stresses that Anonymous is heterogeneous, that there are conflicts and debates about the political direction and that it has a culture of grassroots democracy based on an "anti-leader and anti-celebrity ethic" (Coleman 2011a), "decentralized non-hierarchical modes of interaction" and a "commitment to consensus" (Coleman 2011d).

Coleman (2012) compares Anonymous' humour to movements like the Situationists, the Dadaists, the Yippies or the Yes Men. Based on Ernst Bloch's (1985) principle of hope, she argues that Anonymous gives reason for hope that evading and toppling injustices are "latent possibilities that in certain conditions can be activated and perhaps lead to new political realities" (Coleman 2012). One can add that Anonymous to a certain extent also resembles the Spaßguerilla (fun guerrilla) movement that originated in the German student movement and made use of fun as a political strategy (see

AG Spaß muss sein 1997). Examples have included cake attacks on political opponents, the staging of politically motivated, invisible theatre performances in public spaces, or a planned pudding attack on U.S. vice-president Hubert Humphrey (in the context of the Vietnam War). Other examples include a fake demonstration that pretended to be organized by the German right-wing extremist party Deutsche Volksunion (DVU) and used slogans like "Germans, eat German bananas!" or "I am happy that the earth is a slice" (ibid., 250). They distributed letters to private households during the 1991 Gulf War that stated that Aral Oil provides a voucher for 10 litres free gasoline as part of the campaign "Peace in the Gulf" (ibid., 252).

A central characteristic of Spaßguerilla is that it estranges/distances situations in everyday life from their original context and gives a new meaning to them that has political significance; it tries to publicly uncover and criticise structures of domination (ibid., 74ff.). The Spaßguerilla movement has taken this strategy from Brecht's distancing effect (V-Effekt, or Verfremdungseffekt) in his concept of the epical/dialectical theatre. "The distancing effect is that the thing that shall be brought to comprehension, to which attention shall be directed, is transformed from a common, known, immediately given thing into a special, striking, unexpected thing. The self-evident is made in a certain sense incomprehensible, but this happens only in order to make it then even more comprehensible" (Brecht 1967, 355, translated by the author).

The action performed on stage is brought into "contradiction with handed down beliefs" (ibid., 362, translated by the author). "Conventions are turned into something astonishing, that which is generally present into something peculiar, and that which seems natural shall seem artificial" (ibid., 372, translated by the author). Dialectical/epical theatre shows the "complex, diverse and contradictory relations between individuals and society" (ibid., 922, translated by the author), the "unfixed, volatile, conditional" and "contradictions in all conditions that have the habit to turn into other contradictory conditions" so that the "transformability of the cohabitation of humans and thereby the transformability of the human itself" are shown (Brecht 1967, 923, translated by the author).

The goal is that the audience's attitude is transformed from being passive to being active, as well as that the spectator sees the world as "being available for him and his activity" (ibid., 358, translated by the author) so that a standpoint can emerge that is critical of society (ibid., 346). Dialectical theatre makes use of contradictions of the performed actions and feelings, as well as the transition from quantity to quality (accumulation of incomprehensibilities until comprehension emerges) (ibid., 360, translated by the author). Brecht (ibid., 364) mentions as examples the distancing effect of James Joyce's *Ulysses*, Dadaism and Surrealism.

The text "Fünf Thesen für die Spaßguerilla" (Five theses for the fun guerrilla) concludes that "fun guerrilla has no programme—except: that everyone must become a clown" (AG Spaß muss sein 1997, 200; translated by

the author). Anonymous, just like Spaßguerilla and Brecht's dialectical theatre, aims at disrupting the normal functioning of everyday life and bringing
absurdity into everyday life in order to show the incongruities and absurdi-
ties of the contemporary world itself. Tactics like mass pizza deliveries or the
appearance of Guy Fawkes armies are classical Spaßguerilla tactics themselves. The differences between Spaßguerilla and Anonymous is that the
first is always political, whereas the second is at times political; Spaßguerilla
traditionally originated in offline communities like the Kommune 1,[11] in
which the activists knew each other personally and developed close political, personal, emotional and often sexual relations, whereas Anonymous
is mainly organized online, involves a high level of anonymity and tends
to work to a certain degree from a distance without face-to-face meetings,
although online activism tends to at times turn into offline activism (e.g., in
the Scientology protests). Anonymous, just like Spaßguerilla, brings the
unusual into the common world and thereby tries to estrange everyday life.
Spaßguerilla's strategy is to estrange the estranged world from its estrange-
ment by estranging situations in everyday life, which is a political strategy.
Parts of Anonymous at times share this political strategy, whereas other
parts are simultaneously non-political.

Quinn Norton (2011) sees Anonymous as a culture organized around
"doing weird things" that embarrass and separate, and collective attacks
("raids"). It is diverse and leaderless but does still somehow "succeed in
speaking with a single voice, demanding freedom for the network that is their
home" (Norton 2012b). Norton (2012a) describes how a typical Anonymous
operation originates in an IRC chat (such as Anonops or Anonnet), where
special channels are set up, in which press releases and videos are presented
and where activists gather for planning a joint action. When "some offense
to the net is detected, anons will converge on one or more of these 'chans,'
with hundreds or thousands arriving within hours. [. . .] What looks in one
moment like a sad, empty chat room can quickly become the staging ground
for a major multi-pronged assault" (Norton 2012b). The operations against
credit card companies that blocked payments to WikiLeaks were organized
via the AnonOps IRC channel #operationpayback, where almost eight thousand users together planned the action (Olson 2012, 424). Norton (2012b)
argues that since 2008, Anonymous became subsequently more political
and a threat to governments and corporations; it became "a self-appointed
immune system for the Internet, striking back at anyone the hive mind perceived as an enemy of freedom, online or offline." Especially the support
for the Tunisian revolution and the Occupy movement featured a "radical
new generation of members that eschewed pure lulz in favor of focused,
disruptive action" (Norton 2012b). The Occupy movement had special relevance for Anonymous because Anonymous activists "could culturally connect with the local Occupys" (Norton 2012a). Both collectives were bound
together by "being the kinds of people who never found a comfortable place
in society" (ibid.). As a result, Anonymous "became bolder, stranger, more

threatening, and more comforting in turns" (ibid.). Anonymous is a leaderless "do-ocracy," "rul[ing] by mere doing": individuals propose actions, others join in (or not) and then the Anonymous flag is flown over the result. "There's no one to grant permission, no promise of praise or credit, so every action must be its own reward" (Norton 2012b).

Donatella della Porta and Mario Diani define social movements as "(1) informal networks, based (2) on shared beliefs and solidarity, which mobilize about (3) conflictual issues, through (4) the frequent use of various forms of protest" (della Porta and Diani 1999, 16). Diani, in another definition, says social movements are "networks of informal interactions between a plurality of individuals, groups and/or organizations, engaged in political or cultural conflicts, on the basis of shared collective identities" (Diani 1992, 13). Based on these and other definitions, one can identify important aspects of social movements: societal problems; the negation of dominant values, institutions and structures; dissatisfaction; adversaries; shared collective identities; orientation toward social change; triggers of protest, contagion effects; mobilisation, protest practices and collective action; protest methods; and extra-parliamentary politics (Fuchs 2006).

A specific characteristic of Anonymous is that it is at the same time social movement and anti-movement; it is collective political action based on a shared identification with some basic values (such civil liberties and freedom of the Internet) that results in protest practices online and offline against adversaries and, at the same time, for many of those engaging on Anonymous platforms, individual play and entertainment. For most of the time, Anonymous exists "for the lulz," as fun for the users, but from time to time—and in the past years the frequency has increased—individual action turns into collective political action. Many people joining Anonymous' political actions share some basic political values that have been expressed in the text "5 Principles: An Anonymous Manifesto."[12] These values include struggle for an "open, fair, transparent, accountable and just society," in which information is "unrestricted and uncensored," and the upholding of citizens' "rights and liberties." Also, there is a guarantee of the "privacy of citizens" so that "citizens shall not be the target of any undue surveillance." Anonymous says that it is based on three principles: (1) the media should not be attacked; (2) critical infrastructure should not be attacked; and (3) one should work for justice and freedom.[13] Activists have their own interpretations of these basic values of freedom and justice. The overall principles are very loose, unlike a political party's programme, which is much more formalised. This looseness is also characteristic of social movements, but Anonymous differs from them by maintaining a high level of anonymity of its activists and practices.

The chosen protest methods are unconventional and take place online (hacking websites, publishing personal data, DDoS) and/or offline (street protests). The first require temporal synchronicity but are distributed actions conducted over the Internet from a spatial distance; they are collective online action at a distance. The latter are coordinated and planned online but make use of temporal and spatial co-presence. Traditional social movements (just like political parties) tend to encourage and be based on personal relations, face-to-face meetings, discussions and actions. In contrast, anybody who shares some basic values can declare an action to be part of Anonymous. In conventional social movements, campaigns are often focused on strategic adversaries. The highly decentralised and informal character of Anonymous in contrast often results in multiple independent and parallel campaigns that can become networked and coordinated but can also exist independently.

Anonymous activists often do not know each other and have not met but act in concert as a collective. Anonymous is easier to join and leave than other movements. According to Anonymous, "Anonymous is everyone. Anonymous is no one. Anonymous exists as an idea. You can also be Anonymous. Becoming Anonymous is simple. Just take action."[14] So one specific quality of Anonymous is that it has no clearly defined membership—anybody can join it. Anonymous therefore defines itself as an open idea:

> Now first and foremost, it is important to realize that ANONYMOUS—in fact—does not exist. It is just an idea—an internet meme—that can be appropriated by anyone, anytime to rally for a common cause that's in the benefit of humankind. [. . .] This means anyone can launch a new ideological message or campaign under the banner of ANONYMOUS. Anyone can take up a leading role in the spreading of the ANON-consciousness. [. . .] ANYONE anywhere can initiate an Anonymous operation, action, or group—and so long as they adhere to these [3] basic principles they are as much Anonymous as anyone. EVERYONE is Anonymous.[15]

At the same time, this high level of informality can also result in a lack of trust, stability and cohesion and can result in problems once the movement faces state repression or other challenges.

Anonymous, more than other movements, permanently transgresses the boundaries between individual and collective action, online and offline, movement and non-movement, spatial distance and presence, anonymity and knowledge, play and protest work, entertainment and politics, presence and absence, appearance and disappearance, the mundane and the uncommon, normality and absurdity, the real and the symbolic, conventional and unconventional behaviour. But one should not be mistaken; although everyone can join, Anonymous is not a pure leaderless, decentralised network.

James Surowiecki (2005) has argued that large groups of people are smarter than an elite few and that collective intelligence works better than leadership structures. "Even if most of the people within a group are not especially well-informed or rational, it can still reach a collectively wise decision" (Surowiecki 2005, xiii–xiv). The wisdom of the crowd faces three problems concerning (1) cognition, (2) coordination and (3) cooperation (ibid., xvii–xviii). These three dimensions can be mapped to a model of information that shapes information processing on the Internet. It conceives information as a threefold process of cognition, communication and cooperation. Anonymous therefore seems to be a distributed and networked information structure that involves cognition, communication and cooperation processes. Anonymous has all three dimensions: a mass of people gathers its collective knowledge about certain targets and shares it on the Internet, they coordinate their actions online in IRC channels by communicating, and take joint actions (such as DDoSing, etc.) at certain points in time.

The wisdom of the crowd has four characteristics: diverse opinions, independence of the actors, decentralisation and aggregation of actions (ibid., 10). Anonymous seems to satisfy these conditions: its activists have diverse opinions and motivations, they act anonymously without personal knowledge of each other, they are spatially distributed and their actions are aggregated to form a whole. Surowiecki argues that such structures are collectively smart. He argues that Internet phenomena such as Google, Slashdot and Wikipedia—and he would probably add Anonymous—are "the products of the wisdom of the crowds" (ibid., 275) and that the Internet is

> antihierarchical. It provides a vivid demonstration every day that systems can work smoothly and intelligently without traditional hierarchies and without having any one person in charge. Similarly important is the fact that the Internet simply makes it much easier to aggregate information from many different sources than ever before. (ibid., 276)

So the question is whether Anonymous is such a form of distributed intelligence that makes use of the wisdom of the crowd. My argument is that on the one hand Anonymous is a distributed and networked form of intelligence and collective action, and that on the other hand there are hubs of knowledge and action in this network, that there are contradictions of power (just like in all organizations that are embedded into modern society) and that there are power asymmetries immanent in modern society that allow powerful organizations such as state institutions (the FBI in the case of Anonymous) to monitor and try to control networked structures.

There are core activists with specific technical skills, media skills and organizational skills who carry out the core of hacking activities (Olson 2012). According to Parmy Olson (ibid.), they often meet in secret IRC channels, in which they plan campaigns. Olson (ibid., 9) argues that in many actions, there were several hundred activists, but a group of about ten who "managed most of the decisions" (ibid., 74–75, 113–122). She argues that in many DDoS attacks carried out by Anonymous, only a minor share of the participating computers was made up of the thousands of activists that simultaneously used the LOIC or other software tools (such as Gigaloader, JMeter), but that rather around 90 per cent (e.g., in the attack on PayPal.

com) of the "firepower" came from botnets, which are large networks of tens or hundreds of thousands of "zombie" computers that are controlled by single activists (such as Civil and Switch), with the help of malware that was injected into the computers of users without their knowledge in the form of downloads or viruses so that temporary remote control over these computers was enabled. Anonymous is a rhizomatic network of distributed activists (Coleman 2011a), but this network is neither non-hierarchical nor without internal conflicts and power structures. There are activists that have strategic skills and roles and form hubs in the activist network.

The existence of hubs and conflicts in the network seems to also have implications for state action. According to Olson (2012), Jennifer Emick, a former Anonymous activist, started to search for identifying information on Anonymous activists that she collected in lists and provided to the FBI, which as a result used the information to track down and finally arrest hackers like Sabu, Topiary, Kayla, Tflow and Pwnsauce. Since 2011, dozens of alleged Anonymous activists, including on the one hand AnonOps activists who were engaged in Operation Payback (e.g., Fennic, Nerdo) and on the other hand LulzSec and AntiSec hackers (Anarchaos, Kayla, Palladium, Pwnsauce, Sabu, TFlow, Topiary) were arrested (Olson 2012). This circumstance shows that Anonymous is not an invulnerable, mystic network, but made up of relations between real people that can, like all social movements, be monitored by the police and subjected to the violence of nation states and their coercive state apparatuses. Repression is a reality of all social movements, and Anonymous is no exception from this circumstance. The history of the modern state is also a history of the policing of social movements. Policing Anonymous is different from the policing of communists in the McCarthy era or the activities conducted in the COINTELPRO programme, but nonetheless it shares the aspect of the use of state power against politically motivated movements. The FBI has identified Anonymous as a threat and has defined it as not-for-profit cyber criminals that "undertake protests and commit computer crimes as a collective unit. [. . .] Anonymous has initiated multiple criminal Distributed Denial of Service attacks."[16] In contrast, Gabriella Coleman argues that Anonymous' use of DDoS has brought up the consideration about whether such tactics, although illegal, are ethically legitimate protest tactics (Coleman 2011a, 2011b, 2011c, 2011d).

The employment of symbolic means of expression as symbolic power is particularly important for Anonymous. When Anonymous activists join or organize street protests, they wear Guy Fawkes masks. Guy Fawkes was involved in the Gunpowder Plot in 1605, in which activists tried to bomb the British House of Lords. The Fawkes mask became popular in Alan Moore's comic "V for Vendetta," in which the revolutionary V struggles against a fascist regime. The use of the masks is a media strategy itself because it aims at directing the media and the public's attention to Anonymous. Symbolic expression is important for Anonymous, which relies on videos that are created in a crafty manner and often reflect an expression of artistic creativity.

They contain political messages, announcements of campaigns, statements about broader goals, etc., and are spread on user-generated content platforms like YouTube or Vimeo.

4. ANONYMOUS: LIBERALISM AND SOCIALISM

Stuart Hall (1986) argues that there are different variants of liberalism: conservative, social democratic and radical liberalism. Neo-liberalism as the dominant form of liberalism today blends cultural conservatism with nineteenth-century economic liberalism. Hall says that the dominant form of liberalism is grounded in the thought of John Locke and Adam Smith, whereas a radical form of liberalism that historically blended with socialism has grounds in feminist rights arguments of thinkers like Mary Wollstonecraft, struggles for female suffrage, the reliance of the Chartists and Owenites on liberal parliamentary democracy for socialist goals and the works of Tom Paine. These elements "flowed into working class radicalism and later became a key element in the formation of English socialism" (Hall 1986, 57). Linguistically this ambivalence can be observed in the fact that the term "liberal has often been a group term for progressive or radical opinions, and is still clear in this sense, notably in the USA" (Williams 1983, 181). Liberalism is a contradictory ideology. Anonymous is an expression of liberalism's contradictions. The late twentieth and early twenty-first centuries have seen the political rise of the neo-liberal ideology that stresses radical individualism, entrepreneurialism, individual responsibility, the ideology of the homo œconomicus, markets and competition as governing principles, and laissez-faire. This ideology aims at the "formalization of society on the model of the enterprise" (Foucault 2008, 160), the "economization of the entire social field" (ibid., 242) and the creation of an "enterprise society" (ibid.). Anonymous to a certain degree aligns itself with the language of the free individual that characterises contemporary liberalism, but at the same time expresses the contradictions of liberalism. To a minor extent it productively works on those elements that Hall stresses have historically had a potential to turn liberalism into socialism.

Jodi Dean (2002) points out that the culture of computing has always related to the relationship of publicity and privacy, as well as secrecy and transparency. She argues that in the 1950s and 1960s programmers were seen as a kind of priest-like elite that held a secret knowledge. In the 1970s, hackers would have challenged this aura of secrecy by arguing that information wants to be free and that computing can serve the people and the public. With the rise of neo-liberalism in the 1980s, this countercultural ethos of public information became the ideology of communicative capitalism, so that "net freedom is the freedom of the market, the freedom of corporations to extend market forces throughout the domain of the social" (ibid., 110). Although Anonymous functions as a covert organization, it shares the value of public information and a free Internet that comes from the hacker counterculture and has become a new ideology of capitalism, the new spirit of capitalism (Boltanski and Chiapello 2005; Fisher 2010). This does not mean, however, that Anonymous necessarily supports capitalist ideology, but rather that the complex relations of Anonymous to capitalism are crucial for its political values. The neo-liberal ideology of public information benefits a small elite: there is 'free' access to services like Facebook, YouTube, Google and Twitter, but monetary profit for private owners; there are information production capacities for everyone, but visibility on the Internet for the few; there calls for discussions, the voicing of political opinions, the sharing of user-generated content, innovative ideas, etc. in the 'online public,' but material and political benefits for an elite, etc. Anonymous (and WikiLeaks; see Fuchs 2011) has a contradictory role in this context: on the one hand they reproduce the language of Internet freedom, and on the other hand, the private and capitalist appropriation of benefits at the expense of the public is to a certain degree also questioned.

Coleman (2009) shows how the arrests of Jon Johansen, who programmed a software that unlocks the digital rights management on DVDs so that they can be played on Linux computers, and Dmitry Sklyarov, who developed a software that unlocks Adobe's e-book access control, resulted in protests and the politicisation of hackers. From a rather apolitical culture the liberal political attitude that source code is free speech emerged. The parallel between Anonymous and the politicised free software movement that Coleman describes is that both movements are political and stress the liberal value of freedom. Another parallel is that both have engaged with the corporate domination of the Internet and the software industry (digital rights management and proprietary software in the case of the free software movement; ACTA, PIPA and legal claims against file sharers in the case of Anonymous). Both the free software movement and Anonymous tend to stress freedom of speech. The same liberal value of freedom is at the heart of the idea of the freedom of private ownership that drives the culture industry's interest in commodifying software, culture and the Internet and defending its interests with legal means against those who argue that culture, code and technology is a commons that should be available to all. It was therefore consequent that both the free software movement and Anonymous give up the stress on individual rights and liberalism and consequently see the contradiction that freedom under capitalism benefits private owners of capital, which requires questioning capitalism and liberalism and stressing the collective rights of humans to own knowledge and technology, which is more a socialist than a liberal strategy.

Christopher Kelty (2005) argues that geeks (IT producers, the free software movement, Internet users, etc.) form a recursive public, "a group constituted by a shared, profound concern for the technical and legal conditions of possibility for their own association" (ibid., 185). Kelty expresses with the notion of the recursive Internet public the idea that geeks all have an interest in the Internet staying free from corporate and state control because such control negatively impacts their own existence in their various roles as workers, consumers, friends, activists, etc., which rely on the Internet for organizing their everyday social relations. As a consequence, they are "concerned to protect" the Internet and to keep it "as radically open as possible—for it is now the sine qua non of any other software or network they or anyone else might build" (ibid., 202). The Internet is a tool through which this public constantly comes into being. Applied to Anonymous, the idea of the recursive public allows us to argue that Anonymous has a special interest in Internet politics because the Internet is an existential medium for the movement and its members that enables and organizes their everyday interactions. This is just another way of saying that Anonymous is made up of people who come from a younger generation, whose lives are shaped by the Internet, who cannot imagine a life without it and for whom Internet politics is therefore of particular relevance. Saying that Anonymous is a recursive public, however, does not automatically tell us something about the kind of politics that the movement aligns itself with. Opposition to intellectual property rights, ACTA, PIPA, the prosecution of file sharers, and the corporate and state censorship of the Internet and the advocacy of free software, creative commons, open access, commons-based peer production, etc. does not necessarily have to be framed as individual liberal freedom of opinion and expression, but can rather also be conceived as the collective right of humanity to the common goods (such as knowledge, technology, nature, health and social care, education, nutrition, etc.) that all produce in common and need to exist and lead a good life and that thereby should not be controlled and owned by a specific class, but rather be open to, owned and controlled by all. The fact that geeks tend to frame Internet politics in liberal terms of freedom and individual rights has to do with the circumstance that neoliberal culture and politics permeate our societies so heavily, whereas the notions of collective rights and the commons come from a socialist political tradition that has been politically marginalised during the decades of neoliberalism, but is today (among other phenomena in the form of the Occupy movement) making a return. Many Anonymous activists and contemporary movement activists come from a younger generation of people, who have experienced precarious work and life, as well as temporary or long-term unemployment (Norton 2012). They are the generation that is hailed by neo-liberalism's values, such as individualism, self-responsibility and self-help, but has at the same time suffered under neo-liberalism's intensification of inequality that has benefited corporations and the rich so that they have a more objective interest in questioning liberalism and negating it.

The focus on liberalism and socialism is a contested issue within Anonymous. In August 2011, one Anonymous video called for a campaign (Operation Facebook) to "kill Facebook for the sake of your own privacy,"[17] which was the initiation of an operation directed against a capitalist organization that some perceive as exploiting and commodifying users.

Questioning this operation, other Anonymous activists stressed in another video, "Though we do not agree with Facebook's privacy procedures, we understand that such an attack would not only hurt the people, but also weaken our cause. We would ask any such hacktivists and crackers do not do this attack in the name of Anonymous. Facebook allows friends and families to connect with one another. Anonymous understand the importance of this."[18] A more socialist politics stressing corporate domination was questioned by liberal politics, stressing that it is the users' individual choice to use Facebook and that attacking Facebook means limiting freedom of information. In November 2011, another operation was launched that called on users to delete their Facebook accounts on December 24 (#OpDeleteFB). This operation also took a rather liberal position: "We respect Facebook's right to host a website free from hacking attempts, and any attacks aimed at defacing or taking control in any way of the Facebook website are in no way associated with Anonymous, its members, or those promoting #OpDeleteFB."[19] In contrast to this operation, another faction announced in the same month that it would attack Facebook by spreading the Guy Fawkes virus on the platform (#55).

Support for the attack on the New York Stock Exchange (NYSE) has also been contested within Anonymous: "I am here to clarify that factions of Anonymous are going with the operation. Other factions are opposing it" (#33). Some within Anonymous hold that the NYSE is representing the power of the 1 per cent, whereas others maintain that its website "does not control or contribute to any stock trade or exchange of bonds within the one percent" (#32). This conflict shows that socialist politics and goals are disputed within Anonymous.

Liberal ideology postulates individual freedoms (of speech, opinion, association, assembly, the press) as universal rights, but the particularistic and stratified class character of capitalism undermines these universal rights and creates inequalities and as a consequence unequal access to the public sphere. Jürgen Habermas (1991) in his theory of the public sphere has not idealised the bourgeois public sphere but has rather stressed that there are two immanent limits of the bourgeois public sphere that capitalism poses and cannot overcome: (1) the limitation of freedom of speech and public opinion—individuals do not have the same formal education and material resources for participating in the public sphere (ibid., 227); (2) the limitation of freedom of association and assembly—big political and economic organizations "enjoy an oligopoly of the publicistically effective and politically relevant formation of assemblies and associations" (ibid., 228).

The bourgeois public sphere creates its own limits and thereby its own immanent critique. Liberalism postulates individual freedoms as universal values, but in its own reality permanently undermines these values. Anonymous broaches the issue of the limits of liberalism in contemporary capitalism. On the one hand, it to a certain extent affirms liberal values; on the other hand it constitutes an immanent critique of these values by showing how liberal institutions violate the liberal values of the system that they represent—for example, in the form of police violence against protests, the implementation of intellectual property rights laws that question freedom of information, U.S. support of political regimes that violate liberal rights of the individual, laws that censor the Internet or independent media, and the restriction of freedom of speech and information by the criminalisation and repression of WikiLeaks. The internally contested combination of liberal and socialist world views constitutes a threat for liberal societies that proclaim liberal values, but in their economic and political practices violate these values.

5. CONCLUSION

Horkheimer and Adorno (2002, 28) argue that the liberal enlightenment ideology turns into its own opposite that it initially questioned so that "irresistible progress is irresistible regression." "Once harnessed to the dominant mode of production, enlightenment, which strives to undermine any order which has become repressive, nullifies itself" (ibid., 73–74). Although "freedom in society is inseparable from enlightenment thinking," the negative dialectic of freedom in capitalism is that the very concepts of enlightenment thinking, such as freedom, "no less than the concrete historical forms, the institutions of society with which it is intertwined, already contain the germ of the regression which is taking place everywhere today" (ibid., xvi). The freedoms proclaimed by liberal enlightenment ideology find their actual violation in the practice of capitalism: the ideal of freedom turns into an opposite reality—unfreedom. Marx (1867, 272–273) described this unfreedom as an immanent feature of capitalism when he spoke of the worker's role in capitalism and stressed that the worker is

> free in the double sense that as a free individual he can dispose of his labour-power as his own commodity, and that, on the other hand, he has no other commodity for sale, i.e. he is rid of them, he is free of all the objects needed for the realization *[Verwirklichung]* of his labour power.

Marx speaks of the "freedom" of the worker in a cynical way in order to stress that the worker is unfree in a double sense: he or she must sell his or her labour power as a commodity in order to survive and is the non-owner of the means of production and the produced commodities. The existence of classes guarantees liberal freedoms only for those in power and deprives the subordinated of these freedoms. Class inequality and capitalism's immanent monopoly tendency constitute the necessary regression of the ideals of freedom into unfreedom.

Anonymous describes itself as "the 21st century enlightenment" (#35). It is even more than this; Anonymous is the dialectic of the enlightenment of twenty-first-century informational capitalism. It demonstrates and discloses the contradictions of freedom and liberal ideology by demanding the very rights and values that capitalism, its constitutions and politicians proclaim and that in economic and political reality turn into their opposites. Anonymous shows the difference between the proclaimed essence and actual existence of liberalism. If Anonymous, for example, argues in favour of the freedom of assembly and expression of the Occupy movement and criticises police violence against activists, then it, on the one hand, stays within the categories of liberal thought. At the same time it shows how within the U.S., the country in the world that most stresses the liberal value of freedom, freedom is actually limited by state action, which drives liberal values ad absurdum and shows their actual contradictory existence. Anonymous thereby conducts a practical immanent political critique of liberalism. It, however, frequently misses taking this form of critique to the next step and advancing from immanent critique towards a transcendental critique that sees the limits of the realization of liberal values within capitalism and calls for the establishment of an alternative to capitalism, in which individual and collective values can exist through each other, which is just another formulation for saying that true liberalism can be achieved only in a democratic form of communism. In the case of the Occupy movement, Anonymous has managed to a certain degree to formulate transcendent values by taking up issues of socio-economic inequality, class and capitalism.

One can understand Anonymous not only as an immanent critique of liberalism but also as a parody and absurd theatre of liberalism. A connection between Anonymous and the Spaßguerilla (fun guerrilla) movement becomes clear: humour is to a certain degree used as a political weapon. Anonymous makes fun of its political opponents and uses clownery (in the form of Guy Fawkes armies) as a symbolic strategy to attain the media's and public's attention. There is also a connection of Anonymous to Brecht's (1967) absurd theatre: by proclaiming liberal values and criticising how they become violated in capitalist reality, Anonymous shows the contradictory dialectic of liberalism.

The freedoms that capitalism negates can be realized only in a society of equal owners and participants, a participatory democracy. Anonymous is a theatre of liberalism, and in its own political demands complexly articulates the conflict between liberalism and socialism that is expressed in the presence of the three political positions analysed in this chapter. Liberal enlightenment ideals negate themselves in turn in capitalism and turn into their opposite. Only negating the negative dialectic of the enlightenment by establishing a new society can overcome the consequences of the negative dialectic. Establishing a new society is the only way to address the failings of the enlightenment dialectic. This requires building a new socialism that aims at "an association of free men working with the means of production held in common, and expending their many different forms of labour-power in full self-awareness as one single social labour force" (Marx 1867, 171).

Freedom requires appropriation, joint control and production of the commons, including the communication commons.

NOTES

1. http://boards.4chan.org/b, accessed on 15 April 2014.
2. http://guerrillanews.wordpress.com/2010/12/08/operation-payback, accessed on 15 April 2014.
3. For example, http://www.youtube.com/watch?v=JRm98gFaXgM, http://www.youtube.com/watch?v=_4LU7piK9X4, and http://www.youtube.com/watch?v=fxT3Bn7_-Ig, accessed on 15 April 2014.
4. http://anonnet.org, accessed on 4 December 2012.
5. http://www.anonops.org, accessed on 4 December 2012.
6. http://www.voxanon.org, accessed on 4 December 2012.
7. http://www.anonplus.com, accessed on 4 December 2012.
8. http://site.anonnet.org, accessed on 4 December 2012.
9. See https://encyclopediadramatica.se/Boxxy, accessed on 15 April 2014.
10. https://encyclopediadramatica.se/Lulz, accessed on 15 April 2014.
11. Commune 1; see http://en.wikipedia.org/wiki/Kommune_1, accessed on 15 April 2014.
12. http://anonnews.org/press/item/199, accessed on 15 April 2014.
13. http://occupywallst.org/article/anonymous-joins-occupywallstreet, accessed on 4 December 2012.
14. http://anonnews.org/press/item/199, accessed on 15 April 2014.
15. http://www.youtube.com/watch?v=7cqP8qqqfI0, accessed on 15 April 2014.
16. http://www.fbi.gov/news/testimony/cybersecurity-responding-to-the-threat-of-cyber-crime-and-terrorism, accessed on 15 April 2014.
17. http://www.youtube.com/watch?v=Q6crH8qmyZ8, accessed on 15 April 2014.
18. http://www.youtube.com/watch?v=-Ig4bZawisQ, accessed on 15 April 2014.
19. http://anoncandyman.blogspot.com/2011/11/opdeletefb.html?m=0, accessed on 15 April 2014.

REFERENCES

AG Spaß muss sein, ed. 1997. *Spaß Guerilla*. 3rd ed. Münster: Unrast.
Bloch, Ernst. 1985. *Das Prinzip Hoffnung*. Frankfurt: Suhrkamp.
Boltanski, Luc, and Eve Chiapello. 2005. *The New Spirit of Capitalism*. London: Verso.
Brecht, Bertolt. 1967. *Gesammelte Werke, Band 15: Schriften zum Theater 1*. Frankfurt: Suhrkamp.
Coleman, E. Gabriella. 2009. Code Is Speech: Legal Tinkering, Expertise, and Protest among Free and Open Source Software Developers. *Cultural Anthropology* 24 (3): 420–454.
———. 2011a. Anonymous: From the Lulz to Collective Action. In *Politics in the Age of Secrecy and Transparency*, edited by Gabriella Colleman. http://mediacommons.futureofthebook.org/tne/pieces/anonymous-lulz-collective-action.
———. 2011b. The Ethics of Digital Direct Action. *Al Jazeera*, September 1. http://english.aljazeera.net/indepth/opinion/2011/08/20118308455825769.html.
———. 2011c. Hacker Politics and Publics. *Public Culture* 23 (3): 511–516.
———. 2011d. Is Anonymous Anarchy? *OWNI*, August 22. http://owni.eu/2011/08/22/is-anonymous-anarchy.

———. 2012. Our Weirdness Is Free. *Triple Canopy* 15. http://canopycanopycanopy.com/15/our_weirdness_is_free.

Coleman, E. Gabriella, and Alex Golub. 2008. Hacker Practice: Moral Genres and the Cultural Articulation of Liberalism. *Anthropological Theory* 8 (3): 255–277.

Dean, Jodi. 2002. *Publicity's Secret*. Ithaca, NY: Cornell University Press.

Deleuze, Gilles, and Félix Guattari.1987. *A Thousand Plateaus: Capitalism and Schizophrenia*. Minneapolis: University of Minnesota Press.

della Porta, Donatella, and Mario Diani. 1999. *Social Movements: An Introduction*. Malden, MA: Blackwell.

Diani, Mario. 1992. The Concept of Social Movement. *Sociological Review* 40 (1): 1–25.

Fisher, Eran. 2010. *Media and New Capitalism in the Digital Age: The Spirit of Networks*. New York: Palgrave Macmillan.

Foucault, Michel. 2008. *The Birth of Biopolitics: Lectures at the Collège de France 1978–1979*. Basingstoke: Palgrave Macmillan.

Fuchs, Christian. 2006. The Self-Organization of Social Movements. *Systemic Practice and Action Research* 19 (1): 101–137.

———. 2011. The Political Economy of WikiLeaks: Power 2.0? Surveillance 2.0? Criticism 2.0? Alternative Media 2.0? *Global Media Journal—Australian Edition* 5 (1): 49–76.

Habermas, Jürgen. 1991. *The Structural Transformation of the Public Sphere: An Inquiry into a Category of Bourgeois Society*. Cambridge, MA: MIT Press.

Hall, Stuart. 1986. Variants of Liberalism. In *Politics and Ideology*, edited by James Donald and Stuart Hall, 34–69. Milton Keynes: Open University Press.

Horkheimer, Max, and Theodor W. Adorno. 2002. *Dialectic of Enlightenment*. Stanford, CA: Stanford University Press.

Kelty, Christopher. 2005. Geeks, Social Imaginaries, and Recursive Publics. *Cultural Anthropology* 20 (2): 185–214.

Marx, Karl. 1867. *Capital*. Vol. 1. London: Penguin.

Norton, Quinn. 2011. Anonymous 101: Introduction to the Lulz. *Wired Magazine Online*, November 8. http://www.wired.com/threatlevel/2011/11/anonymous-101.

Norton, Quinn. 2012a. 2011: The year Anonymous took on cops, dictators and existential dread. *Wired Magazine Online*. http://www.wired.com/threatlevel/2012/01/anonymous-dicators-existential-dread/.

Norton, Quinn. 2012b. How Anonymous picks targets, launches attacks, and takes powerful organizations down. *Wired Magazine Online*. http://www.wired.com/threatlevel/2012/07/ff_anonymous/all/.

Olson, Parmy. 2012. *We Are Anonymous*. New York: Little, Brown.

Ralph, Michael, and Gabriella Coleman. 2011, September 29,. Is it a crime? The transgressive politics of hacking in Anonymous. OWNI. http://owni.eu/2011/09/29/is-it-a-crime-the-transgressive-politics-of-hacking-in-anonymous/.

Reissmann, Ole, Christian Stöcker and Konrad Lischka. 2012. *We Are Anonymous: Die Maske des Protests. Wer sie sind, was sie antreibt, was sie wollen*. Munich: Goldmann.

Stryker, Cole. 2011. *Epic Win for Anonymous*. New York: Overlook Duckworth.

Surowiecki, James. 2005. *The Wisdom of Crowds*. New York: Anchor Books.

Williams, Raymond. 1983. *Keywords*. New York: Oxford University Press.

Civil Counter-Power Against Austerity

Section Three

Civil Counter-Power
Against Austerity

5 The Rise of Nazism and the Web

Social Media as Platforms of Racist Discourses in the Context of the Greek Economic Crisis

Panos Kompatsiaris and Yiannis Mylonas

1. INTRODUCTION

On October 1, 2012, in an interview for a local Greek TV channel, Ilias Kasidiaris, one of the most widely exposed and recognisable MPs of the Greek Nazi 'Golden Dawn' (GD) party, made the following statement: "Thankfully we have in our disposal an enormous weapon; this is the internet, where hundreds of thousands of our compatriots managed to learn who we are."[1] In another interview a couple of months later the same MP admitted once more that, "we [GD] used Facebook as a platform to disseminate our views, since no other TV channel has given us a platform."[2] On September 25, 2013, a few days after the killing of the anti-fascist rapper Pavlos Fyssas and the arrest of several members of GD, an anonymous witness and ex-party member warns in his testimony to the trial examiner, "So as to protect the unsuspected and especially the youth, I want to say that it would be good that social media (Facebook etc.) be controlled, because through them activities like calling for protest, propaganda and communication take place."[3]

Undoubtedly, as the foregoing statements imply, in the past few years the party has been particularly active in social media landscapes. Its members have effectively initiated official and fan pages, personal profiles and closed groups in Web 2.0 platforms, such as Facebook, YouTube and Twitter, enabling visibility and relatively uninterrupted circulation of their material. Although GD also used (and was used) by mainstream media to catch public attention, providing interviews to a variety of hosts and journalists of talk shows, new bulletins, tabloid press and newspapers, within social media it found the opportunity to directly share and potentially validate its version of history and politics, bypassing official communication channels. Indicatively, the circulation of hate speech and calls for violence against all GD's enemies, racist and anti-Semitic discourse, open praises of former Greek dictators, direct references and praises to less publicly known fascist ideologues, and more concealed praises to Hitler and the Third Reich found an unexpected host in social media networks. As we will see ahead, GD's strategic use of the Internet and social media can be seen as part of an ideological war that aims to construct localised "regimes of truth" (Foucault 1980) related to national identity, to enable sympathisers to find each other and to build bonds between members.

In this chapter, we examine the strategic use of social media by GD, focusing on the ways it attempts to legitimise its social imaginaries, tactics, strategies and reality constructions, taking advantage of the social turbulence that austerity politics and neo-liberal restructuring have brought since late 2009. While GD's public legitimisation has been closely interweaving with established state power, manifested in its close relation and frequent collaboration with police forces, its political vision is also distinct from the latter to the extent that it wishes to enable a constituent counter-power, aiming both to disarticulate its liberal dimensions and occupy its apparatuses. GD treats the liberal state apparatus as both a partner and an adversary to be infiltrated and subjugated. This idea of state power as being both a partner and adversary for fascist politics is associated with New Marxist approaches to fascism (Poulantzas 1970; Vajda 1976) that see fascism more as a "relatively autonomous" force and an outcome of specific historical conditions and less as an "inevitable stage" of capitalist development (Kitchen 2003, 58). In reverse, while liberal power often instrumentalises fascist discourse and practices in the form of an "authoritarian governmentality" (Dean 2010), at specific moments—as in the case of the recent persecution of GD members in Greece—it can also explicitly denounce and suppress fascism.

As our analysis indicates, Web 2.0 platforms, which have enhanced possibilities for easy access and spread of decontextualised information, can be particularly effective for giving visibility and potentially constructing an aura of 'righteousness' in fascist practices and discourses. GD's engagement with social media bears similarities with what Meg McLagan and Yates McKee have recently coined as "sensible politics" (2013)—that is, political practices that aim to become visible by claiming a part in a given "distribution of the sensible" (Rancière 2006).[4] While McLagan and McKee mainly refer to how these kinds of politics are performed by left-wing and social movements, we draw attention to how the generation of emotion, affect and sensualised responses is also crucial for explicitly fascist politics. GD's politics in social media, in the form of the circulation of highly aestheticised forms within social networks and contexts, seem to be easily facilitated by social media's openness and participation, offering possibilities to connect and network without the mediation of established institutions, state or otherwise. This is a point that needs to be stressed, as in the first stages of GD's appearance, when established media monopolies would not willingly risk being directly or indirectly associated with Nazis, social media were the only channels of communication capable of distributing an explicitly Nazi discourse.

After introducing the political climate that gave rise to a Nazi party in Greece, we develop this thesis by discussing how GD's utilisation of social media shares explicit similarities with the propaganda principles of Joseph Goebbels. In particular, our understanding of Goebbels' conception of propaganda comes from the paper "Goebbels' Principles of Propaganda" by Leonard W. Doob, published in 1950 and based on the 6,800 manuscript pages of Goebbels' diary found in Berlin by American authorities in 1945. Among other sources we use Bramsted's paper "Joseph Goebbels and National Socialist Propaganda 1926–1939," written in 1954, which describes in a very concise way the pre-war propaganda principles, as well as the differences between the period preceding the Nazi succession in power and the one succeeding it. Our aim in this chapter is to show how social media can be used as a tool to promote and effectively contribute to building fascist communities under unstable social conditions that can both exploit and pose a threat to the foundations of the liberal state. Following from this, we also wish to point to the danger of treating social media and Web 2.0 technologies as inherently liberating and revolutionary (Dean 2009), suggesting instead to view them as platforms that enable forms of general social antagonism.

The propagandistic material examined here generally follows the principles of what Walter Benjamin described as the "aestheticization of politics" (2008), meaning the inscription of political affairs to affective representations, or a "spell-binding spectacle and phantasmagoric illusion" (Jay 1992, 45), aiming to sidestep rational argumentation and curb political thinking on social affairs, by giving way to blunt, sensory seduction. The central medium through which aestheticisation takes material form is generally the image, moving or still, usually accompanied by an authoritative quote. Goebbels also saw visual media such as films and posters as possessing greater credibility for the Nazi scope, providing "proof" that spoken or written words could not provide (Doob 1950, 427). According to the visual culture theorist J. Mitchell, the representational clarity of images provides "a direct, unmediated, and accurate representation of things, rather than an indirect, unreliable report about things" (quoted in Jay 2002, 269). Images not only possess this kind "evidential force" (Barthes 1981; Tagg 1988) but also are much better suited to provide simple explanatory narratives in the distractive contexts of the webscape. The ostensible purity and communicational uncomplicatedness of Nazi imagery can thus offer sensory orientation in a chaotic world of crisis where complexity prevails. Similar to the image, the 'slogan' and the 'heading' are other forms of sensible politics that provide a condensed and largely uncomplicated understanding of political affairs. The slogan, the heading and the image have been the principal media through which GD mediated its discourse across the Internet's endless and largely decontextualised environment of information flow.

1.1 Methodology: Multi-sited Ethnography in Virtual Communities

Our research material has been drawn from a variety of platforms, most importantly from Facebook and YouTube, which are the two most popular Web 2.0 sites that Greek Nazis use. These sites largely differ from each other in terms of the possibilities they offer for content generation and interaction (Fischer, Smith and Yongjian 2012); however, they are brought together on the basis that they are services inspired by Web 2.0 principles, "enabling the users to create and share digital contents" (Giglietto, Rossi and Bennato 2012, 145). As organizations that are relatively autonomous from instituted state power, Web 2.0 services offer possibilities for networking, sharing, interacting and more intense group bonding. Social media foster ties and enable friendships and other "mediated intimacies" (Chambers 2013), with the users' interactions being both "what is produced in the moment of being social, as well as the object around which sociality occurs" (Fischer, Smith and Yongjian 2012, 102). Our analysis then focuses on how social media are used and by extension give shape to power relations within the particular social-historical setting (Patelis and Hatzopoulos 2013a). Power relations are always in a process of negotiation (Foucault 1980) and, in this case, a precarious outcome of the ways that offline and online practices and events are articulated, distributed, affirmed or possibly contested. These practices and events require translation and interpretation from users, and as a result there is an ongoing deterritorialisation and reterritorialisation of community's identity and self-understanding.

The method we employ to examine Nazi online activities can be best described as 'multi-sited virtual ethnography,' a practice that involves tracing the ways that the cultural phenomenon under examination is manifested, communicated and reproduced across virtual sites. According to George Marcus multi-sited ethnography "is designed around chains, paths, threads, conjunctions, or juxtapositions of locations" (1995, 105), and is suitable for exploring abstract connections between sites, capturing heterogeneity and multiplicity as well as studying difference over time. Here, as part of our ethnographic practice we have spent a considerable amount of time on sites where Greek Nazis communicate their material and perform their identities, mostly in Facebook groups, such as the very popular GD-affiliated "Ellinon diktyo" (Greeks' network), and YouTube accounts, such as that of 'iwannis metaxas' and 'parkadoroi,' both proliferate GD users, observing and participating in online conversations. As mentioned, Facebook and YouTube are platforms with rather different architectural structures. Facebook, as a social network, is much more effective in keeping with a flow of information, as well as in mobilising action through event invitations. Although YouTube has social networking capacities too, its function has to do more with archiving and documenting material, which is then potentially circulated around the web.

Following Marcus' suggestion, we are tracking "the argument, the debate, the controversy, the metaphor" (Hamilakis 2007, 24; Marcus 1995) arising from the dissemination of the material itself. While traditional ethnography takes place over a long period of time in a single location or place, multi-sited ethnography emerges as a method attempting to make sense of the ways identities are performed in a networked world and how our multiple, everyday, virtual or 'real' presences inform the ways of behaving, relating and acting. The objective is to give an account of "social phenomena that cannot be accounted for by focusing on a single site" (Falzon 2009, 1) by following their interrelatedness and association. For analysing the content of GD's online recitations, images and texts, and for mapping the conceptual linking between the traditional Nazi ideology and GD, we employ analytical categories from discourse theory (Laclau and Mouffe 1985).

2.   THE RISE OF NAZISM IN CRISIS-STRUCK GREECE

In his 2012 book *The black bible of GD*, Dimitris Psarras, a researcher, author and journalist studying the far-right phenomenon in Greece for the last thirty years, argues that the most adequate way to describe GD's ideology, organization and methods is that of a 'Nazi party,' as all other terms, fascist, far right or even neo-Nazi, are inadequate. The two national elections of Greece in May and June 2013 gave nearly 7 per cent of the votes to GD, enabling its entry to the Greek parliament as a legitimate political player. Up until then, GD had a very small base of supporters and never obtained above 0.5 per cent in previous national elections (2009). GD was known as an outspokenly Nazi organization, notorious for its violent acts and its relations to para-state forces in Greece. Up until recently, polls suggested a continuous rise in GD's popularity despite its irrational rhetoric, falsehoods, violent practices and its appalling overall image. While after the aforementioned murder and the mass anti-fascist movement that followed (leading to GD's persecution as a criminal organization) polls suggested a downward trend in GD's popularity, in the municipal elections of May 18, 2014 the party seemed to consolidate and expand its electoral power.

The exponential growth of contemporary Greek Nazism seems to emerge together with the symbolic and material disturbances of the economic crisis caused by austerity policies. To start with, the economic crisis triggered disturbances in a national narrative linked to lasting national expectations. As Tsoukalas (2012, 34) argues, western modernity historically fetishised 'Greekness,' in its attempt to shape itself through the perceptions and romantic myths of classical Greece. In turn, mainstream modern Greek identity was formed in relation to this European imagination, often being loaded with the burden to fulfil the expectations of a 'glorious' past culture (Hamilakis 2007). Especially in the initial stages of the crisis, Greeks were often treated as a *sui-generis* case, an irrational collective whole that was somehow 'known' and explained through tourist and consumer culture stereotypes (Mylonas 2012). The international public mockery brought about a sense discomfort and anxiety in and beyond the mainstreams of Greek society that contributed to opening a void in identity and thus the need for new narratives.

As a matter of fact, in the initial stages of the crisis until around 2011, there was a strong radicalisation and desire for social and political change in Greece, challenging the legitimacy of the sociopolitical and economic establishment and the correlation of main political agents in power (Nea Dimokratia and PASOK) since 1974 (Bosco and Verney 2011, 141). Mass participation in demonstrations, as well as the development of new social movements and forms of protest, which included the Left but also nationalist elements, such as the 'Indignados' (Αγανακτισμένοι) movements in Greece, was indicative of the popular desire for political and social change. The state's response was the violent repression of such mass movements, which was also accompanied by their defamation in mainstream media discourses (Mylonas 2012), which often portrayed them as the main reasons behind the crisis and the failure of the harsh reforms.

Furthermore, strikes and political and social rights, as well as a supposed ideological hegemony of the Left in society, were usually presented as the real sources of Greece's weaknesses. In this sense, the reaction of the political and financial authorities towards resistance was to displace the roots of the capitalist crisis by blaming those most affected by it, a strategy that is an important part of neo-liberal restructuring processes (Wacquant 2012, 73). Gradually, as unemployment among the youth and the lower and middle classes swiftly rose together with the pitting of Greek labourers against immigrant ones, so did an ethno-populist understanding of social affairs that was key to GD's rise in popularity.

GD's rise was also fuelled through practices by Greek governments that since 2009 articulated xenophobic and racist public discourses and policy agendas. These agendas pushed biopolitical measures of 'law and order' and 'public health' issues—identifying migrants with crime, HIV-positive women and drug users with hygienic threats and Leftists and anarchists with 'lawlessness'—were soon captured and amplified by mainstream media, while the repressive mechanism of the state organized massive operations of persecution of migrants, with or without work permit and papers (Áthanasiou 2012, 33). Moralistic and nationalist discourses became central in the public articulation of austerity for constructing social discipline and the fashioning of neo-liberal social subjects (Brown 2003). In this sense, the broader neo-liberal restructuring process that is engineered under the so-called debt crisis pretext facilitates a shift towards a soft totalitarian state with minimal rights that are fluid and subject to continuous change.

In addition, after Syriza's rise to the country's leading opposition party after the May 6, 2012, national elections, the country's economic, social and cultural established power mainly saw the possibility of a left-wing government with anxiety and fear. In the months that followed, the Conservative and the Social Democrats and most mass media, often supported by EU leaders, launched systematic attacks against the 'Left' so as to curb its rise both as a material and symbolic entity. This attack triggered a deepening dichotomy in Greek society, reintroducing themes, passions and traumas connected to the civil war era that were thought to have been reconciled during the post-dictatorship period after 1974. Together with the attack against the Left, however, another rhetoric appeared in public discourse, mainly adopted by the patriotic Right and in part by elements of the patriotic Left, that symbolically identified 'politicians' and the 'establishment' with national traitors.

GD surfaced in this context by attempting to make both ends meet: the Left was to blame for the crisis, yet so too were the bankers, the bourgeois politicians and other national traitors. GD put both ends in the same box under a conspiracy theory mantra where other groups, such as the 'Jews' and the 'homosexuals,' were also involved. GD also attempted to forge political alliances with big businesses, voting, for example, against the taxation of shipowners, or by attacking Leftist unions, while advocating for low-wage labour on the premise of creating "jobs for Greeks [sic]." In this way, the regressive class role of GD, which according to Poulantzas is intrinsic to all fascist movements (1970), publicly emerged.

The rise of Nazism in Greece is also rooted in far-right legacies and establishments in the country's institutional apparatuses. The political history of Greece throughout the twentieth century suggests the existence of far and extreme right enclaves affiliated with the Church, the military, the police and the conservative Right. This legacy has ties to the anti-communist hysteria of the regimes during the 1940s and 1950s, as well as to the military junta of the late 1960s and early 1970s. This legacy was also an outcome of the hegemony of the extreme Right that emerged shortly after the end of the country's Nazi occupation in late 1944 and the civil war that followed it, with the subsequent military defeat of the communist and leftist forces of the country at the end of 1949 (Mazower 2000, 2001; Voglis 2002; Makrides 2004; Dordanas 2011). The geopolitical interests of the emerging 'western block' aimed for a 'western Greece' in order to curb Soviet geopolitical influences in the southeastern Mediterranean.

Furthermore, the rise of Nazism in contemporary Greece is connected to the strong presence since the late 1990s of a far-right, nationalistic discourse in popular private television networks and later in social media, which then found representation in the Greek parliament through the far-right party of 'LAOS' (People's Orthodox Alert), basing much of its power in publicity (Ellinas 2010). LAOS participated in the unelected, technocratic government of Lucas Papademos, formed by the Troika and supported by the German government. Prominent members of that particular party, some of whom are now ministers in the current government of Antonis Samaras, include the former associate of Jean-Marie Le Pen, Makis Voridis.

3.   SOCIAL MEDIA, GOLDEN DAWN AND NAZI PROPAGANDA PRINCIPLES

By looking at the content of GD's propaganda material in social media we can see that it resembles in significant ways, if not directly copies from, traditional Nazi propaganda as described and implemented mainly by

Goebbels before the Nazis' succession to power in 1933. As we will see in this section, from Goebbels' idea that "making noise is an effective means of opposition" (Bramsted 1954, 72) to the dissemination of affective 'anti-systemic' visual material and the constant relativising of the accusations directed against them, GD and its supporters employ propaganda tactics in social media similar to the traditional Nazi propaganda principles. Social media offers the possibility of preserving material traces that support Nazi ideology—for example, in the form of YouTube videos, which can be made visible through their circulation in other social media platforms, such as Facebook or Twitter. As these documents enter the perceptible everyday reality of users, bypassing mainstream channels of communication and gaining attention due to interest around GD after its entrance to the parliament, they become objects of discussion and possible objects of emotional investment and identification.

The content that we examine refers either to, strictly speaking, ideological pieces or to informative pieces intending to respond to and describe specific events. In some cases there is a combination of both, where the recounting of events is combined with theory or vice versa. Here our analysis is based on two main tactics of Nazi propaganda—namely, 'spectacularisation' and 'relativisation.' Ahead we describe such forms of GD propaganda tactics, following their distribution through social media platforms and stressing the ways that they become legible documents as they enter the realm of politics.

3.1.   Identifying the Nation with Golden Dawn's Ideas: Signification, Goebbels and the Making of National Enemies

An important element of GD rhetoric refers to the systematic promotion of the idea that the party represents the 'pure' national community and that those disagreeing with these views are degenerates and corrupt and consciously work for the destruction of the nation. Thus, GD attempts to colonise the signifier 'Greece,' equating it entirely with what the party represents. The individual members of the 'Greek community' in this arrangement should be totally obedient to the party and ready to sacrifice themselves for the benefit of the nation (Welch 2004). This equation of the Nazi party with a pure and cleansed national community was exactly what Nazi propaganda principally aimed for (ibid., 217). As Ernest Bramsted argues, Goebbels' 'attack on the system' and the existing state of things in the period 1926–1933 in the years of Weimar Republic had as its purpose to brand his political enemies as enemies of the general 'national community' (Volsgemeinschaft). In his public propaganda material Goebbels promoted the idea that "everything in the Republic . . . was sham" and that the Nazi Party "would expose and unmask the sham values" (Bramsted 1954, 72).

As our daily monitoring of GD Facebook pages indicates, such ideas came to be widely circulated in the public sphere. They became the object of attention and of extensive commenting through social media channels associated with the party, such as "Ellinon diktyo" (Greeks' Network), which before its first banning after Fyssas' assassination had reached more than seventy-five thousand likes.[5] "Ellinon diktyo" reposts daily tens of articles from GD's official webpage and other extreme right-wing sources, such as the militaristic blog 'defenceNet.gr,' and thus constantly reaches users' updates in Facebook, who in turn often post them on their walls. Here it is important to mention, following McLagan and McKee's idea of "sensible politics," that irrespectively of how strongly each user identifies with the content of such posts, Nazi propaganda becomes visible, occupying a certain portion of sensible reality and becoming an object of debate around which discursive encounters occur.

Another element of Goebbels' propaganda approach is that "propaganda must label events and people with distinctive phrases and slogans" (Doob 1950, 435) and that these slogans should be easy, "a verbal cliché" and "must be capable of being easily learned" (ibid., 436). In accordance with this idea, and following Goebbels' doctrine of "using a concise and graphic language" (Bramsted 1954, 77), labelling as a practice has been very important in GD's rhetoric. The main identifiable targets are expressed linguistically more or less with the same words as in Hitler's Germany: the immigrants, the Jews and the Bolsheviks, who are all impure and threaten to corrupt the nation. This propaganda tactic is easily facilitated in social media, where within the immense flow of information slogans and labels can more easily catch users' attention than extended pieces.

The tactic of tarnishing the image of the enemy is manifestly evident in the main slogan that GD extensively employed before the June 2012 elections: "*So to rid the filth from this land.*" The slogan became viral in social media to a degree that supporters and opponents would immediately identify it with the party. It started gaining popularity when it appeared in a self-titled post in GD's website after the elections in May 2012, which gave them for the first time a surprising 7 per cent. In this short article, accompanied by a photograph of protesting crowds waving Greek flags before the Greek parliament, GD constructed an affective and spectacular representation of the elections inspired by war fantasies and a rhetoric of the supposed coming national liberation:

> In a moment when Greek society suffers from recession, insecurity and uncertainty ALL the sub-parties care only about how they will come to power and will serve their vested interests . . . Outside of this rotten establishment, ALONE AGAINST EVERYONE, remain the Greek Nationalists.[6]

Furthermore, according to their official anthem, which currently has over one hundred thousand views on YouTube, they appear as "the followers of great ancestors, sons of glorious fighters," who "want a new Greece which will cover the whole earth."[7]

The initial target of the slogan "*So to rid the filth from this land*" was the 'immigrants,' who according to GD's rhetoric are considered 'filthy,' 'scum' and 'dirt,' pollute the Greek neighbourhoods and have to be 'wiped' off the land. Gradually, however, hate slogans are meant to include anyone who disagrees with the party, now labelled as 'national traitors.' GD's "enemies discourse" forms a "chain of equivalence" (Laclau and Mouffe 1985, 127) that can extend to include anyone who in particular contexts would appear as an enemy to the party. This chain of equivalence starts with the migrants, who are racialised and denied humanity, and further extends in including 'corrupt politicians,' 'bankers,' 'homosexuals' and 'faggots'—a vague category attributed in order to emphasise militarist and macho identities. Besides, the strategy of feminising the interlocutor and reaffirming masculine superiority in a patriarchal society is another way to demoralise and humiliate the opponent. As such, sexist remarks are commonly used by GD members and supporters in order to rhetorically discredit others.

Most crucially the main nodal point of GD's enemy is the 'Left,' which is related to all previous categories of enmity and summons all their despised features,[8] which in the Nazi rhetoric are Jewish, Islamic, capitalist, Stalinist, criminal, degenerate, homosexual and part of the 'corrupt establishment.' The broadness of the signifiers constructing the enemies of the Nazis in 'anti-national' terms shows that anyone can be included in the category of enemies by the Nazis according to their strategies and tactics. The construction of enemies is meant to curb critical thinking, to alienate the Nazi sympathisers from 'others' and to subordinate society through symbolic (but also physical) terror, as Hannah Arendt (1976) discussed in her *Origins of totalitarianism*. The lack of stable and rational definitions of opponents also guarantees constant alertness and mobility, which, according to Arendt, Nazi movements rely upon.

This mobility relates to unclearly defined civic rights that are permanently exceptional due to (supposed) permanent risks of eschatological threats to the nation that Nazi discourses enact. GD's leader, Nikos Michaloliakos, has explicitly addressed his voters not as civilians but as soldiers of his organization's 'military battalions.' In a known interview on mainstream television after his party's election in the parliament, he stated, '*Thank God, we were voted by four hundred thousand Greeks, which amounts to thirty or forty divisions.*'[9] The supporters of GD are therefore supposed to be in a permanent state of militarisation in which their rights are exempted, and those who disobey or question orders, like real soldiers, can be subjected to penalties of 'treason,' as the September 2013 persecution of GD as a criminal organization revealed.

GD's romanticised war fantasy was re-enacted and recited in numerous contexts across social media. It was used in images, posters, video clips and short films where GD, incarnating the 'Greek nationalists,' was represented as a 'pure' force, 'alone against everyone,' that will punish the enemies and regenerate the nation from its ashes.[10] This visual material regularly includes crowds waving Greek flags and computer-generated representations of ancient Greek warriors, mainly Spartans, in order to anachronistically construct visibility and to virtually realize heroic and 'purist' fantasies.[11] For instance, a regular pattern in GD's heroic and sentimentalised war representations of itself as the incarnation of the nation is the use of images taken from the famous blockbuster film *300*. This ultra-macho imagery aims to demonstrate GD's 'antique' ties to a heroic moment pivotal to discourses on western identity: the battle at Thermopylae against the Persian army in 480 BC. The film is recontextualised to modern-day Greece in order to stress a need to fight heroically for the fatherland's salvation, following the example of heroic Greek ancestors. Through the recitation of computer-generated imagery of the film, the fantasy of Greeks as the 'ultimate warriors' is dispersed around social media so as to create identities and consolidate bonds to GD. A number of fan pages and closed pages in Facebook directly or indirectly linked to GD use variations of the slogan "*So to rid the filth from this land*" as their title and extensively employ visual imagery from the film (using the keyword 'ξεβρομίσει ['to rid'] in a Facebook search in June 2013 we came up with more than ten results of closed groups and fan pages sympathetic to GD). The ties between the slogan and the film enable a desire to network on the basis of a popular imagination for an ultimate salvation, a 'final solution' to redeem the 'national community.'

Furthermore, GD aims at making itself the centre of a strong identification, a 'sacred' entity to be loved and worshipped by fanatic supporters. As we found out through our research, the posts on social media pages such as "Ellinon diktyo" cultivate this cult image by sharing and advertising events, rituals and activities, such as the tattoo engraving of GD symbols on supporters' bodies, the embodiment of GD's ideology through specific outfits, haircuts, lifestyle habits and ways of speaking or the use of material or fetish objects that reify GD. All the foregoing strive to construct and maintain identities through the creation of common sets of beliefs, values, morals and attitudes among GD supporters. Thus, GD becomes something much more than a political party, representing an idea and identity that have to be secured with lifelong devotion. Critique or introspection in this regard are resented and met with rage as a loss and corruption of the fascist sublime. GD's affective tactics attempt to generate in supporters a narcissistic euphoria in the midst of crisis depression, alienation and resentment.

3.2. "Making Noise Is an Effective Means of Opposition": Events, Communication and Spectacularisation

As Goebbels declared, "Making noise is an effective means of opposition" for propaganda purposes (Bramsted 1954, 72). According to Bramsted, Goebbels was constantly preoccupied in inventing "new stunts and tricks to attract the masses," which ranged "from mysterious aggressive posters to the use of white mice and snakes which disturbed the elegant public" (ibid.).

Similarly, apart from the anti-systemic character that GD wishes to cultivate through the everyday propaganda in social media, one of the organization's main tactics is to produce noisy and spectacular events. These events can guarantee publicity for the group as they provide 'phantasmagorias' to all possible audiences in Greece and abroad, whether supportive, ambivalent or oppositional. In addition they are meant to demonstrate force and, within the particular climate of the crisis, to show that GD is 'doing something'— because a general banal and apolitical claim that appears is that people should 'do something' to restore the crisis-struck country. Through social media GD seemed able to remediate staged events in favourable ways by easily bypassing state or other institutional dependencies. Here it should again be noted that through posting these 'shocking' events, followed by spectacular titles on Facebook pages such as "Ellinon diktyo," GD attempts to present them as natural, as 'practices of friends,' by taking advantage of the 'mediated intimacy' that it cultivates routinely with fans.

A number of these events that members of GD provoked in the Greek public sphere and that were subsequently excessively communicated in social media have become rather fundamental for GD's public image and sociopolitical trajectory. One of the most remarkable events took place on June 7, 2012, in the days between the two elections that led to GD's parliament entry, in a talk show panel on the popular ANT1-TV channel. Halfway through the show, GD MP Ilias Kasidiaris, who was invited to the programme, threw water from a drinking glass in the face of the Syriza MP Rena Dourou and subsequently struck an MP from the Communist Party of Greece, Liana Kaneli, three times in the face. After the incident a warrant was issued for Kasidiaris, who disappeared; he finally turned up in a police station forty-eight hours later, filing a lawsuit against Liana Kanneli and accusing her of attacking him first. This event, which was meant to appear as a 'spontaneous act,' was modelled, as Psarras (2012) has showed, on the tradition of producing televisual spectacles. As Psarras discusses, the event has striking similarities with an event that took place in Russia in 1995 that was praised by GD, when the far-right politician Vladimir Zhirinovsky threw a glass of orange juice at one of his political opponents.

This was the first event that exposed the violence and notoriety of GD to society, and was condemned by all other political parties. Due to its spec-tacular character the incident became viral in social media, making GD a very popular subject of discussion across the Greek webscape. The video has been uploaded on many different channels and was viewed more than two million times (counted by results generated by searching the keywords 'kasidiaris kanelli' or 'κασιδιάρης κανέλλη' [in Greek] in October 2013). The most viewed video (currently with almost 910,000 views) is uploaded to a Nazi sympathiser channel called "SuperBestvidzGr" and carries the milita-ristic title 'KANELLI IS BEATEN BY KASIDIARIS IN A SHOW!'[12] Despite the widespread belief that after the exposure of this incident GD would not maintain its popularity in the following June 17 elections, GD managed to maintain the same percentage, proving how under certain circumstances negative popularity is equally crucial as positive popularity for extremist groups to amplify their marginal voice and establish their presence publicly.

Immediately after the event, a Facebook page titled "Kasidiaris, blessed is your hand" was created and received more than six thousand likes within a few days (Hatzopoulos and Patelis 2013b) (currently, in October 2013, the particular fan page is down and a closed group took its place with 687 members). The moderators of the page and its members thought of Kasidiaris as a popular hero who was brave enough to challenge the hypocrisy and political correctness of politicians, mainstream media and journalists. The incident also sparked popular imagination and cultural production. A hip-hop remix of the event, claiming to be the hit of 2012 summer, appeared on YouTube (in October 2013 it had almost four hundred thousand views) and got quickly reproduced on other YouTube channels as well as websites, generally receiving very positive comments.[13] The song remixes phrases that the participants said during the incident, emphasising in particular Kasidiaris' phrase, "*bloody-commie*," which was directed against Kaneli, as well as "αντε βρε νούμερο," a slang phrase which could be freely translated into 'enough with your silly acting,' addressed to Dourou. A more traditional musical interpretation of the event, composed in the Greek folk musical style of rembetika by the songwriter Paris Mavromatis, was also presented a few months later. This song was titled "Ilias Kasidiaris," and again it was relatively widely reproduced on social media (around twenty-five thousand views on YouTube in October 2013). The refrain of the song, which was accompanied by the traditional Greek instrument the bouzouki, which has working-class associations, says, "Kasidiaris, blessed is your hand; the entire world shouts that you are a brave lad."[14]

At another staged event that was reproduced thousands of times on social media (more than three hundred thousand views using the keyword 'Χυτηριο' [Chytirio] in October 2013), outside Chytirio Theatre a GD MP named Ilias Panagiotaros shouted to the audience and actors of a play the following sexist and racist hate-utterances, in what appears on camera as a performance of delirium:

> You little cunt, wrap it up. Did you get that? Wrap it up you little faggots. You 'sticking-it-in-the-ass' fuckers, actors-my-ass. Yes, just keep staring at me you little hooker. Your time is up. Film, go ahead film [me] you are fucked by the Pakistanis. You fucking Albanian assholes, eh, you fucking Albanian assholes.[15]

Other nodal events that brought GD to the centre of social media publicity in Greece and abroad include the staged attacks on migrant merchants at flea markets across Greece, mainly on September 7–8, 2012, and GD's protest outside the major private Greek TV station Mega Channel' for showing

Turkish soap operas on March 25, 2013. In the latter event, GD's now imprisoned MP Christos Pappas urinated outside the station's main entrance as a form of protest, an action that was filmed and circulated around social media and subsequently discussed in the parliament. Events were also created through staged protests on anniversaries and commemorations, such as at the funeral of the junta military officer Nikos Dertilis on January 31, 2013, or the anniversary of the so-called Imia crisis (February 2, 2013). Simultaneously, GD was creating noise in parliament, mainly by swearing at other MPs or by making provocative claims that often relied on conspiracy theories, which are generally adored by Nazis (Taguieff 2004). Indicatively, on October 24, 2012, Ilias Kasidiaris read in parliament an excerpt from the proven anti-Semitic hoax "The Protocols of the Elders of Zion" as if it were a valid document, to make his point that the "global centres of power systematically fight GD."

GD media networks are quick to create big titles of such staged performances and to fuse them with YouTube. Simultaneously, the group's media activists are quick to post comments and respond to oppositional ones with violent, vulgar and divertive utterances. Comments seem to target viewers who may have a certain level of undecidability, in order to dazzle them and to have impact on them through the exhibition of rhetorical power and offence. Apart from the comments, the titles of posts or videos are also important in creating an effect of righteousness. Some YouTube video titles, taken from a popular GD channel belonging to frequent user 'iwannis metaxas,' are indicative of the tone and content of GD's political discourse and the one-way, affective message that the Nazi spectacle seeks to create (the following videos currently have between 50,000 and 150,000 views):[16]

- Arrest of 35-year old anti-authoritarian—drug dealer (16/06/2012)
- CONFLICTS IN CORFU BETWEEN INHABITANTS AND GYPSIES (10/06/2009)
- Trial of an Albanian animal torturer (26/12/2011)
- Anarcholeftists beat up girls + burned a flag (17/06/2012)
- Jobs for Greeks by Golden Dawn (29/09/2012)

Overall, GD social media channels are constantly and systematically feeding their audience and the general public with the spiteful spectacles they create. In this way they attempt to normalise their violent and racist attitudes and agendas, hero-worshipping their own members and vilifying their enemies. In such videos the public persona of the Nazi is constructed in order to serve as a role model for the groups' supporters, accompanied by an aura of the righteous and the undefeatable. As Adorno (1991, 133) argued in his analysis on the mediatisation of fascism, monotony, the constant reiteration and the scarcity of ideas are indispensable in the technique of mass mobilisation against democracy. In a period of crisis when identities seem to be more malleable and thus more easily attracted by supposed 'ruptures' in ordinary politics, social media prove to be particularly effective in facilitating noise-making propaganda by offering extended visibility to the group.

3.3.   Relativisation of Accusations and Constant Attack

Relativisation is a strategy that GD publicly follows, similarly to Nazis. This involves iterating the response that the acts they commit are nothing compared to those of the politicians that ruled Greece so far. As Doob puts it, relativising the accusations directed against them was another Nazi strategy that intended to vilify the opponents, as well as to intensify the propaganda against them. For instance, Goebbels thought that when Germany was accused of the mistreatment of Jews the best strategy was to fight back against its opponents in the name of humanity. As Doob puts it,

> As Germany was attacked for her treatment of Jews, the policy of "complete silence" seemed unwise: "it is best to seize the offensive and to say something about English cruelty in India or the Near East" (M3064) and also to "intensify . . . our anti-Bolshevik propaganda." (M32'25) (1950, 430)

This is a strategy that GD follows systematically. Indicatively—only one case among many—in an interview done a few days after the first elections in May 2012 and viewed over half a million times on YouTube (the count based on search results from the title of the TV show *στα άδυτα της χρυσής αυγής* [Deep in Golden Dawn]), another now imprisoned MP, Giannis Lagos, when asked if GD regards the colonels' military dictatorship of Greece during 1967–1974 as 'junta,' replied, "I will reverse the question and ask you whether what we live today is junta, because for me what we live today is junta."[17]

Indicatively such relativisation tactics are found in post titles that the Facebook page "Ellinon diktyo" shared on October 7–8, 2013, after the arrest of many GD members and its legal charges for being a criminal organization:[18]

- Why is the Communist Party that wants to break down the constitution no [sic] arrested?
- Criminal organization or Political Party?? 90+1 crimes of the criminal organization 'PASOK'
- A query: Is it criminal if you declare to be a nationalist? What is the sentence it entails?

The relativisation strategy is very important for GD, as crucial terms for their discourse, such as 'Nazism,' 'Hitler' or 'dictatorship,' bear very negative connotations in the Greek public sphere. Thus from the moment of its election and its elevation to a mass organization, GD attempted to hide its

Nazi identity by saying that they are 'Greek nationalists,' but also by being playful with it, constantly attempting to trivialise the meaning of Nazism. In this way Nazi crimes are relativised in statements such as "history will judge Hitler in due time" or "we do not think that Hitler is the one responsible for the problems of the world."[19] Nikos Michaloliakos known to have 'zieg-heiled' his audience in a mass rally of his organization, said that "these hands may sometimes wave this way, but they are clean hands, they never stole anything."[20] GD also tries to present the fascist salute as a 'Doric,' 'ancient Greek' salutation, and accordingly to claim an ancient Greek patronage of the swastika. Such a rhetorical tactic lessens and trivialises Hitler's crimes, preparing the audience for a Nazi reading of Hitler and a Nazi historical revision, where the meanings of the Second World War are discredited as fabricated by 'Jewish conspiracies.'

Kasidiaris' (and other GD members') mode of argumentation violates the rules of reason through the use of arbitrary generalisations, unproven 'facts' and positions, and conclusions not supported by evidence or data. The Nazis attempt to destroy conversation, while giving the illusionary impression to a viewer that their opponent is defeated. Furthermore, GD public performances are usually accompanied by an emphatic voice and bodily attitude that is meant to stupefy and dazzle the viewers into aporia and fascination. The point of such tactics is for GD's public personas to construct themselves as superhumans (Horkheimer 2004). The public cultivation of a personality cult is a classic Nazi-fascist strategy, where the fascist subjects make themselves into a spectacle, an image.

By not being explicit about Nazism, GD manages to maintain its connection both to its hardcore Nazi followers, who understand this as a necessary strategy because society is not yet 'radicalized enough,' and to broader masses of conservative or indignant people who may regard GD as an honest political party because they are not 'thieves.' Simultaneously, GD's declared denunciation of violence and proclaimed faith in the constitution aim at fabricating its position as a legitimate party.

On GD's English webpage, where its programme is posted, "free of Western Marxist propaganda" in the group's own words, the approved comments are only those from like-minded people across the world, accompanied by explicitly Nazi expressions, so as to create the illusion of international solidarity with their cause:

- Anonymous December 29, 2012 at 12:56 AM. Hail GD!!!! once you take your country back, others i think will follow
- slovenski domoljub March 7, 2013 at 12:21 PM Heil the GD, i hope soon that you will be able to open one of your offices in Slovenia becouse we need one, every european country needs one but we have to work hard on our own first so that can happen so as a NS i say: Comrades, get to work:)

- Anonymous March 1, 2013 at 4:23 AM Respect to GD from Sweden! May the good forces annihilate the evil Zionist ideology.
- Glenn M. February 5, 2013 at 12:07 AM (2/4/2013) Your 50,000 strong Athens demonstration was awesome, bone-chilling, and super inspirational to White Nationalists the world over. After 42 years an American activist, I never thought I'd live to see anything like it. You've given us all pride and much hope. Bravo to Greece, and bravo to the Greek people everywhere.[21]

Social media are thus used reflexively by maintaining communication with hardcore Nazi supporters and by adjusting newcomers to Nazi jargon and ideology, discrediting the post–Second World War consensus on the evils of Nazism.

The relativisation strategy usually works alongside the promotion of a positive image of the party, mainly related with 'social work,' such as staged blood and food donations 'only for Greeks' and animal rights and ecological activism (including the setup of a 'bureau' that seeks employment 'only for Greeks,' proposing an average daily wage of eighteen euros, when even austerity laws guarantee a daily income of about twenty-five euros!).[22] As regards to ecology there have been numerous ecological actions organized by the party that were advertised online in an attempt to create an image of responsibility. In a recent interview widely promoted on Golden Dawn webpages, we can notice how the MP Panagiotaros (who was shouting the racist and sexist rants outside the theatre protest) is transformed from a 'brutal warrior' to a pet-loving, sensitive man who sincerely cares about engendered species, animal rights and ecology. These occasions, however, become also an opportunity to tarnish the image of the immigrants and the Left. Panagiotaros, for instance, in the foregoing interview creates another sensualised spectacle by attacking immigrants for 'eating dogs,' further accusing animal rights NGOs for protecting them as they are affiliated with the Left.[23] GD's positive action is regularly invoked when the party is accused of employing military tactics or being cruel to immigrants. In this regard, positive action mostly has a 'balancing role' between Nazi extremism and the petty-bourgeois sensibility of a large part of the public. Overall, in terms of social media communication, the positive image cultivated by GD works to provide arguments in the relativising strategy, while further sketching an 'evil' image of their opponents.

4. CONCLUDING REMARKS

Despite its monstrosity and banality, GD managed to mobilise people from various social strata for its cause. In this chapter we demonstrated that social media played an important role in this mobilisation, making visible extreme discourses and practices that would not so easily be promoted by mainstream media. We also showed how the techniques used by GD in the digital media context, such as spectacularisation, relativisation and the creation of noise, are identical to the ones used by Goebbels. Social media can provide a fertile ground for the fast circulation of affective images and slogans and can contribute to the legitimisation of Nazi discourse, especially in periods of crisis. Social media, then, through party member accounts that attempt daily to create an 'mediated intimacy,' can become an instrument of the broader scope of Nazis to both disarticulate and occupy liberal power and the state apparatus in its existing form.

The decontextualised effect of social media, as we saw with the employment of the Hollywood film *300*, whose imagery is constantly reproduced in the nationalist webscape, is very important for communicating and making abstract connections between periods, populations and ideas. These abstract connections work to constitute possible 'regimes of truth' (Foucault 1980) that provide particular frameworks of looking at and discussing things. As we found throughout our research, Facebook and YouTube allow GD to perform a number of actions which would be unimaginable to carry out on such a scale through existing media, such as producing history, mobilising action, becoming an intimate and trusted organization and commenting daily on current political affairs.

In the precarious times of neo-liberalism, the ideas of the Greek Nazis seem to be filling a void by providing goals, organizing social relations and giving some kind of illusionary meaning to an otherwise chaotic environment. Along with its horrific side, GD's propaganda also strives towards community and identity building in moments of social depression and institutional delegitimization. Both sides work supplementary to each other and social media are very important in both regards; through the easy accessibility and anonymity they offer to users, they give GD the opportunity to make its discourse visible and engage in argumentation with other interlocutors. By rendering the social realm as a state of permanent war through an engagement with (hyper-) 'sensible politics,' the Nazis try to create an army of fanatics satiated with simplified answers to complex questions. The utilization of social media for an effective Goebbels-style propaganda has marked a dangerous territory within the Greek social and political landscape that calls for the intensification and expansion of antifascist action."

NOTES

1. This is heard at 'Interview with Ilias Kasidiaris at TV 10 of Trikala, January 10, 2012', published in YouTube on the October 3, 2012 by the user 'MelitaInsula' http://www.youtube.com/watch?v=ZqCa81BNAPk. The particular phrase can heard at 7:40 (in Greek, our translation).
2. 'There are good communists too. . . !' An interview with Ilias Kasidiaris at 'Sportdog', on 2 October 2013. http://www.sportdog.gr/article/153736/yparxoyn-kai-kaloi-kommoynistes%E2%80%A6 (in Greek, our translation).

3. 'Witnesses that 'burn' Golden Dawn: How they fish supporters, how they beat foreigners' at 'Parapona Rodou.' http://parapona-rodou.blogspot.com/2013/09/blog-post_7141.html#.UlFOcxBFqYQ. Accessed on 20 October 2013 (in Greek, our translation).

4. For Rancière the distribution of the sensible refers to "the system of self-evident facts of sense perception that simultaneously discloses the existence of something in common and the delimitations that define the respective parts and positions within it. A distribution of the sensible therefore establishes at one and the same time something common that is shared and exclusive parts" (Rancière 2006, 12).

5. The original page "Ellinon diktyo," which had more than seventy-five thousand likes, was censored by Facebook some days after the murder of Fyssas. Currently there is "Ellinon diktyo II," which has many fewer likes. http://www.hellinon.net/ Accessed on 18 April 2014.

6. The text is found in the official GD website on 15 May 2012 (in Greek, our translation). http://www.xryshaygh.com/index.php/enimerosi/view/chrush-augh-janagia-na-jebrwmisei-o-topos#.UXPIEMqf-So. Accessed on 23 October 2013.

7. The official song of GD. Uploaded on YouTube, published on 25 July 2012 by the user 'Sereosoo8.' http://www.youtube.com/watch?v=I3_g8oSm3MY (in Greek, our translation).

8. The 'Left' as a material and symbolic space is usually perceived as a barrier to the Nazis' 'anti-systemic' profile and in this sense it is the central enemy of GD. GD has thus declared that it is 'today's Left' in order to attract supporters who could follow the Left. This technique involves appropriating the anti-systemic language of the Left only to attract the attention of those protesting against corruption. Similarly, Bramsted cites how Goebbels in 1927 published "glaring posters in red, screaming in Communist fashion 'THE BOURGEOIS STATE IS APPROACHING ITS END'" (1954, 71) so as to neutralise the communist slogans by appropriating their language in order to attack the system.

9. The particular quote comes from the video 'The Unknown Leader of GD,' which is an excerpt from an interview with Nikos Michaloliakos given to the journalist Stavros Theodorakis at Mega TV Channel. The video was published online by the user 'Zappitvideo' on 11 April 2012 at http://www.youtube.com/watch?feature=player_embedded&v=Sk7aoZ1JOrQ (in Greek, our translation).

10. Some YouTube videos that use the particular slogan are the following: 'Golden Dawn to get rid of the filth,' published by the user 'iakxos serraios' on 6 April 2012. http://www.youtube.com/watch?v=cWBkCE7iaLc&no redirect=1 'CRITICAROOM.COM to get rid of the filth' published by the user 'LeonidasAT300' on 23 May 2012. http://www.youtube.com/watch?v=_Y4bg1CIoQs (in Greek, our translation).

11. The photograph that can be found in the link below reads: '*Giannis Lagos—a modern Leonidas*', published by the user 'Ethnikr' on 12 May 2012. The picture is posted in a blog in English, devoted on 'Greek issues' (sic), that is clearly about neo-Nazi issues and propaganda. The GD MP Giannis Lagos appears in a photo-collage to walk alongside Gerald Butler as 'Leonidas' in an image taken by the film '300' http://ethniko.net/blog/%CE%B3%CE%B9%CE%B1%CE%BD%CE%BD%CE%B7%CF%82-%CE%BB%CE%B1%CE%B3%CE%BF%CF%82/.

12. 'Kaneli gets beaten up by Kasidiaris in a TV show!' published in YouTube by the user 'SuperBestVidzGR', on 7 June 2012 http://www.youtube.com/watch?v=2Hk2FqoZoOQ.

13. The 'remix' of the event can be found, among other YouTube channels, here: 'Άντε βρε νούμερο (summer 2012 hit) by the user ZLow' published by the user 'Melitalnsula' on 15 June 2012 http://www.youtube.com/watch?v=3q2ODAbVjdY and 'Άντε βρε νούμερο' published by 'Zlow' on 22 June 2012 http://www.youtube.com/watch?v=n6Vjw2yWjWw

14. The song 'Paris Mavromatis – Ilias Kasidiaris', is published in YouTube by the user 'parismavros' on 25 December 2012 http://www.youtube.com/watch?v=B8w0f_9ZhJM (in Greek, our translation).
15. The video where the particular figure swears the quoted text: 'MAT –Chytirio Theater', published by the user 'elsabeh5318' on 11 October 2012 http://www.youtube.com/watch?v=JDzptwor6ps. The translated text is published on 11 October 2012 in the link http://www.twitlonger.com/show/jk3k7s.
16. Here we should also say that Ioannis Metaxas, from whom this channel borrows its name, was a Greek dictator. The channel can be seen here: https://www.youtube.com/channel/UCsAbvgQlvEGQzzjm_C-IIXQ.
17. 'Video Shock: Deep in Golden Dawn'. Published by the user 'Radio9gr' on 9 May 2012. Lagos says the particular phrase at 4:30 http://www.youtube.com/watch?v=3etEoYRLI3I. Accessed on October 23, 2013.
18. The reposted articles can be found here: 'Why is the Communist Party that wants to break down the constitution not arrested?' Published in the official GD page on 8 October 2012 at http://www.xryshaygh.com/index.php/enimerosi/view/giati-den-diwkontai-oi-kkedes-enw-dhlwnoun-aperifrasta-oti-einai-antisuntag. 'Criminal organization or Political Party?? 90+1 crimes of the criminal organization 'PASOK." Published in the official GD page on 7 October 2013 at http://www.xryshaygh.com/index.php/enimerosi/view/ta-901-kakourghmata-ths-egklhmatikhs-organwshs-pasok#.UlRbdxBFqYR. 'A query: Is it criminal if you declare to be a nationalist? What is the sentence it entails?' Published in the nationalist website 'Greek alert' http://www.greekalert.com/2013/10/blog-post_5932.html. Accessed on 23 October 2013.
19. 'Golden Dawn: PM stated that History will judge Hitler.' Published in the news portal 'Pinikio' at http://www.pinnokio.gr/arthro/xrysh-aygh-boyleyths-dhlwse-o-xitler-tha-krithei-en-kairw-apo-thn-istoria-vid (in Greek, our translation). Accessed on 23 October 2013.
20. 'N. Michaloliakos: These hands are clean.' Published in YouTube by the user 'serreosoo8' on 21 October 2012 at http://www.youtube.com/watch?v=Jh5-c7IiGe8 (in Greek, our translation).
21. Here is the link for the webpage of 'GDGD-International Newsroom' where these discussions can be found http://golden-dawn-international-newsroom.blogspot.gr/p/the-program-of-golden-dawn.html (in Greek, our translation). Acessed on 23 October 2013.
22. In the article 'KKE: Slave trade in the employment offices of Golden Dawn' the journalist Dimitris Galanis of the newspaper 'Vima' explains how the Communist Party of Greece accuses Golden Dawn for engaging in modern 'slave trade' practices by suggesting a daily wage of 18 euros. http://www.tovima.gr/politics/article/?aid=476918. Published 28 September 2012. Also, the class role of the GD is further revealed by the group's support of the tax free status of ship-owners as well as the discrete support of the scandalous gold-mining activity of the Canadian multinational 'Eldorado Gold', in Northern Greece, despite mass protests across the country against it.
23. This phrase is taken by an interview that Ilias Panagiotaros gave to the online news portal 'Madatofors' titled 'Interview of the Golden Dawn MP Ilias Panagiotaros' that can be found at https://vimeo.com/64226460#at=0. Panagiotaros says the particular phrase at 11:25 (in Greek, our translation) Accessed on 23 October 2013.

REFERENCES

Adorno, Theodor. 1991. *The Culture Industry.* London: Routledge.
Arendt, Hannah. 1976. *The Origins of Totalitarianism.* New York: Harcourt.

Áthanasiou, Athena. 2012. *Η κρίση ως «κατάσταση έκτακτης ανάγκης: κριτικές και αντιστάσεις* [The crisis as a state of emergency: Critiques and resistances]. Athens: Savvalas.

Baird, Jay W. 1982. Goebbels, Horst Wessel, and the Myth of Resurrection and Return. *Journal of Contemporary History* 17 (4): 633–650.

Barthes, Roland. 1981. *Camera Lucida: Reflections on Photography.* New York: Hill and Wang.

Benjamin, Walter. 2008. *The Work of Art in the Age of Mechanical Reproduction.* London: Penguin Books.

Bosco, Anna, and Susannah Verney. 2011. Electoral Epidemic: The Political Cost of Economic Crisis in Southern Europe, 2010–11. *South European Society and Politics* 17 (2): 129–154.

Bramsted, Ernst. 1954. Joseph Goebbels and National Socialist Propaganda 1926–1939: Some Aspects. *Australian Journal of International Affairs* 8 (2): 65–93.

Brown, Wendy. 2003. Neo-liberalism and the End of Liberal Democracy. *Theory & Event* 7(1): 1–25.

Chambers, Deborah. 2013. *Social Media and Personal Relationships: Online Intimacies and Networked Friendship.* Houndmills, UK: Palgrave Macmillan.

Dean, Jodi. 2009. *Democracy and Other Neoliberal Fantasies: Communicative Capitalism and Left Politics.* Durham, NC: Duke University Press.

Dean, Mitchell. 2009. *Governmentality: Power and Rule in Modern Society.* London: SAGE.

Doob, Leonard W. 1950. Goebbels' Principles of Propaganda. *Public Opinion Quarterly* 14 (3): 419–442.

Dordanas, Stratos. 2011. *Η γερμανική στολή στη ναφθαλίνη. Επιβιώσεις του δοσιλογισμού στη Μακεδονία, 1945–1974* [The German uniform in mothballs: Survivals of collaborationism in Macedonia, 1945–1974]. Athens: Estia.

Ellinas, Antonis. 2010. *The Media and the Far Right in Western Europe: Playing the Nationalist Card.* Cambridge, UK: Cambridge University Press.

Falzon, Mark-Anthony. 2009. *Multi-sited Ethnography: Theory, Praxis and Locality in Contemporary Social Research.* Aldershot: Ashgate.

Fierke, Karin. 2007. *Critical Approaches to International Security.* Cambridge, UK: Polity Press.

Fischer, Eileen, Andrew Smith and Chen Yongjian. 2012. How Does Brand-Related User-Generated Content Differ across YouTube, Facebook, and Twitter? *Journal of Interactive Marketing* 26 (2): 102–113.

Foucault, Michel. 1980. *Power/Knowledge: Selected Interviews and Other Writings, 1972–1977.* New York: Random House Digital.

Giglietto, Fabio, Luca Rossi and Davide Bennato. 2012. The Open Laboratory: Limits and Possibilities of Using Facebook, Twitter, and YouTube as a Research Data Source. *Journal of Technology in Human Services* 30 (3–4): 145–159.

Hamilakis, Yannis. 2007. *The Nation and Its Ruins: Antiquity, Archaeology, and National Imagination in Greece.* Oxford: Oxford University Press.

Horkheimer, Max. 2004. *The Eclipse of Reason.* London: Continuum.

Jay, Martin. 1992. "The Aesthetic Ideology" as Ideology; Or, What Does It Mean to Aestheticize Politics? *Cultural Critique* 21: 41–61.

———. 2002. Cultural Relativism and the Visual Turn. *Journal of Visual Culture* 1 (3): 267–278.

Kitchen, Martin. 2003. Fascism and the Capitalist System: A Marxist view. In *The Fascism Reader,* edited by Aristotle Kallis, 57–63. London: Routledge.

Laclau, Ernesto, and Chantal Mouffe. 1985. *Hegemony and Socialist Strategy: Towards a Radical Democratic Politics.* London: Verso.

Makrides, Vasilios. 2004. Orthodoxy in the Service of Anticommunism: The Religious Organization Zoë during the Greek Civil War. In *The Greek Civil War: Essays on a Conflict of Exceptionalism and Silences,* edited by Phillip Carabott and Thanasis Sfikas, 159–175. London: King's College.

Marcus, George E. 1995. Ethnography in/of the World System: The Emergence of Multi-sited Ethnography. *Annual Review of Anthropology* 24: 95–117.

Mazower, Mark. 2000. *After the War Was Over: Reconstructing the Family, Nation, and State in Greece, 1943–1960.* Princeton, NJ: Princeton University Press.

_____. 2001. *Inside Hitler's Greece, the Experience of an Occupation 1941–1944.* New Haven, CT: Yale University Press.

McLagan, Meg, and Yates McKee, eds. 2012. *Sensible Politics: The Visual Culture of Nongovernmental Activism.* Cambridge, MA: MIT Press.

Mylonas, Yiannis. 2012. Media and the Economic Crisis of the EU: The "Culturalization" of a Systemic Crisis and Bild-Zeitung's Framing of Greece. *tripleC—Cognition, Communication, Co-operation: Open Access Journal for a Global Sustainable Information Society* 10 (2): 646–671.

Patelis, Korinna, and Pavlos Hatzopoulos. 2013a. The Comrade Is Violent: Liberal Discourses of Violence in Anti-austerity Greece. *Theory & Event* 16 (1).

———. 2013b. Introduction: Understanding Social Media Monopolies. *First Monday* 18 (3–4). http://journals.uic.edu/ojs/index.php/fm/article/view/4614/3418.

Poulantzas, Nicos. 1970. *Fascism and Dictatorship: Third International and the Problems of Fascism.* London: Verso.

Psarras, Dimitris. 2012. *Η μαύρη βίβλος της χρυσής αυγής* [The black bible of the GDGD]. Athens: Polis.

Rancière, Jacques. 2006. *The Politics of Aesthetics.* London: Continuum

Sevastakis, Nicolas. 2008. Φιλόξενος μηδενισμός: μια σπουδή στον homo democraticus [Hospitable nihilism: A study on homo democraticus]. Athens: Estia.

Tagg, John. 1988. *The Burden of Representation: Essays on Photographies and Histories.* Minneapolis: Minnesota Press.

Taguieff, Pierre-Andre. 2004. *Conspiracy Theories, Esoterism, Extremism.* Athens: Polis.

Tsoukalas, Constantinos. 2012. *Greece of Oblivion and Truth: From a Prolonged Adolescence to a Violent Maturation [Ελλάδα της λήθης και της αλήθειας, από την μακρά εφηβεία στην βίαιη ενηλικίωση].* Athens: Themelio.

Vajda, Mihaly. 1976. *Fascism as a Mass Movement.* London: Allison & Busby.

Voglis, Polymeris. 2002. *Becoming a Subject: Political Prisoners during the Greek Civil War, 1945–1950.* New York: Berghahn Books.

Wacquant, Loïc. 2012. Three Steps to a Historical Anthropology of Actually Existing Neoliberalism. *Social anthropology* 20(1): 66-79.

Welch, David. 2004. Nazi Propaganda and the Volksgemeinschaft: Constructing a People's Community. *Journal of Contemporary History* 39 (2): 213–238.

6 More Than an Electronic Soapbox

Activist Web Presence as a Collective Action Frame, Newspaper Source and Police Surveillance Tool During the London G20 Protests in 2009

Jonathan Cable

1. INTRODUCTION

In April 2009 the Group of 20 (G20) international summit was held in London, and similar to previous summits was met by a mass demonstration. The protests against the summit fit into a sequence of anti-globalisation demonstrations over the last fifteen years or so. These summit protests first gained international prominence at the World Trade Organization (WTO) meeting in Seattle, Washington, in December 1999 (DeLuca and Peeples 2002). The London protests were spearheaded by G20Meltdown, an umbrella organization representing around sixty groups (G20Meltdown 2009o).[1] The aims of the group were to highlight issues of war, climate change, financial crimes and land borders, and these were all connected by the overarching subject of capitalism. The use of the G20 summit as a protest platform was against a backdrop of press attention on the banking crisis and MPs' expenses scandal (Curtice and Park 2010, 131). The aim of this chapter is to look specifically at the media strategies used by G20Metldown to communicate their messages and mobilise support, and their representation by the press. In doing so the chapter will examine their use of the Internet and explore the interrelationship between protester messages, press coverage and police tactics. This is because the way that activists portray themselves and the messages and images they promote online resonate beyond activist circles. This will be shown to occur in both press reports and police intelligence gathering. The two important questions raised in this chapter are 1) how are online platforms used by activists? and 2) how are activists' online messages used and interpreted by the press and police? Before addressing these questions the chapter will present a brief theoretical background to the research to situate it within broader academic debates.

2.   POLITICAL AND MEDIA OPPORTUNITIES

Protest groups utilise many different modes of communication and pro-test tactics, each of which provokes a variety of reactions from the press and dominant institutions.[2] The actions and reactions to protest provide an opportunity to gain a deeper understanding of the processes that shape collective action. To theoretically contextualise the influences on collective action is to consider political opportunities. The definition of political opportunities ties the relative success and failure of protest groups to political, institutional and environmental variables that shape collective action (Eisinger 1973; Gamson and Meyer 1996; Meyer 1993; Meyer and Minkoff 2004; Sireau 2009). The role of the media in political opportunities has not previously been granted sufficient theoretical prominence. It needs to because today the media is the focal point and site of political debate. The theory of political opportunities has come under more scrutiny and been moved towards a more mediated framework. This is where the media gains increased prominence in the success and failure of protest groups to publicise their messages (Cammaerts 2012; McCurdy 2012). The basis of this power relationship is effectively described by Wolfsfeld: "[t]he relative power of either side—a given news medium and a given antagonist—is determined by the value of its services divided by its need for those offered by the other" (2003, 84). Power in this quote refers to "relative dependence" (ibid., 84), or more simply who needs who more. This power equation is weighted towards the media, because they are not obliged to cover a protest group. It follows that the media's power and involvement in contentious politics are their ability to signal to dominant institutions what issues should be granted increased salience. This means the media agenda is significant not only because of its influence on the political and public agenda but also because of its ability to increase the prominence of issues (Behr and Iyengar 1985, 38). This is where media opportunities are important to the promotion of protester messaging, because if a group is able to highlight an issue in the press it will potentially move up the media agenda. Furthermore, if the issues under protest are already on the media agenda they are more likely to be reported favourably. However, protest groups are competing with other, more institutionally powerful sources attempting to make their framing of an issue the dominant definition.

2.1.   Protest Group Messages and Self-Representation

This approach puts an increased focus on the messaging and mode of communication used by protest groups and follows Diani's political message approach towards political opportunities. He argues that successful protest group messaging occurs within many different media and political contexts (1996, 1067). Investigating the messages of protest groups is to examine the collective action frames contained in protester communications. These represent a protest group's interpretation of an issue that is unfiltered by the mainstream media. The function of collective action frames in this context is to diagnose and define an issue as an issue, highlight the issues and suggest potential solutions to a grievance (Gamson 2003; Sireau 2009; Snow and Benford 1992; Entman 1993). To bring these issues to public attention, protest groups utilise a number of different protest and media tactics (McAdam and Su 2002; Lipsky 1968; Eisinger 1973). Rucht argues that in response to a lack of media coverage activists can use a combination of the Quadruple A, referring to abstaining from the media, attacking the media, adapting to the media and the creation of mainstream media alternatives (2004, 36–37).

In the case of G20Meltdown the communications tactics were a mixture of adaptation and the creation of alternatives, in particular online. To contextualise this use of digital media further Hands provides an exploration of the use of digital technology in activism and its relationship with power (2011). Hands specifically talks about capitalism as the overarching power that online activism targets and aims to dissolve power relations with (ibid., 8). Furthermore, Hands states that one of the key uses of online activism is in the mobilisation and coordination of protest actions. This has meant that in the run up to and on the day of protest participants can be moved around more effectively, and adjust protest tactics to perhaps instigate a more direct action approach (ibid., 124–125). This chapter will demonstrate how G20Meltdown used online communications to promote their messages, but it will also emphasise how these messages were interpreted by the press and police.

2.2. Mass Demonstrations and Media Coverage

The transition of protester messages into media coverage brings in Entman's concept of framing, in which media texts construct and put forward an "imprint of power" (1993). In this respect the media plays the role of 'validator' of competing frames and influences "whose views need to be taken seriously" (Gamson and Meyer 1996, 290). Furthermore, a group's choice of protest tactics has a major impact on the content and amount of media coverage. The repertoire of tactics available to protest groups ranges from direct democratic events, such as voting, to heavy violence or arson (Kriesi et al. 1992, 228). The more spectacular and confrontational the protest tactics the greater the publicity a group will receive, but consequently the press will critically divorce the protest from the underlying issues, removing the context as to why a group is protesting (Rosie and Gorringe 2009a; Wykes 2000; Gitlin [1980] 2003; DeLuca 1999; Wahl-Jorgensen 2003). The use of confrontational tactics, such as stunts and image events, by protest groups both recognises and manipulates news values.

Gamson and Meyer argue that the image and spectacle created by protest are its primary news value, and this is particularly true when protests turn more aggressive, even violent: "Burning buildings and burning tires make better television than peaceful vigils and orderly marches" (1996, 288). This is what Wahl-Jorgensen found in her research of the Mayday demonstrations in London in 2001. The early newspaper articles in the run-up to the protest set the tone with predictions of violence (2003). This resulted in the coverage falling into three different categories: 1) law and order, where protesters are a problem of policing; 2) the economy and the negative impact of protest on it; and 3) the spectacle—a focus on the processes and consequences of protest (ibid., 131). There is always the potential that confrontational protests will be covered in the press with dominant themes of disruption and an anticipation of violence.

3.   METHOD

To fully investigate G20Meltdown's collective action frames, press coverage and the reaction of the police and dominant institutions, a range of different empirical methods were used. First, G20Meltdown's official website, Twitter feed, Facebook pages and electronic copies of leaflets found on their official website were examined. More specifically, these sources were examined to deduce the key issues at the heart of the protest, the attribution of blame for the issues, suggested solutions, the framing of the protest opportunity or, more bluntly, why now is the time to act, the expectations of success and the mobilising of resources. These aspects of protest communications are at the core of collective action framing (Sireau 2009, 136–137, 162; Gamson and Meyer 1996, 286). Second, to create a detailed picture of how G20Meltdown were presented in the press a content analysis of British national press was carried out. The debates around the issues and protest found in newspapers reveal the "strategies of power or strategies for defining the rational and the commonsensical" (Wahl-Jorgensen 2003, 133–134). The sample was taken from British newspapers between January 2009 and June 2009 and included tabloids, middle market and broadsheets spread across political ideologies. The online newspaper database LexisNexis was used to collect the press reports. The focus was placed on articles that contained the name of the group, G20Meltdown, and the names of five high-profile members involved in the campaign.

The emphasis on the name of the group rather than the G20 protests in general allowed for the inclusion of a wider range of publications, and a concentrated targeting of the group's messages and protest tactics. This method yielded ninety-seven newspaper reports in the time frame. In order to examine the press samples' visual framing of the protest, the images accompanying articles were sourced from physical copies of the newspapers and analysed. This was to uncover any patterns in the imagery used, how these images complemented or contrasted to the written articles, and whether these images contributed to the overall framing of the protest. The interplay between text and image provides valuable insight into the dominant framing of protest events. Finally, following the G20 protests a number of governmental and police reports were produced; these were examined in order to build a picture of dominant institutional reactions to the protest. This chapter will now move on to detail the results of the empirical methods, and the implications of the findings for protest groups and future academic research.

4. THE MEDIA AND POLITICAL OPPORTUNITIES OF THE G20 SUMMIT

The actions of G20Meltdown are situated within the political and media context of the G20 summit in London. These types of international summits represent a large political and media opportunity for protest groups to get attention because international summits attract a lot of media focus, which groups like G20Meltdown can exploit. The G20 summit occurred in the aftermath of Britain's banking crisis and the global economic crisis in 2008, and followed a summer of political scandal in 2007, with the release of members of Parliament's expenses (Curtice and Park 2010, 131). The place of the banking crisis and the G20 summit for G20Meltdown's political and protest opportunities is detailed in an interview with one of the more prominent members of the network, Marina Pepper, in *Shift Magazine*: "With the crunch and the bail outs enough people could finally see the bleeding obvious: don't ask the problem for solutions. We are the solution" (2009).

This quote places capitalism as the main issue at the heart of the protest, and G20Meltdown as the alternative. The press' focus on the banking crisis presented the opportunity for the group to highlight their issues and played a large part in G20Meltdown's protest. The other variable affecting G20Meltdown's media and political opportunities was the lack of competition for attention. The only potential distraction was a coalition of non-government organizations (NGOs), trade unions and other campaign groups who protested under the banner of Put People First. They staged their protest on the weekend before the summit started (Put People First 2009), and did not directly compete with G20Meltdown's protests a week later. This meant that for G20Meltdown the political, media and protest opportunities were arguably open, and, as the foregoing quote demonstrates, the activists recognised the political and media context of their protest actions.

4.1. G20Meltdown's Use of the Internet

This section will explore G20Meltdown's collective action frames through the examination of their use of online communications. This will show that the different communication methods used by G20Meltdown attempted to create a coherent narrative. The majority of their online communications occurred through G20Meltdown's official website and on the social networks Twitter and Facebook. The Internet represents an alternative media opportunity for protest groups to reach the public that is unfiltered by the mainstream media. These online platforms were a place where G20Meltdown could fully explain their issues and present their preferred framing of the potential solutions to the issues. G20Meltdown's use of the Internet falls into four main categories:

1. Mobilise and advertise events
2. Provide details of protest targets and tactics
3. Explain the impetus and issues behind the protest
4. Respond to press coverage and police tactics

Each of these will now be discussed individually. The mobilising and advertising of events sees the Internet being used as an organizational tool and aids in the construction of a broader communicative narrative. The following tweet is an example of G20Meltdown encouraging participation and advertising pre-protest preparation: "Meltdown meets today. Check out website and Facebook for updates" (G20Meltdown 2009i). Alongside encouraging protest participants, G20Meltdown's communications attempted to produce a sense that anyone who took part in the protest would be part of something larger, and contained the optimism that G20Meltdown would succeed. The prospect of success is central to protest group communications, because negativity would ultimately be self-defeating and discourage people from participating.

The second and third facets of G20Meltdown's online communications are inextricably linked. This is because the protest tactics are inherently linked to the underlying issues of protest. The name of the group, 'Meltdown,' hints at a connection to the underlying issues, and represents economic, ecological and political 'meltdowns.' The march itself was constructed around four feeder marches converging on the protest target of the Bank of England. Each of the feeder marches represented a different issue and was led by a large horse puppet to create Four Horseman of the Apocalypse. The horses and the issues they were said to represent were as follows:

1. Red Horse—War
2. Black Horse—Homelessness, also cited as land enclosures/borders to "celebrate the 360th anniversary of the Diggers"[3]
3. Silver Horse—Financial crimes
4. Green Horse—Climate change (G20Meltdown 2009e)

Although these four issues are seemingly diverse and unrelated, G20Meltdown would use capitalism to connect the issues to each other and broaden the overall narrative. These issues are presented as an entry point to criticising capitalism; as Pepper says, "people will come to understand it's all part of the same problem" (2009). This part of G20Meltdown's collective action framing was a consistent part of everything they did. For example, the Facebook event for the G20Meltdown Party had the tagline, "Capitalism isn't in crisis, capitalism IS crisis!" (G20Meltdown 2009d). What is also clear from the group's communications is that they did not see an alternative to capitalism being offered by the mainstream political system, and that G20Meldown represented the alternative. Their Facebook group states, "We don't see any choice on offer except between bankers, bankers and more bankers, between capitalism, capitalism and more capitalism" (G20Meltdown 2009h).

Alongside their online communications G20Meltdown produced several leaflets. When examining the leaflets themselves the term 'protest' is avoided and the idea of a carnival is promoted. British demonstrations have historically used the term carnival—for example, the protest against the G8 in Scotland in 2005 was called the Carnival for Full Enjoyment, and the Carnival against Capital was held in London in 1999 (Molyneaux 2005, 109, 111). The noticeable characteristics of the leaflets are their use of humour, irreverent language and imagery, and a mixture of militaristic and confrontation language (G20Meltdown 2009k; 2009l; 2009c). The humour was contained in the name of the demonstration 'Financial Fools Day,' and in the imagery of subverted bank notes and maps of feeder marches (G20Meltdown 2009k). The two leaflets that resonated most with the press were a lot more confrontational and aggressive in their language. The first contained the slogan "storm the banks" (G20Meltdown 2009l), and it is this sentiment that was seized upon by the press. In addition, the leaflet talks of a "Spring Offensive," and a "fight back." The imagery accompanying the text adds to the aggressive talk with a mocked up image of a hanging banker (ibid.). The final leaflet re-emphasises this sense of militaristic foreboding with an image of the Bank of England and a superimposed image of a horseman of the apocalypse (G20Meltdown 2009c). The language again pushes the confrontational edge to the demonstration, stating that "thousands of people will lay siege" to the Bank of England (ibid.).

However, when these leaflets are compared to G20Meltdown's official press release for the protest there is still talk of revolution, but this sentiment is tempered by an emphasis on peaceful protest:

> head to the Bank of England for a 'Very English Revolution.'
> The 'Revolution' will take the form of an openly organized free assembly in public space outside the Bank of England, a peaceful and fun street party! (Barrett 2009)

The final use of social media by G20Meltdown was to react to events and press coverage before, during and after the G20 protests. Twitter was used to give immediate reactions to events, as well as publicise and plan further protests. The following list represents select tweets from the official

G20Meltdown feed and covers the build-up, day of and aftermath of the protests:

- March 19th—12:54 AM—Conspirators are everywhere. . . . who tells the truth? Which is genuine warning? What scare tactics? Who are these armchair generals? (G20Meltdown 2009b)
- March 26th—12:36 PM—When asked about predictions of violence we say: "We would hope the police can keep their truncheons in their belts, but who knows?" (G20Meltdown 2009n)
- April 1st—3:23 PM—Teabags arrived. Kettle went on. [. . .] Rozzers now in riot gear: Totally wrong outfits (G20Meltdown 2009m)
- April 1st—3:51 PM—In all fairness. cops ARE behaving. Well why wouldn't they be? Did I miss something? G20 leaders take note: we've taken the power back (G20Meltdown 2009g)
- April 2nd—1:59 PM—100s have gathered outside the Old Exchange at the Bank of England. Come down and join us. Chants of shame on you to the police. (G20Meltdown 2009a)
- April 8th—10:53 AM—Momentum gathers apace for silent demo: assemble Bethnal Green Police Station 11.30 Saturday. Events prior to Ian Tomlinson's death vex all (G20Meltdown 2009j)

What this timeline demonstrates is that social media allowed G20Meltdown a platform to respond to statements in the press and react to police tactics. These instant comments on Twitter aid in communicating what is happening on the ground during a protest, and highlights the protester's perception of the demonstration. However, as the last tweet in the timeline shows, the death of Ian Tomlinson came to dominate G20Meltdown's communications. The representation of the protest and issues in G20Meltdown's communications points towards the group's collective action frames. It demonstrates what issues concerned them, how they wanted to tackle these issues and what the aims of their protests were. The words activists use to describe their protest actions become increasingly important when considering press coverage and interpretations of the protest. The activists clearly presented a narrative of a demonstration with a confrontational edge, but their intention was for peaceful protest, as evidenced by G20Meltown's aforementioned press release which emphasises the protest as "a peaceful and fun street party" (Barrett 2009). It is this difference between activist and press representations of protest that highlights discrepancies in the framing of mass demonstrations and contentious politics.

4.2. Press Coverage of G20Meltdown

The interpretation of G20Meltdown's communications by the press and police will be discussed in this section. The major themes found from the content analysis and their importance will be discussed. In addition, the effect of G20Meltdown's communications and protest tactics on press coverage and the police will be unpacked. First, the press coverage was characterised by themes of law and order and the spectacle of protest. In other words press attention focused on the impact of the demonstration and the construction and nature of the protest. The dominant framing used in the press coverage was, in part, created by a Metropolitan Police briefing published in the *Guardian* in February 2009 (Lewis 2009a, 1). The briefing evokes two particular scenarios: (1) the protest was going to be as violent as the 1990 Poll Tax riots; and (2) activists would be coming out of retirement with the intention of causing maximum disruption (ibid., 1). The report also mentions the prospect of a "summer of rage," predicting that the G20 protests would be part of an ever-increasing series of confrontational protests (ibid.). The frames put forward in the article provided a narrative template that would be frequently utilised in press reports. This represents the definitional power of the police. The Metropolitan Police as an authoritative source were taken at their word, and there was no rebuttal provided by any of the activist groups mentioned. The following statistics reflect these themes. The top-level categories could appear multiple times in an article, but the subcategories only once. From the sample of ninety-seven articles, the major themes found in ten articles or more are shown in Table 6.1.

What Table 6.1 shows is that the themes of the spectacle of protest and law and order appeared in the sample in much higher frequencies compared to the other categories. These two categories taken together represent 81 per cent of all the story themes. This is further emphasised when the most frequent subcategories are dominated by the impact of protest and acts of protest. Table 6.2 shows the subcategories that appeared in fifteen or more press reports (5 per cent of the sample).

What this table demonstrates quite clearly is how the themes found in the Metropolitan Police briefing created a powerful template that resonated in the press. This is reflected in the three most frequently occurring themes in the coverage: (1) fear and an anticipation of violence; (2) references to historical protests that were disruptive and violent; and (3) a focus on the

Table 6.1   The overall categories of newspaper stories

Top-Level Story Categories	N	%
Spectacle of protest	136	45.0
Law and order	114	35.9
Economy	39	12.6
Recognition of protest	11	3.6
Total (including categories not listed)	309	100

Table 6.2　The top subcategories in newspaper articles

Subcategories	N	%
Anticipation of violence	53	17.2
Structure of protest	37	12.0
Police operation	35	11.3
Historical protest evoked	22	7.1
Cost of policing	20	6.5
Disruptions for commerce	19	6.1
Disruption to the public	17	5.5
Protester violence	15	4.9
Total (including categories not listed)	309	100

disruption and violence. It must be emphasised, however, that this was not due to a lack of protesters' voices in the press reports. Quite the opposite—as the following statistics demonstrate, when protesters'[4] sources are added together they appeared most frequently in the press coverage (129, or 41 per cent of total sources). This compares favourably to the institutionally powerful news sources of politicians[5] (51, or 16 per cent) and the police (50, or 16 per cent).

Although activists were used in the creation of the stories this does not mean that quantity equals quality of representation, nor that the protester frames will become the most prominent. Instead, it is clear that the press coverage of the G20 protests was the creation and promotion of an anticipation of violence that appeared in fifty-three of the ninety-seven articles (or 54 per cent). This anticipation of violence helps to separate a group from the underlying messages and issues at the heart of the protest, and distracts the press from debating the positives and negatives of a protest's arguments. To give an example of how an anticipation of violence is constructed in the press, the *Mirror* headline "Countdown to chaos" was printed in the build-up to the protests (Anon 2009, 5). The images accompanying articles helped to reinforce this narrative with depictions of boarded-up shopfronts, safety barriers and the police performing security checks in sewers and rivers (O'Neill 2009d, 16–17; Penrose 2009, 9). This preparation can partly be accounted for by the threat of terrorism to international summits, but these particular images were used in conjunction with articles specifically about the protest.

The protesters' role as a news source in the press coverage manifests itself through the simultaneous depiction of activists as an invisible threat and a visible menace. This type of portrayal creates both a hidden threat of protesters planning mass chaos and substantial disruption, and an overtly aggressive amorphous mass of people intent on violence (Rosie and

Gorringe 2009a). Portraying protesters in this way ensures that the press includes the protest in news coverage while excluding the issues. The role of online media in these press depictions highlights a major disadvantage of groups using an open media platform, such as the Internet or leaflets, as a part of their messaging. This is because the statements written on these platforms can easily be taken and reinterpreted by journalists, and in doing so remove their original meaning. The use of these resources takes them out of their original context, and the quotes and images made the most prominent point towards the press' preferred framing of a protest. This could fall into either a concentration on aggressive statements or an emphasis on more moderate voices.

To further illustrate this point the press used protester websites and leaflets as a source twenty-five times (8 per cent of all sources), with the web acting as an electronic distribution network for information. The attribution of these sources would vary between identifying them as online sources, but perhaps not name the website. For example, "One website urges demonstrators to 'express their rage' and promises 'a day of f***ing up the summit'" (O'Neill 2009e, 5). On the other hand, other news stories would not attribute statements to online sources, even though they can be traced back to G20Meltdown's website and leaflets. This was no more prevalent than the graphical maps and protest routes that accompanied the articles because these were clearly taken from online sources. This included information relating to protest event locations and the various routes of the feeder marches being incorporated into maps of potential 'flashpoints' (Edwards and Gammell 2009, 5; O'Neill 2009b, 3). Furthermore, the press produced timelines of protest, a breakdown of protester demographics and number of people in the protest. These elements of coverage were recorded as the structure of the protest in the content analysis, and related to the planning, construction and processes of the protest appearing in thirty-seven articles (or 38 per cent of the total). This reprinting of activist plans helped to do some of G20Meltdown's media promotion for them by advertising and informing the public about the protests.

The language of the articles replicated the phrases found in the leaflets and online. Especially the term 'storm the banks': The *Times*, for instance, reported that "violent sentiments" discovered on websites were encouraging activists to "'Storm the Banks' and 'Bash a Banker'" (O'Neill 2009a, 8). The *Express* went further, interpreting the leaflets as prompting "Fears of bloodshed" and reporting that the imagery used was "murderous" and "spread a message of hate" (Dixon 2009, 27). The protesters' messages in these examples were used as evidence by the press for an increased fear of violent protest. The very use of online media and social networking by G20Meltdown was incorporated into the press' narrative of fear. It meant that the protests were portrayed as highly organized with military levels of planning and precision. The *Times* referred to "Twitter tactics" and the use of social media to evade the police (O'Neill 2009c, 5). The *Daily*

Mail went further, describing the use of online resources as "Google anarchists targeting the city," and stating that social media was being used to provoke "mayhem" at the G20 protests (Wright 2009). This heightened sense of potential violence and disruption was aided by how the G20 protests were contextualised. A historical context was frequently mentioned in news reports and appeared in twenty-two articles (23 per cent of total). However, these historical references were characterised by protests that ended in violence and disruption, such as the WTO in Seattle in 1999, the 2001 G8 summit in Genoa, the 2000 London May Day protests and the Poll Tax riots in 1990.

The *Daily Telegraph*, for instance, discussed the 1999 Seattle protests, saying, "It is a decade since the anti-capitalist movement exploded on to the streets of Seattle" (Pitcher 2009, 24). It added to this by mentioning the G8 protests in Genoa in 2001 as an "insurrection" that ended in a protesters death (ibid.). The mention of historical protests was often accompanied by the names of the groups involved, and doing so further enhances the idea of activists 'coming out of retirement' to protest. The following quote from the *Sunday Mirror* includes both historic protests and the groups involved to enhance its storyline: "Anarchists from the 1990 Poll Tax riots are coming out of retirement to plot mayhem," and "notorious groups such as Class War, the Wombles and the Whitechapel Anarchist Group have secretly ganged up" (Penrose 2009, 9).

The press' depiction of protest from within this historical context does give the G20 protests a thematic context. This is further advanced by mentioning historically prominent groups and aids in placing the protest into a sequential narrative, but, as already mentioned, this is from within the frame of disruptive and violent protest. The violence of previous protests in this case acted as a historical anchor for the press to attempt to contextualise the G20 protests. This dominant framing of an anticipation of violence and fear meant that all of the demonstrators involved in the protests were judged within this frame. The framing helped create a preconception of how the protests should be interpreted before they had happened, and this in turn distracted from the underlying issues and reasons for protest. This is not to say that G20Meltdown were completely blameless in this portrayal, because their choice of words in online communications and leaflets became part of an ongoing press narrative. Their communications had the second consequence of influencing police intelligence gathering and the public order tactics deployed.

4.3.   Police Interpretations of G20Meltdown's Messages

This section will examine the police intelligence of the demonstration to show that protesters' online communications were used in a way similar to how the press used them. These similarities relate to anticipations of violence and situating the G20 protests into a historical context of disruption and violence. The documents drawn on for this section were produced following the death of bystander Ian Tomlinson.(Lewis 2009b, 1). The inquiries into public order tactics were held by Her Majesty's Inspectorate of Constabulary (HMIC) and the Joint Committee on Human Rights and the Home Affairs Committee. The official documents highlight the influence of protester communications on the police and the briefing of this intelligence to and by the press. The HMIC document "Adapting to protest" states that activist websites were an important source of information for police intelligence (HMIC 2009, 42). This echoes the press reporting of the demonstration, in which the aspirations for the protest were interpreted from online materials. The police intelligence was therefore limited, and illustrates the potential influence protester communications can have on police tactics. The report states that police intelligence had revealed "unprecedented levels of communication between disparate protest groups" and "a large number of un-notified[6] protests were expected" (ibid., 42). The police document goes on to explain that the intelligence for any 'un-notified' protests was garnered from "open source materials" such as activist websites and leaflets (ibid., 101). The use of online media by protest groups does, perhaps, hand the tactical initiative to the police and removes the element of surprise. The maps that are publicised online, for instance, allow the police to plan according to the convergence points and routes detailed in protester communications.

Subsequently, when mentioning the intentions of the protesters the police estimated that only "a small number of extremists" were planning violence (ibid., 42). The report also talks of a "recurring theme" in the police intelligence which claims that protesters were aspiring to "bring the City to a halt" (ibid., 42). The police did not know what the protest would be like or how many people would attend. Metropolitan Police Commander Simon O'Brien admitted not knowing how big the protest would be, but did acknowledge that police were "monitoring chatrooms, emails, and open sources of information" (Metropolitan Police 2009). The use of protest websites by police and press means the content of protesters' online communications took on increased representational importance. The protesters' own communications were being taken and interpreted beyond their control.

The final similarity between police and press perceptions of the G20 protests is the placing of the protest into a historical context. The HMIC report uses historical protest in a similar way to the press by containing a timeline of international summit protests and noting details of the number of arrests, whether there was disorder and the structure of the protests (HMIC, 2009). Again, this use of protester communications and historical context creates an overriding preconception of what will happen at a protest. The police preparations were geared towards an expectation of violence, and this perception is what they communicated to the press.

5. CONCLUSION

The fundamental point to be made is that "radical ideas require more space than events" (Doherty, Plows and Wall 2003, 675), and that G20Meltdown attempted to open this space through the use of a mass demonstration. Although the use of the spectacle by a protest group plays into what Gamson argues is the press' need for drama and entertainment (2003, para. 69), what the G20 protests turned into meant that scenes of violence and property damage came to dominate the press reports. The press' pre-frame of anticipating violence, fear and historical context is difficult for protest groups to overcome. A secondary issue is the timing of protest. The date of the summit and consequently the date of the demonstration were known well in advance. This creates a 'news hole' between the announcement of a summit and when the protest will occur. The hole is then filled by the press' expectations of how a protest will unfold, and this creates the frame through which a protest will be perceived and reported on. There was a month between the printing of the police's press statement in the *Guardian* and when the protest took place. The impact of the pre-coverage of protest is, "if anything[,] more important than how an event itself is reported" (Rosie and Gorringe 2009b, 2.9). The anticipatory coverage of protest helps to create the media context which is "essential to a full understanding of any given protest" (ibid., 2.9). The influence of G20Meltdown's communications is particularly evident in this respect because their aspirations, slogans and images were taken out of context and placed into an overriding frame of fear and predictions of violence. The impact of the protesters' own communications only added to the press' sense of fear and influenced police tactics as their intentions were interpreted as being inherently violent.

The use of the Internet by G20Meltdown is more than just a question of pessimism/optimism because there are mixed implications for protesters, the press and police. The Internet does allow activists a media opportunity on a potentially global platform to connect with like-minded people, but this should be tempered by the fact that the Internet's openness means anyone can view publicly available information. There are two main concerns that stem from this; the first centres on the power of activists to control their messages and representation. The public nature of G20Meltdown's communications meant that both the press and the police seemingly took and reinterpreted these messages to either fit a news narrative or dictate police tactics. The second concern is about activist media strategies—information published online has become an easily accessible source of information for press and police. This use of activist online communications diminishes the effectiveness of protesters to become more integral to the news story because the information required has been taken from other sources. The case of G20Meltdown demonstrates the limitless potential the Internet gives groups to publicise their concerns and actions, but these same groups must be aware that online communications exist as a readily available source for the press and police intelligence.

NOTES

1. The website for G20Meltdown no longer exists. A cached version can be found on the Internet Archive Wayback Machine (G20Meltdown 2009f).
2. Dominant institutions in this chapter are taken to mean centralised political institutions and the police.
3. The Diggers appeared in 1649 after the English revolution and demanded that land be given back to the people and held as "common treasury for all."
4. This is a combined total that includes members of specified protest groups, unspecified protesters, NGOs and protester leaflets/websites.
5. This included members of Parliament, the House of Lords, London Assembly members, councillors and anonymous government sources.
6. The police divided groups into categories of 'notified' and 'un-notified,' depending on whether they had informed the police of their demonstrations before they took place (HMIC 2009, 99–101).

REFERENCES

Anon. 2009. Countdown to Chaos; Anarchists' Warning as We Track Down Fred the Shred after Attack on His Home. *Daily Mirror*, 26 March. p. 5.

Barrett, Mark. 2009. G20 Meltdown Movement Calls for "Very English Revolution" to Start Debate for New Future. *Google groups*. http://groups.google.com/group/21st-century-network/browse_thread/thread/f829ef334d3c3f9b/8739430126d0ed49?q&hl=en.

Behr, Royl L., and Shanto Iyengar. 1985. Television News, Real-World Cues, and Changes in the Public Agenda. *Public Opinion Quarterly* 49 (1): 38–57.

Cammaerts, Bart. 2012. Protest Logics and the Mediation Opportunity Structure. *European Journal of Communication* 27 (2): 117–134.

Curtice, John, and Alison Park. 2010. A Tale of Two Crises: Banks, MPs' Expenses and Public Opinion. In *British Social Attitudes: The 27th Report: Exploring Labours Legacy*, edited by Alison Park, 131–152. London: SAGE.

DeLuca, Kevin M. 1999. *Image Politics: The New Rhetoric of Environmental Activism*. New York: Guilford Press.

DeLuca, Kevin M., and Jennifer Peeples. 2002. From Public Sphere to Public Screen: Democracy, Activism, and the "Violence" of Seattle. *Critical Studies in Media Communications* 19 (2): 125–151.

Diani, Mario. 1996. Linking Mobilization Frames and Political Opportunities: Insights from Regional Populism in Italy. *American Sociological Review* 61 (6): 1053–1069.

Dixon, Cyril. 2009. Alert after Threats of G20 Mayhem. *Daily Express*, 27 March. p. 27.

Doherty, Brian, Alexandra Plows and Derek Wall. 2003. "The Preferred Way of Doing Things": The British Direct Action Movement. *Parliamentary Affairs* 56 (4): 669–686.

Edwards, Richard, and Caroline Gammell. 2009. Demonstrators. *Daily Telegraph*, 1 April. p. 5.

Eisinger, Peter K. 1973. The Conditions of Protest Behaviour in American Cities. *American Political Science Review* 67 (1): 11–28.

Entman, Robert M. 1993. Framing: Toward Clarification of a Fractured Paradigm. *Journal of Communication* 43 (4): 51–58.

G20Meltdown. 2009a. 100s Have Gathered outside the Old Exchange at the Bank of England. Come Down and Join Us. Chants of Shame on You to the Police. Someone. . . . *Twitter.* Posted 2 April. http://twitter.com/#!/Meltdown2010/status/1438094602.

———. 2009b. Conspirators Are Everywhere. . . . Who Tells the Truth? Which Is Genuine Warning? What Scare Tactics? Who Are These Armchair Generals?. *Twitter.* Posted 19 March. http://twitter.com/#!/Meltdown2010/status/1351739785.

———. 2009c. *G20 Meltdown in the City* [leaflet].

———. 2009d. G20 Meltdown Party 1st & 2nd April. *Facebook.* 1 April. http://www.facebook.com/events/69116968752/.

———. 2009e. Home—On April 1st, We'll Show the G20 What Meltdown Means. *G20Meltdown.* http://web.archive.org/web/20090325233413/http://www.g-20meltdown.org/.

———. 2009f. Home—SUMMER OF RAGE HOTS UP!. *G20Meltdown.* http://web.archive.org/web/20100124044929/http://www.g-20meltdown.org/.

———. 2009g. In All Fairness. Cops ARE Behaving. Well Why Wouldn't They Be? Did I Miss Something? G20 Leaders Take Note: We've Taken the Power Back. *Twitter.* Posted 1 April. http://twitter.com/#!/Meltdown2010/status/1431755448.

———. 2009h. Meltdown. *Facebook.* http://www.facebook.com/groups/53674491031/.

———. 2009i. Meltdown Meets Today. Check Out Website and Facebook for Updates. The Black Horse Group Meets Ramparts, March 16th 8.00pm. Details Follow. *Twitter.* Posted 8 March. http://twitter.com/#!/Meltdown2010/status/1296112810.

———. 2009j. Momentum Gathers Apace for Silent Demo: Assemble Bethnal Green Police Station 11.30 Saturday. Events Prior to Ian Tomlinson's Death Vex All. *Twitter.* Posted 8 April. http://twitter.com/#!/Meltdown2010/status/1475629868.

———. 2009k. *Party in the City!—Fake Money* [leaflet].

———. 2009l. *Storm the Banks!* [leaflet].

———. 2009m. Teabags Arrived. Kettle Went On. Lovely Few Cuppas.. Billy Bragg Singing. Reggae Music Too. Rozzers Now in Riot Gear.:Totally Wrong Outfits. *Twitter.* Posted 1 April. http://twitter.com/#!/Meltdown2010/status/1431586790.

———. 2009n. When Asked about Predictions of Violence We Say: "We Would Hope the Police Can Keep Their Truncheons in Their Belts, But Who Knows?" *Twitter.* Posted 26 March. http://twitter.com/#!/Meltdown2010/status/1394027742.

———. 2009o. Who's Who. *G20Meltdown.* http://web.archive.org/web/2010010 8022457/http://www.g-20meltdown.org/node/5.

Gamson, William A. 2003. Bystanders, Public Opinion, and the Media. In *The Blackwell Companion to Social Movements*, edited by David A. Snow and Sarah A. Soule, 242–261. Oxford, UK: Blackwell.

Gamson, William A., and David S. Meyer. 1996. Framing Political Opportunity. In *Comparative Perspectives on Social Movements: Political Opportunities, Mobilising Structures, and Cultural Framings*, edited by Doug McAdam, John D. McCarthy and Mayer N. Zald, 275–290. New York: Cambridge University Press.

Gitlin, Todd. (1980) 2003. *The Whole World Is Watching: Mass Media in the Making and Unmaking of the New Left*. London: University of California Press.

Hands, Joss. 2011. *@ is for Activism: Dissent, Resistance and Rebellion in a Digital Culture*. London: Pluto Press.

HMIC. 2009. *Adapting to Protest*. Her Majesty's Inspectorate of Constabulary. 5 July. http://www.hmic.gov.uk/media/adapting-to-protest-20090705.pdf.

Kriesi, Hanspeter, Ruud Koopmans, Jan Willem Duyvendak and Marco G. Giugni. 1992. New Social Movements and Political Opportunities in Western Europe. *European Journal of Political Research* 22 (2): 219–244.

Lewis, Paul. 2009a. Britain Faces Summer of Rage—Police: Middle-Class Anger at Economic Crisis Could Erupt into Violence on Streets. *Guardian*, 23 February. p. 1.

———. 2009b. Revealed: Video of Police Attack on Man Who Died at G20 Protest: Footage Shows Man Thrown to Ground by Officer: Guardian Hands Dossier to Police Watchdog. *Guardian*, 8 April. p. 1.

Lipsky, Michael. 1968. Protest as a Political Resource. *American Political Science Review* 62 (4): 1144–1158.

McAdam, Doug, and Yang Su. 2002. The War at Home: Antiwar Protests and Congressional Voting, 1965 to 1973. *American Sociological Review* 67 (5): 696–721.

McCurdy, Patrick. 2012. Social Movements, Protest and Mainstream Media, *Sociology Compass* 6: 244–255.

Metropolitan Police. 2009. Operation Glencoe Policing and Security for the G20 London Summit. [press release]. 2 April.

Meyer, David S. 1993. Protest Cycles and Political Process: American Peace Movements in the Nuclear Age. *Political Research Quarterly* 46 (3): 451–479.

Meyer, David S., and Debra C. Minkoff. 2004. Conceptualizing Political Opportunity. *Social Forces* 82 (4): 1457–1492.

Molyneaux, Lydia. 2005. The Carnival Continues. . . . In *Shut Them Down!: The G8, Gleneagles 2005 and the Movement of Movements*, edited by David Harvie, Keir Milburn, Ben Trott and David Watts, 119–126. Leeds: Dissent! and Autonomedia.

O'Connor, Gavin. 2007. Is There Still Room for Our Best-Loved Old Pubs? *South Wales Echo*, 21 July. p. 20.

O'Neill, Sean. 2009a. Bankers Seek Security as Vandals Strike at Sir Fred. *Times*, 26 March. p. 8.

———. 2009b. City Told to Expect Week of Protests; Hundreds of Anti-G20 Activists to Converge on Bank. *Times*, 21 March. p. 3.

———. 2009c. G20 Activists Hope Twitter Tactics Will Keep Them One Step ahead of the Police. *Times*, 28 March. p. 5.

———. 2009d. Hospital All Set for Victims of G20 Violence: London Is Braced for Riots in City Streets as Protesters Vent Anger. *Times*, 27 March. pp. 16–17.

———. 2009e. Summit Police Fear Attacks on Hotels Used by the G20 Leaders: Security Will Be Bolstered against "Guerrilla" Raids. *Times*, 18 March. p. 5.

Penrose, Justin. 2009. Anarchy Back in the UK; Exclusive the London Summit 2009 Countdown to World Leaders' G20 Summit Meeting Rioters Come Out of Retirement Secret Plans to "Take Over" City. *Sunday Mirror*, 29 March. p. 9.

Pepper, Marina. 2009. Interview with Marina Pepper/G20 Meltdown. *Shift Magazine*. http://libcom.org/library/interview-marina-pepperg20-meltdown.

Pitcher, George. 2009. Violent Class War Must Be Condemned, Not Understood. *Daily Telegraph*, 27 March. p. 24.

Put People First. 2009. Put People First: March for Jobs, Justice and Climate ahead of the London G20 Summit. http://www.putpeoplefirst.org.uk/.

Rosie, Michael, and Hugo Gorringe. 2009a. The "Anarchist World Cup": Respectable Protest and Media Panics. *Social Movement Studies* 8 (1): 35–53.

———. 2009b. What a Difference a Death Makes: Protest, Policing and the Press at the G20. *Sociological Research Online* 14 (5). http://www.socresonline.org.uk/14/5/4.html.

Rucht, Dieter. 2004. The Quadruple "A": Media Strategies of Protest Movements since the 60s. In *Cyberprotest: New Media, Citizens and Social Movements*, edited by Wim Van De Donk, Brian D. Loader, Paul G. Nixon and Deiter Rucht, 29–56. London: Routledge.

Sireau, Nicolas. 2009. *Make Poverty History: Political Communication in Action.* London: Palgrave MacMillan.

Snow, David A., and Robert D. Benford. 1992. Master Frames and Cycles of Protest. In *Frontiers in Social Movement Theory*, edited by Aldon D. Morris and Carol McClurg Mueller, 133–155. New York: Vali-Ballou Press.

Wahl-Jorgensen, Krain. 2003. Speaking Out against the Incitement to Silence: The British Press and the 2001 May Day Protests. In *Representing Resistance: Media Civil Disobedience, and the Global Justice Movement*, edited by Andy Opel and Donnalyn Pompper, 130–148. Westport, CT: Praeger.

Wolfsfeld, Gadi. 2003. The Political Contest Model. In *News, Public Relations and Power*, edited by Simon Cottle, 81–95. London: SAGE.

Wright, Stephen. 2009. Google Anarchists Targeting the City. *Daily Mail*, 2 April.

Wykes, Maggie. 2000. The Burrowers: News about Bodies, Tunnels and Green Guerillas. In *Environmental Risks and the Media*, edited by Stuart Allan, Barbara Adam and Cynthia Carter, 73–90. London: Routledge.

7 Assemblages

Live Streaming Dissent in the 'Quebec Spring'

Elise Danielle Thorburn

1. INTRODUCTION

On March 22, 2012, a massive demonstration snaked through the downtown streets of Montreal. It was the largest in a series of escalating demonstrations taking place as the winter turned to spring, in protest of proposed tuition fee hikes in the province. The hikes in question—$325 annually for five years, for a total increase of $1,625—spurred the biggest student strike in the province's history; more than 150,000 students were on strike at the highest point. Roving marches marked the nights; economic disruptions marked the days. Demonstrations featuring at least a quarter of a million people celebrated the strike's anniversary each month. Striking students attended daily general assemblies in their departments and faculties, and sent representatives to the monthly assemblies of the province-wide coalition spearheading the strike, CLASSE.[1] Through all of this, both bluster and contemplation, riot squads chased students through the streets and by mid-summer almost five thousand people had been arrested over the course of the strike.[2] Amid this relative calm of general assemblies and chaos of the street demos, a group of students and media activists undertook a project to revolutionise journalism, surveillance culture and the use of technology in popular movements. Using the latest in live streaming technology, teams of media activists from Montreal's CUTV (Concordia University Television) took to the streets, marching alongside protesters, filming the demonstrations and instantly live streaming those images to the Internet, beaming them to computers across the province, country and in fact the world. Mixing human and machinic, politics and journalism, technology and technique, CUTV's live stream creates out of varied and heterogenous components a Deleuzian assemblage, an assemblage of minoritarian becoming. This assemblage points to possible emergent political forms and gives insight into the dangers and possibilities inherent in a highly mediated and surveilled society and social movement, complicating easy analyses of social media's role in struggle.

This chapter takes the Deleuzo-Guattarian concepts of becoming-minoritarian, weapons and tools, and puts them together with their closely aligned concept of the assemblage. These concepts are then put into conversation with the concrete example of a social movement and social media. It is important to avoid resigning ourselves to either a technological fetishism (believing that the Internet and social media are the key to successful activism in the current conditions) or a technological fatalism (believing that technology has only negative repercussions on social movements, offering us only weak links and surface-level engagements with struggle[3])—what Christian Fuchs has called the "normative dimensions of technological determinism" (Fuchs 2012, 387). These determinisms proffer a one-dimensional view of technology and provide a causal relationship between media, technology and society, assuming that "a certain media or technology has exactly one specific effect on society and social systems" (Fuchs 2012, 387). It is important to develop an analysis of social media and social movements, then, that is complex, complicated and dialectical, developing critical theories of technology and social change.

This chapter attempts, then, a dialectical and critical analysis of live streaming technology at play in movements. It seeks to imagine the ways in which a specific convergence of social media and social movement can open up sites of state power and a state surveillance apparatus, but can also circumvent state power, create sites of resistance and construct counter-powers. In order to develop this balanced view, I propose a theory of assemblages coming out of Deleuze and Guattari, but speculating on what these assemblages could look like as specifically political, specifically radical configurations. What are assemblages of radical politics and what possible assemblages arise when activists take up new media technologies, platforms and devices? What weapons or tools are created? I argue that the tool or weapon status of projects like CUTV's live stream is entirely a consequence of the collective machinic assemblage in which they arise. In order to understand this argument fully, we will begin with a brief elaboration of the concepts in play in this chapter, and then operationalise these concepts in relation to the CUTV coverage of the student strikes.

In the spring and summer of 2012 I participated in the Quebec student movement. I volunteered with CUTV's live stream team, walking the streets of Montreal as part of a human-machinic assemblage, a backpack filled with a wireless uplink system transmitting full HD video strapped to my back, a thick black firewire connecting myself to a camera operator. An assemblage that at times resembled an octopus with disconnecting-reconnecting tentacles, at other times a cybernetic organism with human bodies and machinic addendum, the live stream team found itself often in the front and centre of police attacks, running chaotically through the streets, chased by riot police, or stopped for hours in the middle of a police kettle. CUTV members were gassed with pepper spray, had ribs broken by police batons or swift kicks and were arrested on more than one occasion (although ultimately all were released).[4] The CUTV live stream team, the demonstrators and the viewers of the CUTV broadcasts engaged in a collective process akin to becoming-minoritarian, and grounded locations for the possible becoming-minoritarian of participants and viewers. CUTV's live stream opened the possibility of composing new subjects, a new social field and new modes of resistance.

The project of creating new subjects and a post-capitalist social field is not something that can be determined or planned in advance. As Marx (1976) suggested, the future world is not held in a recipe that can be drafted for the cookshops of the future. Rather the world is constituted in variable and mutable relations of force, a world of flows and flux that can be channelled into various assemblages of becoming, various politics of majority, minority or minoritarian. The task is to draw forth a new socius, new liberatory assemblages of minoritarian becomings, which will arise from engagement with both the technological and capitalist relations in which we live, and put our minoritarian politics in clear association with class struggle. This struggle must be a becoming, and all becomings are, by Deleuzian definition, minoritarian. Hence class struggle in the contemporary, digital age must be a struggle of minoritarian becoming.

2. BECOMING-MINORITARIAN

In the political philosophy of Deleuze and Guattari, all human becomings are political. Becoming is neither mimicry nor similitude—if one is to become-rat, for example, one does not mimic a rat. Rather one adopts the relations of a rat, makes one's "organism enter into composition with *something else*" (Deleuze and Guattari 1987, 274). Although ethereal, in a political sense becomings can be concrete. They are about a dismissal of liberal politics as a mere mimicry of relations of power and domination, and they forward a politics of creative engagement and constitution. For Deleuze and Guattari there are three political options: majority politics as an identification with the face of power or a standard; minority politics as the identity politics of a subordinated social group, and the affirmation of power and life of that group, necessarily involving a struggle to stabilise said minority; and finally, a minoritarian politics which is non-identarian and is a process of becoming (that which negates both the standard and its deviation, but in the process constitutes something entirely new). The minoritarian not an entity or identity but rather is "*processes* and *treatments* of life" (Thoburn 2003, 6). The minoritarian is not the minority, then, but rather a *becoming* over which no one fixed identity has ownership. A politics of becoming-minoritarian is not about representation but about constitution, about the creation of a people rather than their representation, the constitution of something new.

These "becoming-minoritarian" politics reflect the recent struggles of the 2011 "movement of the squares,"[5] wherein a politics of representation has waned, replaced by a constitutive politics of assembly. Assemblies and their directly democratic processes are not brand new—they have a long history on the left[6]—but have been directly connected to the impacts of the Internet and its modes of communication and organization, especially Web 2.0. Often, though, social media is given far too much autonomy in the development of these movements. For example, Spanish academics Jose Manuel Sánchez and Victor Sampredo Blanco have "interpreted the actions of the Indignados movement [in Spain] as a sort of *transfer* to the streets of practices of cooperation first developed on the web" and claim that "the Net was the square" (Gerbaudo 2012, 96). The logic of the Internet that has been transferred to public life, according to these theorists, includes the practices of "self-summoning, forum deliberation, consumption of counter-information, the weaving of affective and effective networks" (ibid.). As well, traits of communication such as "cooperation, instantaneity, self-nurturing, horizontality, decentralisation, flexibility, dynamism, and interconnection" (ibid.) are present in communication in the digital sphere, but not exclusive to it. These directly democratic and horizontal forms of communicating, organizing and understanding politics have their own vaunted history in radical movements—especially those of workers engaged in struggles for democratic self-management—that must not be ignored.[7] That being said, analysing the role of social media in social movements can deepen an understanding of the myriad possibilities that these movements possess. The project of CUTV's live stream does not demand particular identities or ideological alliances and instead proffers a politics of the minoritarian through its convergence of human and machinic technologies.

3.   THE HUMAN AND MACHINIC IN CONCORDIA UNIVERSITY TELEVISION

CUTV is a student- and community-run television station based out of Concordia University in Montreal, Quebec, broadcasting via a closed-circuit TV network, DVD releases, Internet distribution networks and public access TV channels. It is the oldest university television station in Canada, founded in 1969. Undergoing a series of changes during 2009–2010,[8] the station emerged into a wider public spotlight with the decision, in the winter of 2012, to obtain high-definition live streaming equipment, and to begin streaming video footage of the demonstrations underway in Montreal and across the province as part of the Quebec student strike.[9]

   The station leased equipment from LiveU—the apparatus provider—and purchased platform space from Livestream at livestream.com. LiveU provided CUTV with an LU60 backpack, which contains the technology necessary to stream live video to a web platform. This includes encoding hardware, a firewall cable, and a built-in wireless connection with six load-balanced 3G modems that deliver data over 3G and 4G cellular networks. The LU60 backpack contains a transmission system that is connected via a lengthy wire to any shoulder-mounted camera. The transmission system takes video images, disassembles them, bonds them and sends them over cellular networks to the Livestream platform, where they are reassembled and uploaded. The backpack also contains its own modem and router, making it a mobile Wi-Fi hotspot, allowing again for constant connectivity but also permitting other mobile devices to connect to the Internet. The transmission system also simultaneously analyses conditions in the field, and recommends the most suitable video settings for the prevailing conditions.[10]

While live streaming video is not immediately considered among the platforms considered 'social media,' in this case I want to connect the devices, practices and outcomes at work in CUTV's live stream project to 'social media' as it has been previously defined and considered, especially with regard to social movements. Defining social media is a difficult endeavour because all media are, by necessity, social. Conventionally considered, though, as the series of online communicative applications that developed out of the theoretical and technological foundations of Web 2.0, 'social media' as a specific term describes online sites and spaces for the convergence of disparately located human beings, text, images and video (Joseph 2012). 'Web 2.0' is a term and concept developed by Tim O'Reilly and describes an Internet highly reliant on user-generated content. Web 2.0 is a "set of principles and practices that tie together a veritable solar system of sites that demonstrate some or all of those principles" (O'Reilly 2005). In the Internet of Web 2.0, then, social media are the platforms through which users and participants can interact, communicate, create and share text, images and video. Social media, then, is part of the highly participatory Internet—sites where the communication platform is provided, but content is created by participants. Live streaming technology adheres to this particular definition of social media in some ways, and departs from it in others. Streaming media is generally visual data content constantly received by and presented to an end user while being delivered by a provider. Delivered live, over the Internet, live streaming "refers to the synchronised distribution of streaming media content to one or more clients" (Padmanabhan et al. 2002). This involves video imaging sent through an encoder to digitise the content, a content delivery network (the distributed systems of servers encompassing multiple data centres of the Internet) and a media publisher or platform, such as Livestream.

The platform for streaming media relies on users to provide the content, but live streaming video is far less participatory or interactive than other forms of social media—for instance, Twitter, and Twitter's new video sharing application, Vine. Some live streaming platforms—for example, Livestream and Veetle—offer chat boxes below or beside the streaming media, and so interaction is possible, but not in precisely the same way as with other social media platforms. That being said, live stream is considered here a variant of 'social media' primarily because it connects to several of the definitions of Web 2.0 provided by O'Reilly (2005). Using new, digital technology, live streaming video permits users to generate content and instantly upload it to the Internet, and viewers and producers can communicate with each other via the chat boxes provided, thus fitting into the "architecture of participation" (O'Reilly 2005). It is not reliant on a professional class in order to communicate to large audiences, and because it is live and uploaded to the Internet it becomes accessible to broader swathes of people. Mostly, though, live streaming technology can be considered 'social media' through its interactions and convergences with *other forms of social media*. For example, in my experience with CUTV's live stream, our ability to communicate with the viewers came through our simultaneous connection to other social media platforms, such as Twitter. Thus, live stream can be seen as social media on its own, but it becomes even more clearly so as it becomes part of a network of possible modes of communication that contemporary activists and media makers utilise.

In the winter and spring of 2012 CUTV broadcast live each night from the midst of the demonstrations. The camera and crew were on the ground and in the crowd, regardless of whether the demonstration was a peaceable (though speedy) walk through Montreal's city streets or in the near war-zone of Victoriaville, where tear gas canisters and rubber bullets assailed protesters, injuring some and hospitalising others. CUTV did not remain at a distance from struggle, but was a part of it, and thus established itself not simply as passive, objective, sidelined media but as co-constructing new minoritarian subjects. The technological and human components of the CUTV assemblage converged, so that the social media form became a part of human transformations underway in the Quebec student strike.

The CUTV crew and the perspective they provided are a fundamental component of making this live streaming assemblage possible. Although the LiveU backpack and shoulder-mounted camera can be worn by a single operator, CUTV chose to engage with the demonstrations as a unit, like a small affinity group of their own.[11] Live stream teams were assembled with a rotating cast of volunteers, each playing a different role. On the ground there were two technical positions—a camera operator and a technical operator carrying the backpack. There was also a reporter, a researcher and a director. On occasion there was also a spotter.[12] The camera operator and the technical operator were physically connected via a firewire cable running from the backpack to the camera. The technical operator, then, is also engaged in supporting the camera operator through tight crowds or around obstacles, alerting her to changes in the street's topography or to the dangers out of the camera operator's line of sight.[13] The reporters roam free with wireless microphones, interviewing participants and providing commentary in both official languages. The researcher investigates background information, checking the name of blockaded institutions and possible reasons for a particular institution being blockaded or targeted, for example. The researcher also communicates via social media with live stream viewers and seeks and shares information on Twitter.[14] Finally the director of the shoot attempts to maintain nominal structure, coherency and agreement between the varied parts of the live stream assemblage. She has something like ultimate authority over the team, based on previous collective discussion, and can make calls regarding what is best to film, which direction the crew will move in and when to sign off coverage and return to the studio. She can decide, in the heat of the moment, whether to move to a safer location, run or hold ground. The other component members of the team cede some authority to the director in order to maintain a coherency to the project, and to avoid disassembling into chaos.[15]

The politicised interfacing of human and machines at play in CUTV's live stream team is important for a thorough accounting of social media as an element in assemblages of minoritarian becomings, and for these becomings as models of resistant and constituent structures that challenge and negate the multiple apparatuses of the state. The particularities of CUTV's live streaming during the Quebec student strike also offers us models of constituting alternative subjectivities—transforming students from liberal to revolutionary subjects, in some cases. The next section, then, will discuss CUTV as a component in a process of minoritarian becoming through a representative selection of examples drawn from my own and others' experiences with CUTV. From these, we will then go on to discuss the dangers posed by both minoritarianism as a political strategy, and the specific technologies of live, streaming, digital video.

4.   BECOMING MINORITARIAN THROUGH CUTV'S LIVE STREAM

CUTV's unceasing, uncensored and explicit coverage of state violence contributed to the process of becoming-minoritarian. Live video of police violence challenged the authority and legitimacy of the state and state power for viewers and participants alike, exposing the state, as at its base, fundamentally violent and repressive. This is the violence that configures the majority position; the state itself is defined by "the perpetuation or conservation of organs of power" (Deleuze and Guattari 1987, 357). The deployment of police to quell and crush demonstrations—both prior to but in a far more concerted way after the implementation of Law 78 (or Law 12)[16]—demonstrates the violent lengths to which the state will go to maintain control and order. It also highlights the state's points of weakness and points to openings for rendering its authority illegitimate. This both makes possible the reassessment of minority politics—liberalism—as the default terrain of struggle and develops the possibility of minoritarianism.

For example, CUTV's constant coverage of the demonstrations and the increasing police violence, with some demonstrators losing eyes and being hospitalised, brought many not-already constituted activists into the streets to demonstrate against the state and state violence. As some interviewees and student movement participants noted, already constituted activists of varying tendencies soon were outnumbered by a much broader swath of the population who had witnessed the violence of the state on CUTV and through the mainstream media's use of CUTV's footage. Mobilised by their outrage at police actions, a multitude of Quebec's population—and allies from across Canada—poured into the streets. The modes of organization at use by CLASSE and the student organizers, such as the assembly, soon filtered out from activist groups to the community with the constitution of autonomous neighbourhood assemblies. A year later, these neighbourhood-level direct-democracy institutions still operate in some areas of Montreal. The strongest of those established still meet regularly to discuss and plan events around varied issues, including police repression, migrant rights and gentrification.[17] These autonomous neighbourhood assemblies are the legacy of that moment in Quebec wherein politics and technology merged in productive and powerfully political ways. The assemblies are the legacy of both the strike itself and the coverage of it by CUTV, and by the politics they espoused and inspired.

A more immediate and direct effect of CUTV's live streaming reports was evident on the streets of Montreal in those months of the student strike. That video footage of police actions is seen as a serious threat to the main-tenance of state control is evident in policing theory. Newnham and Bell (2012, 38) note that live or near real-time footage "has significant conse-quences for governments, riot police, and other agencies whose every move can be uploaded for the world to see." The response from the state can often be violent, and can lead to cascading effects among the population. Programming Director Laith Marouf recounted the frequency with which he, while operating the live stream camera, was attacked by the police, and the effect that these live streamed attacks had on the population at large:

> For myself, in like 3 or 4 days in a row they would attack, pepper spray my camera and me, directly into my eyes. There would be no dem-onstrators around or anything like that, at many of those moments. So you'd see these incidents, unwarranted, unprovoked incidents of violence, live on the broadcast . . . This was making people disturbed by what was happening in our society. (Marouf, pers. comm.)

From distress of the populace at the actions of police and the implementa-tion of Law 78 came the nightly *casseroles*,[18] an act of defiance against the authority and legitimacy of the state. While Law 78 demanded that public gatherings be reported in advance to police, the *casseroles* were spontaneous and autonomous: responding to a call on Facebook but led and organized by no one other than those who left their homes nightly at 8 p.m., the *casseroles* saw thousands of Montrealers armed with pots and pans noisily join with their neighbours in the streets. Together they formed a spontaneous orches-tra of defiant noise, walking through city streets towards the city's core, meeting with other collections of neighbours, with individuals, growing larger and wandering for most of the night throughout Montreal. Although not solely responsible for the widening of the uprising against the Quebec state, CUTV made profound contributions to the movement's expansion. The live stream coverage of demos received tens of thousands of hits, mainstream media outlets used CUTV footage in nightly news broadcasts and those watching at home (both on the live stream feed and on mainstream television news) were compelled to take to the streets to protest the actions of police and question the legitimacy of the state. CUTV's live streaming broadcasts, working in concert with and as a component part of the student movement, trespassed the safe territory of the state apparatus and its arm of the police, exposing on live feeds the violent urges of the state and calling into question its legitimacy.

While the student movement was divided on the question of the state, broad elements of the movement and of CUTV can still be seen to have advanced a politics of becoming-minoritarian. In general, the movement held no goal of state power,[19] and CUTV did not seek to mimic or recreate mainstream or corporate media, as station staffers Kneale and Marouf made repeatedly clear.[20] The station did not attempt to construct for itself or of itself a mode of power based on fixed identity; it did not try to constitute itself or its participants as minorities in a dichotomous and subordinated relationship to power as a method of achieving that power. Rather, the attempts of CUTV's live stream were to displace and deterritorialise or decompose the power of the state altogether, and open up space for the creation of something different in its place: the building of constituent powers that lean towards becomings, engagement in a process of creation that would have unexpected, unforeseen, unknowable results in its creation of something entirely new.

Of course, the responsibility of destabilising, disassembling and challenging the despotic face of the majority cannot be held by CUTV alone. CUTV is but one part of a larger assemblage—the student movement, for example—which comes together, dissipates, acts and reacts situationally. CUTV's live streaming broadcasts were, in their criticality, operations against the state, and thus deterritorialising and destabilising for the state and its apparatuses. This deterritorialising process opens up the possibility of a radical shift in the politics of a people and the possibilities for resistance and constituency. The process, though, also opens up dangerous possibilities for the reconstitution of majoritarian power. Benjamin (1986), in his *Critique of violence*, recounted the ways in which strike actions, as acts, called into question the state's monopoly on the legitimate use of force, thus deterritorialising the state. But it was through this very process of deterritorialisation that the state was able to reterritorialise, reconstitute its legitimacy and incorporate the 'right' to strike into the legal paradigm. Similarly, the state has not found the power of the student movement nor the streaming video of CUTV an insurmountable impediment to reconstituting itself as authority: instead the student movement was thwarted by an election call, the removal from power of the offending political party and the election of a party that trumpeted its support for the students until their election, upon which time politics (and state power) as normal was restored.

As well, troubling possibilities persist regarding state surveillance with new technology, social media (especially video footage) and political demonstrations. Machines and technologies, as Hardt and Negri (2000) rightly observe, are not neutral entities, not blank pages upon which we can write whatever script we choose. They are rather "biopolitical tools deployed in specific regimes of production, which facilitate certain practices and prohibit others" (ibid., 406). The "exploitation of social media sites by political activists" is something which should not be "understated" (Newnham and Bell 2012, 42) by police and the state. Thus risks as well as the possibilities of any merger of the political and the technological in a process of minoritarian becoming must be carefully considered. The remainder of this chapter, then, is devoted to thinking through the risks and possibilities of minoritarian becomings proceeding through live streaming technologies. As this requires an encounter with the assemblage it is important to define and operationalise 'assemblages' as a term and as praxis. Then we will centre the rest of the discussion on the notion of surveillance, and the use of live stream broadcasts by the police as a wing of the state apparatus: live streaming technology and the process of becoming that CUTV engaged in as simultaneously a moment of majoritarian assertions of control through the state's use of the live stream to follow, identify and potentially arrest.

5. DANGEROUS LIBERATIONS: MINORITARIAN ASSEMBLAGES IN A SOCIETY OF CONTROL

Assemblage is an English translation of the French word *agencement*. The francophone word seems to better capture a sense of agency, of action, that the term implies—an assemblage as the active linking of disparate things together in their heterogeneity. Assemblages are multiplicities and establish connections *between* multiplicities, between heterogenous components. In this sense they are akin to collectives, to communities.[21] They are compositions of forces, and are the primary form of our social reality—we live in and through assemblages as they are the very structures that populate the sociopolitical world. Assemblages rely on relations of interiority—between multiplicities within—and relations of exteriority—an engaging with external multiplicities. In this way no assemblage nor any component part can be considered in isolation: individuals, institutions and devices all must be considered in relation to each other and with regard to the immanent possibilities that their interminglings create. For example, the invention of the stirrup, Deleuze and Guattari (1987, 90) note, "entails a new man-horse symbiosis that at the same time entails new weapons and new instruments." One element, in relation to another, creates a new assemblage and expands the old. They are not necessarily random, but rather can be calculated or coordinated collections of heterogenous elements. They are "every constellation of singularities and traits deducted from the flow—selected, organised, stratified—in such a way as to converge (consistency) artificially and naturally; an assemblage, in this sense, is a veritable invention" (ibid., 406). Assemblages can be as large as cultures, or even 'ages,' or as tiny as atoms.

Although often considered antithetical to domination, assemblages are not automatically liberatory. For Foucault, some collective assemblages included the school, the army, the factory, the hospital and the prison. These assemblages of power contain micropowers and micro-fascisms. But assemblages of power are more akin to "botched assemblages"; they are destructive, constraining and not creative. Demonstrating an inherent tetravalence, Deleuze and Guattari (1987, 89) describe the feudal assemblage, considering all the interminglings of bodies that define the institution of feudalism:

> The body of the earth and the social body; the body of the overlord, vassal, and serf; the body of the knight and the horse and their new relation to the stirrup; the weapons and tools assuring a symbiosis of bodies—a whole machinic assemblage. We would also have to consider statements, expressions, the juridical regime of heraldry, all of the incorporeal transformations, in particular, oaths and their variables (the oath of obedience, but also the oath of love, etc): the collective assemblage of enunciation.

The four components—territorialisation and deterritorialisation, content and expression—are here demonstrated. Stabilising and destabilising elements, corporeal and incorporeal transformations occur to create the assemblage of feudalism. Feudalism demonstrates the despotic capacity of assemblages, their possibility of imperialism and authoritarianism. What is then needed, conceptually and concretely, is to consider and to create *minoritarian assemblages*, or *assemblages of minoritarian becomings*, those which open specifically onto possibilities of liberation, or lean more heavily towards the liberatory in all four directions of their tetravalence. In its constitution of alternative subjectivities and its enunciation of alternative realities,[22] CUTV's live stream project approached this composition of a minoritarian assemblage during the 2012 Quebec student strike.

6. CUTV AS MINORITARIAN ASSEMBLAGE: PROMISE AND PREDATION

CUTV is itself an assemblage. Made up of human volunteers, digital technologies and institutional structures (the university, as well as mainstream and alternative media), CUTV is connected to the broader assemblage of the student movement in Quebec, and globally. It operated as an assemblage with its component parts in tight integration—individuals, institutions and technologies hanging together in their heterogeneity. The live stream team reflected this in practice, through the team's relatively non-hierarchical structure and focus on consensus-based decision making prior to shoots.[23] The live stream project as an assemblage is not a logical necessity—it is not naturalised as a totality-organism. Instead, its status as assemblage—a minoritarian one—results from careful negotiations, solidarity and the co-evolution of the component parts, machinic and organic, through their work. This signifies that assemblages are the result not of chaos and randomness, but develop from "intersecting layers of organisation" (Due 2007, 132)—from spontaneity, yes, but from organization and a contingently obligatory coherence also. This is a coherency at play, for CUTV, between component parts that are biological—living, breathing human beings and movements—and starkly technological—digital apparatuses as well as the institutions that are one of the conditions of existence for CUTV. Thus assemblages, and CUTV, contribute to an idea of wholeness that does not give way to totalities but rather opens us—participants and observers—onto other, varied possibilities.

Relations of exteriority were made possible and expanded through CUTV's use of digital technologies. The station beamed visual information to other individuals and other assemblages around the world. These relations of exteriority were also expressed through the live stream team's usage of instant messages, SMS messages, chats and tweets to connect with viewers and other movement participants. These relations of exteriority (communication and live imaging) could alter the subjective constitutions of both viewers and movement actors: both could adopt the subjective position of something *other* than subordinated minority, opening the possibility (if not yet the reality) of a powerful, creative minoritarian becoming. For example, then-staffers Kneale and Marouf both asserted that CUTV's mandate was not to speak for student demonstrators, nor to operate 'objectively,' such as mainstream or corporate media does. Rather they sought to allow the demonstrators and students in the street to present themselves to the world. CUTV sought to give voice to "communities that don't have any representation or are misrepresented in the mainstream" and to "give a platform to students to voice their opinions."[24] Like the mounted archer with stirrup and steel opening the possibility of colonial conquest, the particular political trajectory of the live streaming assemblage at CUTV creates the effect of new political possibilities and minoritarian becomings, invoking changes in the way that politics, and subjectivity, is considered.

As well, CUTV offers itself as an example of possible minoritarian becomings through its rotating positions of authority within the live stream team and the organization and structure of the station as a whole. This points towards a politics that does not ossify into striations of power but operates to avoid invocations of micro-fascisms. It is this particular structure of CUTV as an assemblage that holds its heterogenous parts together without then condensing them into sameness or descending into differentiated chaos. Instead of creating a rubric of domination, CUTV opens the assemblage to the possibility of becoming-minoritarian. The CUTV assemblage gives coherency and direction to the heterogenous components wherein these disparate components can cohere with their own carefully constructed, non-hierarchical politics. This offers a challenge to identarian politics, and therein lies its promise.

While such a promise exists, this politics cannot be approached without some trepidation. Elaborating a liberatory politics out of CUTV's live stream project also brings with it the possibility of predation by the state—the live stream can also become embedded in or a part of the surveillance apparatus of the state assemblage. CUTV's assemblage can be used, then, to block minoritarian becomings, thwart resistant or constitutive politics and, more generally, hunt, arrest and jail activists.[25] Although little evidence has been uncovered to suggest this happened during the Quebec strike, a visibility is at work in live video and this makes individuals possibly unwilling partners in state surveillance tactics. As Trottier (2012) has noted, new social media forms amplify policing due largely to their social saturation. In Quebec, police did make active use of Twitter, frequently communicating directly with CUTV's Twitter feeds, suggesting often that the team "pack up and go home," and, via the *manifencours* hashtag, urged others communicating online to do the same. The possibility exists, then, of connecting online social media users with protest participants for the purposes of squelching dissent. Live streaming video then poses the problem of becoming not a liberatory assemblage but rather a surveillance assemblage, a tool in service of the state.

Like all assemblages, the surveillance assemblage is a potentiality. Surveillance is often taken by activists as something to fear: surveillance technologies are used to crush dissent, identify targets and terrify populations. Surveillance assemblages turn human bodies into lines of data, information made available for scrutiny or targeted for intervention. Surveillance assemblages interface between technology and corporeality, and are made up of "the surfaces of contact [. . .] between life forms and webs of information, or between organs/body parts and entry/projection systems" (Bogard 1996, 33). Importantly, they reside at the intersection of varied media forms and thus cannot be dealt with in unmediated ways. Yet surveillance assemblages cannot be dismantled simply by targeting particular technologies— digital cameras or live streaming video, for example—nor by focusing on a single institution or bureaucracy. In fact, there is little activists can do to avoid the possibility that their video footage will be taken up as a tool of the state—as Trottier (2012) noted, social media can make unwitting and unwilling partners of users and the state. To attempt a struggle against particular and isolated manifestations of surveillance is akin to "efforts to keep the ocean's tide back with a broom—a frantic focus on a particular unpalatable technology or practice while the general tide of surveillance washes over us all" (Haggerty and Ericson 2000, 609). Thus, rather than eradicating a technology itself it is the practices within an assemblage of human and machine—the context of the assemblage formation—that must be the source and site for minimising damaging possibilities. CUTV's live stream, for example, could have been simultaneously a weapon and a tool, and more weapon than tool depending on the contours of the assemblage.

'Weapon' and 'tool' as terms serve distinct purposes in Deleuze and Guattari's work. They do not refer to specific objects like a tank or a hammer. Rather, objects are given significance (weapon or tool status) through the context of the system to which they are aligned, the assemblage within which they arise. The tool is aligned to the work-state system, wherein work is a motor cause that "meets resistances, operates upon the exterior, is consumed and spent in its effect, and must be renewed from one moment to the next" (Deleuze and Guattari 1987, 397). The weapon is aligned to the nomad-free activity system, wherein free activity is also a motor cause but one without resistances to overcome, which "operates only upon the mobile body itself, is not consumed in its effect, and continues from one moment to the next" (ibid.). Deleuze and Guattari define work in the capitalist sense, as Marx described wage-labour, and connect it to the assemblage of the tool. Marx's work as free human activity not subsumed by capital is connected to the free activity assemblage of the weapon. A weapon is thus linked to the free activity of activists, and tools to the work (specifically in this case the surveillance work) of the state. The weapon is not magical in comparison to the tool; they are both subject to the same laws, they share a common sphere. Similarly, a technology itself does not determine its own use. Rather it is "the social or collective machine, the machinic assemblage, that determines what is a technical element at a given moment, what is its usage, extension, comprehension, etc." (ibid., 397–398); the particularity of the assemblage gives the context to the object to become either weapon or tool. Technologies and machines are themselves simply component parts of larger social machines—the LiveU hardware a component part of the CUTV social entity—and these larger social machines are themselves "a functionally connected assemblage of human subjects and technical machines, people and tools" (Dyer-Witheford and de Peuter 2009, 70) or, of course, weapons. It is the assemblage that constitutes the system, that determines the characteristic of weapon or tool for an object or activity. Thus the question becomes determining differential traits that open an object to one assemblage over another. The mounted archer, Deleuze and Guattari note, is an assemblage that produces "social projects of colonisation and conquest" (1987, 353), whereas the live streaming assemblage of CUTV can produce, among other things, the possibility of a radically politicised subjectivity, subjectivities of becoming, for those who see themselves on and in its images.

CUTV forms an assemblage of minoritarian becoming, through its specific political direction, but also in the practices it engages in and the way it operationalises the live streaming technology for the benefit of a broad community. The state as an apparatus of capture attempts to make use of the same objects or instruments as tools of surveillance and the stabilisation or territorialisation of the state. CUTV's live stream operated, in the spring of 2012, as a weapon precisely because of the assemblage it was: democratic, open and productive of new alternative subjectivities and narratives. Because demonstrators were interviewed and allowed to tell their stories, express their opinions and explain their motivations without interruption, editing or censoring, they were able to begin to define themselves outside of the narrative of mainstream media descriptions, descriptions which often began from a place of limited understanding. Meanwhile, images of state repression went viral, spread on social media networks beyond the boundaries of Quebec and were even picked up by mainstream news outlets. Aside from the possibilities of self-definition that live streaming allowed, capturing images live also ensured that they would be seen. The police could not confiscate discs, files or hard drives and erase the images; instead the images were simultaneously filmed and transmitted, saved to remote servers. Streaming images of protest live to the Internet also means, of course, that the police can watch, observe and record images, determine who is a frequent participant based on whose images are seen regularly, direct officers to scenes that the live stream crew may be filming, and select individuals for the officers to target, all from a secure and distant location. The possibilities of live streaming go both ways, and thus the use of live streaming for liberation is never simple nor guaranteed.

In sum, weapons and tools become what they are and are altered as they enter into other relations or are taken up by different assemblages. New technologies can permit new assemblages to form, and in these assemblages new technologies take their shape or obtain their traits—impermanent and fluctuating though they may be. The work of the activist, then, is to determine the type of assemblage that will lean new technologies more towards the status of a weapon, and then to use the weapon carefully, with intention, until the point that that weapon ceases to be a weapon, until the assemblages shift and change and one can see the tool status of the object subsuming the weapon system. This means that no technology, especially in this case the technology of live streaming images used by CUTV, can be used without caution, without intention, without constant vigilance and reassessment of the type of assemblage it is used within, and the types of assemblages it connects to, bumps up against, and interacts with in its relations of exteriority. And it means that at a certain point a once-useful technology may have to be immediately discarded.

The weapon/tool distinction and the use of activist technologies by the state—the chaos made possible through becomings and a politics of minoritarianism—cannot ever be completely avoided. We cannot, as Deleuze and Guattari note, simply adopt a new system and deem ourselves saved. But considered carefully, both theoretically and practically, the contours of a liberatory assemblage begin to take shape. We must focus on developing, alongside our technologies, the careful construction of an assemblage with a political directionality we ourselves determine. This is to suggest that the practices through which we organize ourselves and our institutions weigh heavily on how we use the technologies made available to us. Assemblages are much like the politics of the assembly that Quebec activists used in their organizing, and which have a long history in left politics—they too aim at the possibility of creating non-hierarchical organizations which can inhibit the potential of internal micro-fascisms and expand liberation. A politics thoughtfully invested in assemblages of minoritarian becomings, in direct democracy and thoughtful use of technology, contributes to the project of creating an alternative 'patchwork' struggle. It supports our struggle to compose resistance that is also constitutive of something new, a new mode of living, a new socius. This does not mean that we ignore the dangers inherent in our new weapons, but conversely that we interrogate them deeply and tackle their problematics. For CUTV, for instance, it became policy to avoid filming interviewees during the demonstrations if they preferred to not be visually identified. It also meant not filming the occasional and isolated acts of vandalism or, if captured, to avoid filming the faces of those engaged in smashing windows. A minor act, but a beginning. And all revolutions—digital or biological, human or machinic—must have a beginning. Where we take our first steps on that beginning contributes to the determination of our ends.

NOTES

1. Coalition large de l'Association por une Solidarité Syndicale Étudiante.
2. See: The Canadian Centre for Policy Alternatives blogposting by Phillippe Hurteau on 6 Jun 2012 at http://www.behindthenumbers.ca/2012/06/06/the-student-strike-in-quebec/; and a CBC News Montreal report from 22 March 2012 found at http://www.cbc.ca/news/canada/montreal/story/2012/03/22/montreal-student-protests.html. Both accessed 15 June 2013.
3. The idea of social media as an organizational force leading only to weak links and thus weak activism was forwarded by Malcolm Gladwell in a 2012 *New Yorker* article. For a rebuttal based in social movements, see Nunes (2012).
4. For more on this, see Thorburn (2012b).
5. "Movement of the squares" is a catch-all term for the social movements of 2011, marked by the occupation of public space, primarily city squares, parks and plazas. These popularly include Egypt's initial revolution, the Indignados in Spain, and Occupy, but could also count the struggles in Tunisia and Greece, as well as the more recent Turkish and Brazilian uprisings.
6. See Thorburn (2012a).
7. For more on the history of workers' struggles around the creation of institutions of democratic self-management and workers' control, see Ness and Azzelini (2011). For more on the contemporary assembly, see Thorburn (2012a).
8. In 2009 a referendum at the university saw an increase in the student levy directed towards CUTV (up to thirty-four cents per student), which effectively doubled the station's budget. This permitted the station to hire staff. Laura

Kneale was hired as station manager in 2010 and Laith Marouf as programme director.

9. The demonstrations that crossed Quebec and reverberated in the rest of Canada in the winter, spring and summer of 2012 were centred around student opposition to increased tuition fees at Quebec's publicly funded universities. The movement involved almost all university and CEGEP (college) campuses across the province, and was largely led by a coalition of student associations and individual student unions under the umbrella of CLASSE (Coalition Large de l'ASSE), which operated on the basis of directly democratic decision making through regular general assemblies. Soon garnering vast public support, monthly demonstrations sometimes involved 250,000–400,000 people, including labour activists and community groups, and nightly demonstrations began lasting for several months consecutively. "Casserole" protests also began, inspired by the cacerolazos of Chile in the 1970s, and neighbourhood assemblies also began across the city of Montreal, incorporating community members into the organizing and structure of the student strike. The strike had always been, but became clearly then, about much more than simply tuition fees, and instead was a sustained attack on the austerity policies of the Liberal government. With approximately 150,000 students on strike by May of 2012, the Liberal government soon folded and declared an election, which they lost. The fee increases have recently been renegotiated by the victorious Parti Quebecois government, and will, in the long run, amount to greater increases than what the Liberal party was originally proposing. Therefore, although quiet now, student strikes could easily erupt again in Quebec in the coming months and years. For further writing on the student strike of 2012, see parts 1 and 2 of *WI: Journal of Mobile Media* 6, no. 2 (2012).

10. All information about the LiveU LU60 backpack can be found through the LiveU website, at http://www.liveu.tv.

11. Affinity groups are small groups of individuals formed around shared interests or goals. Often affinity groups operate in a non-hierarchical manner, making decisions by consensus. They provide a small, flexible and decentralised mode of organization within larger activities, demonstrations or events.

12. The spotter kept apprised of the movements of police and other demonstrators, and ran errands when necessary.

13. For example, while I was working as a technical operator our team was in a crowd that was attacked by police with flash-bang grenades and tear gas canisters. Along with other demonstrators, and due to the panic that flash-bang grenades induce, our team began to run, over sidewalks, through parks and across uneven ground. While running, I had to maintain visual and physical contact with the camera operator, ensuring that he did not trip on sidewalks or tree roots as his vision was significantly impaired due to the obstruction of the camera and lens. This demonstrates the role of solidarity as integral to the operations of the CUTV live stream 'assemblage' as an example of the possibility of minoritarian-becomings.

14. Because demonstrations are frequently divided and dispersed by police, this function of social media becomes incredibly important in reassembling after dispersal. Although not always effective (because, as will be discussed, the police also make use of these social media sites), using text and social media in this way can help isolated individuals regroup after being charged and divided by police and increase safety.

15. The legitimacy of the director's temporary authority, though, comes entirely through the consent obtained in collective processes of discussion and decision making held beforehand. Teams discuss comfort levels, personal

limitations, arrest aversion and the like prior to heading out to a demonstration so that the director can make informed decisions. To attempt to engage in collective decision making and assess the position of each team member while in the midst of demonstrations would negate the necessarily immediate response times of a *live, streaming* broadcast, and so one component of the team must take a temporary, flexible and rotating position of authority in order to provide coherency and political directionality to the project.

16. Law 78 was passed in May 2012 by the Quebec government, and sought to impede strikers' ability to blockade university entrances. It also made any protest or public gathering of fifty or more people illegal unless notification and march routes were provided to police eight hours in advance.
17. See Lakoff (2013).
18. The *casseroles* come out of the tradition of anti-Pinochet Chilean demonstrators in the 1980s, and in both situations members of the public stood on street corners, on balconies or in front of their homes and banged pots and pans together, in noisy defiance of the authority of the state.
19. Although this is troublesome, some student movement leaders went on to become candidates for political parties and others supported strongly leftist parties. But officially, and in practice, many activists militated against aligning the movement with a particular party or maintaining much investment in the state.
20. "We are biased!" declared Marouf, but a bias that bent towards the disenfranchised, towards those without a voice or access to the levers of power. The goal, for Marouf and for CUTV at the time, was to place their hands on those levers of power and, through the strength of their uncensored live streams, pull.
21. Although Deleuze and Guattari would never use such a descriptor
22. Or rather, realities that differ from those proffered by the mainstream media.
23. This is at least true for the live stream teams, as they assembled nightly. There has been some controversy over the hierarchical nature of the station as a whole over the last year, which has been dealt with through a turnover in much of the staffing and through general assemblies which altered the station's mandate and constitution to a large degree.
24. Marouf, pers. comm.
25. This was seen earlier, in 2010, at the G20 protests in Toronto, Ontario. It has also been discussed in Trottier (2012).

REFERENCES

Benjamin, Walter. 1986. *Reflections: Essays, Aphorisms, Autobiographical Writings.* New York: Schoken Books.
Bogard, William. 1996. *The Simulation of Surveillance: Hypercontrol in Telematic Societies.* Cambridge, UK: Cambridge University Press.
Deleuze, Gilles, and Felix Guattari. 1987. *A Thousand Plateaus.* Minneapolis: University of Minnesota Press.
Due, Reidar. 2007. *Deleuze.* Cambridge: Polity Press.
Dyer-Witheford, Nick, and Greig de Peuter. 2009. *Games of Empire.* Minneapolis: University of Minnesota Press.
Foucault, Michel. 1980. *Power/Knowledge: Selected Interviews and Other Writings.* Ed. Colin Gordon. Random House, New York.
Fuchs, Christian. 2012. Social Media, Riots, and Revolution. *Capital and Class* 36 (3): 383–391.

Gerbaudo, Paolo. 2012. *Tweets and the Streets: Social Media and Contemporary Activism*. London: Pluto Press.

Gladwell, Malcolm. 2010. Small Change: Why the Revolution Will Not Be Tweeted. *New Yorker*, October 4. http://www.newyorker.com/reporting/2010/10/04/101004fa_fact_gladwell.

Haggerty, Kevin D., and Richard V. Ericson. 2000. The Surveillant Assemblage. *British Journal of Sociology* 51 (4): 605–622.

Hardt, Michael, and Antonio Negri. 2000. *Empire*. Cambridge, MA: Harvard University Press.

Joseph, Sarah. 2012. Social Media, Political Change, and Human Rights. *Boston College International and Comparative Law Review* 35 (1): 145–188.

Lakoff, Aaron. 2013. Quiet Streets, Emboldened Hearts. *Canadian Dimension* 47 (5). http://canadiandimension.com/articles/5526/.

Marx, Karl. 1976. *Capital*. Vol. 1. London: Penguin Books.

Ness, Immanuel, and Darid Azzelini. 2011. *Ours to Master and to Own*. Chicago: Haymarket Books.

Newnham, Jack, and Peter Bell. 2012. Social Network Media and Political Activism: A Growing Challenge for Law Enforcement. *Journal of Policing, Intelligence and Counter Terrorism* 7 (1): 36–50.

Nunes, Rodrigo. 2012. The Lessons of 2011: Three Theses on Organization. *Mute Magazine*, June. http://www.metamute.org/editorial/articles/lessons-2011-three-theses-organisation.

O'Reilly, Tim. 2005. What Is Web 2.0? http://oreilly.com/web2/archive/what-is-web-20.html.

Padmanabhan, Venkata N., Helen J. Wang, Philip A. Chou and Kunwadee Sripanidkulchai. 2002. Distributed Streaming Media Content Using Cooperative Networking. *Proceedings of 12th International Workshop on Network and Operating Systems Support for Digital Audio and Video (NOSSDAV)*, May 12–14. Miami, FL. 177–186. New York: ACM. http://dl.acm.org/citation.cfm?id=507670.507695.

Thoburn, Nicholas. 2003. *Deleuze, Marx, and Politics*. London: Routledge.

Thorburn, Elise. 2012a. A Common Assembly. *Interface: A Journal for and about Social Movements* 4 (2): 254–279.

———. 2012b. Squarely in the Red: Dispatches from the Quebec Student Strike. *Upping the Anti*. http://uppingtheanti.org/journal/article/14-quebec.

Trottier, Daniel. 2012. Policing Social Media. *Canadian Review of Sociology/Revue canadienne de sociologie* 49 (4): 411–425.

Contested and Toppled State Power

8 Creating Spaces for Dissent
The Role of Social Media in the 2011 Egyptian Revolution

Sara Salem

1. INTRODUCTION

The 2011 Egyptian uprising constitutes one of the most important sociopolitical events in modern Middle Eastern history. Spanning a mere eighteen days, from January 15 until February 11, the revolution began with street protests calling for social, economic and political reforms, and ended with the resignation of President Hosni Mubarak. The Supreme Council of the Armed Forces (SCAF) came to power temporarily, with promises of parliamentary and presidential elections within the year.

The Egyptian uprising followed the Tunisian one, and has been part of a wave of protest movements across the region, termed the *Arab Spring*. These movements have given rise to a multitude of questions that have looked at the social, economic and political factors that came together to bring about the Arab Spring. In my research, I looked at narratives of protesters in an attempt to understand the various factors that brought about the revolution. Social media was an important part of my theoretical framework, and was a dominant theme in many of the narratives.

Since the beginning of the Arab uprisings that spread across the Middle East in 2011, much attention has been paid to the role of social media in general, and Facebook and Twitter in particular. To argue that Facebook and Twitter were responsible for the revolution is to take agency away from the millions of Egyptians who took to the streets, as well as from the organizations and activists who worked tirelessly for years to mobilise Egyptians. Nevertheless, social media inevitably plays a role in most uprisings today due to the changing nature of contemporary society. The fluid nature of political struggle today demonstrates that social media can be creatively infused within broad sociopolitical movements (Cottle 2011, 651).

The broad aim of this chapter is to demonstrate the role of social media in creating political openings within Egyptian public and political space that eventually allowed for the mass mobilisation that toppled Mubarak. Before the revolution, Egypt was an authoritarian police state, where open dissent was highly regulated and often punished. The spread of new technologies and the rise of social media, however, allowed young Egyptians to communicate and organize in ways beyond the control of the state. This movement began to gain momentum, eventually culminating in the 2011 revolution itself, which in some ways depended on the creative use of technology and social media.

This chapter will use the narratives of Egyptian protesters in order to explore three questions. First, how was social media used during the 2011 revolution? Second, in what ways does social media challenge the state in the public sphere, thus creating new spaces for dissent? Third, how do social identities intersect with social media to produce new relations of inclusion and exclusion? Addressing these questions will shed light on the complex ways in which new media is infused within social movements. It is not my aim to demonstrate the extent to which Egyptians relied on social media, nor the extent to which social media can be credited for the success of the mass mobilisation that was witnessed during the uprising. It is not a question of whether social media allowed or prevented an uprising from occurring in the way that it did; rather the focus should be on the multitude of ways in which social media interacted with the uprising (Cottle 2011, 652).

2. THE 2011 UPRISING

Mass uprisings are among the more complex social phenomena, resulting from an arrangement of social, political and economic factors that combine at a specific moment to result in mass mobilisation. In Egypt, these factors can be traced back to the inception of the modern Egyptian state under Muhammad Ali, as well as the presidencies of both Gamal Abdel Nasser and Anwar el Sadat. Economically, Egypt transformed from state-led socialism under Nasser[1] to free-market capitalism under Sadat, who liberalised the economy through encouraging privatisation and foreign direct investment. This led to rising unemployment, a rising cost of living and a growing gap between rich and poor—despite an annual growth rate of 6 per cent. Politically, Egypt has been an authoritarian state for more than sixty years, with increasing centralisation of power and intensified state repression. As neo-liberal policies multiplied, more coercion was needed to quell the growing social unrest, resulting in the increased power of police forces. At the social level, the education system has been decaying, family structures are under increasing stress, there has been a significant expansion of people under the age of thirty and the majority of Egyptians face insecurity in almost all aspects of their lives (Hudson 2011).

Egypt's uprising resulted from a combination of all of these factors. It was a grassroots movement, unlike the 1952 military coup, popularly understood to have been a revolution, and its main demands were bread, freedom and human dignity.[2] It should be understood within the context of previous modern Egyptian revolutions, including the 1919 revolution to overthrow British colonialism and the 1952 military coup, led by Nasser and the Free

Officers. All of these revolutions included demands for economic and social justice (El Shakry 2011).

Most narratives of the uprising have focused on two dominant conceptualisations: either actors have gained a new consciousness and risen up against injustice or accumulating social issues pushed a population to the edge. In either case, the actions of the population must be contextualised. One explanation of the uprising could be a decline in the ability of the government to coerce: such a shift in power may be evidenced by the street fights between protesters and police during January 25–28 (El Shakry 2011). Another explanation could be that the protests had been building up for years and that two events gave local disputes with the state a national focus: the murder of Khaled Said in 2010 and the heavy rigging of the 2010 parliamentary elections. Both led to state violence and widespread anger among the Egyptian population.

The focus on the state may be what most distinguishes the 2011 Arab uprisings from previous movements in the Middle East (Khalidi 2011). They were all directed inwards at their own societies rather than outwards at imperial powers. In Egypt, action was directed towards the state's constant infringement on the dignity of the individual Egyptian and on the dignity of the collective nation. It countered the state's view of citizens as worthless, previously internalised by Egyptians and manifested in an array of social problems, including sexual harassment, sectarian conflicts, an increase in crime and a general feeling of public frustration.

Dignity, both at the personal and collective level, is a critical issue (Khalidi 2011). The reclaiming of dignity, then, was arguably one of the main aims of the uprising. It can be linked to both French and British colonialism, during which Egyptians suffered decades of subjugation, as well as to the countervailing era of Arab nationalism, which provided an Arab social and political narrative (Kazam 2011, 19). This sense of pride had suffered following the Arab-Israeli war of 1967 (which ended in a massive defeat for Arabs) and again following the events of 9/11. Therefore retrieving a sense of dignity can be seen as the most important change in the Arab consciousness (Kazam 2011, 19).

3. THE RESEARCH

The narratives used in this chapter are drawn from fieldwork conducted in Egypt in June and July 2011, several months after the uprising. The interviews took place in Cairo, predominantly among middle-class Egyptians, most of who participated in the uprising. A total of twenty in-depth interviews make up my sample.[3] I relied on snowballing as a means of creating a sample, which resulted in the sample being quite narrow in terms of social class but balanced in terms of age, occupation and gender. Respondents' ages ranged from early twenties to late sixties, and the sample was equally divided between men and women. While in theory a more representative sample could have led to different findings, this sample can be generalised to the wider population in several important respects, especially given that the uprising had many common goals that bridged social class.[4] These included demands to reform the Ministry of Interior and eliminate police brutality; demands centred on dignity; and demands around freedom and justice. The ways in which Egyptians identified with each demand differed based on class and other characteristics, but the overarching demands were often similar.

The interviews were focused and semi-structured in order to resemble a conversation in which the respondents felt free to bring up issues they saw as relevant or important. It also allowed flexibility in choosing issues to focus on or changing the direction of the interview. I began with a set of interview questions that were completed in most of the interviews. Most of the questions were open-ended. All interviews were conducted in person and most were recorded, except when technical difficulties arose (in two cases). All of the interviews were in English. One drawback of focused semi-structured interviewing is that it is time-consuming, which resulted in a small sample.

Several dominant themes emerged from the narratives of the protesters. These include: social class, the nature of the Egyptian state, generational differences and the role of social media. These themes are all interconnected, and cannot be clearly separated from one another. They all address and are informed by the political, social and economic aspects of contemporary Egyptian society.

In order to analytically approach the complexity of the narratives, I consciously applied the theory of intersectionality to the data. "The intersectional perspective provides a holistic framework for conceptualizing social identity processes" (Thomas et al. 2011, 531). Instead of studying only one concept of identity, it is useful to look at them as influencing one another. This perspective allows the focus to be on the way the different themes interact with one another and allows one to see the links between social media and various institutions, as well as the way social media was used to target different local, regional and global audiences.

4.   SOCIAL MEDIA AND THE EGYPTIAN PUBLIC SPHERE: QUESTIONS OF MOBILISATION, CLASS AND CHALLENGING THE STATE

In order to understand the dynamics of social media use in Egypt, I will employ the overarching concept of the public sphere as a useful way of tying together three important themes: social media and mobilisation; social media and the state; and social media and class. By providing some historical context, the links between these themes will become clear, specifically those between state power and protesters' use of social media to wage a battle over Egyptian public space.

The public sphere can be defined as a space within social life in which public opinion can be formed (Habermas, Lennox and Lennox 1974, 49). Habermas later went on to speak of the impact alternative publics could have on the public sphere, claiming they could "resist mass-mediated representations of society and create its own political interventions" (Downey and Fenton 2003, 187). Although Habermas expressed doubts regarding the extent to which these alternative public spheres—created through new media—could actually impact the political sphere, I will argue that in the case of Egypt, clear inroads were made into the political sphere due to the use of social media. Downey and Fenton argued that the "mass-media public sphere will become more open to radical opinion as a result of the coincidence of societal crises and the growth of virtual counter-public spheres" (ibid., 199). The growth of these counter-public spheres in Egypt has had a marked impact on the mass-media public sphere and the political sphere.

Social media can be viewed as both a technological tool as well as a space within which political acts are played out (Lim 2012, 234). In this sense, the interaction between social media and the public sphere is an especially interesting area of research. Media can be said to constitute part of communication processes within the public sphere (Fuchs 2010, 175). The public sphere in Egypt is a definitive space within which multiple understandings of political and social issues are projected. However, it is also a highly contested space, over which the regime has strong control.

4.1. Media History and Context

Traditionally, the Egyptian state has co-opted much of the media available to Egyptians. These provided legitimacy to the authoritarianism underlying state structures (Cottle 2011, 650). Social media was not the first instance of technology being used to challenge the state's dominance within the public sphere. There appears to be a consensus that satellite television laid the basis for the social media activism that emerged during the last decade. These channels have played a part in creating an Arab public opinion that stretches across geographical space. While some argue that these new types of media are affecting local languages and cultures, it is also the case that they are leading to an opening up of the Arab public sphere (Ghareeb 2000, 399).

The proliferation of satellite television in particular has had dramatic effects on Egyptian audiences (Alterman 1998). Many of these channels, which were privately owned, included programming that was explicitly political. Talk shows in particular were numerous, and the political discussions on these shows led to higher expectations among the population. Moreover, these talk shows acted as spaces in which sensitive subjects could be broadcast, such as freedom of expression, democratisation and economic problems. Nevertheless, it is worth nothing that these new satellite channels often have political agendas of their own. MBC, the most popular satellite channel until Al Jazeera came on air, aimed at spreading the Saudi Arabian government's views throughout the Arab world. While it did address certain taboo subjects, it avoided criticising the monarchies of the Gulf and Saudi Arabia (Ghareeb 2000, 402). Similarly, Al Jazeera Arabic has been accused by some of refraining from criticising Qatar and being pro-Islamist.

Al Jazeera (AJ) in particular has had an extremely influential effect on the Egyptian media sphere. AJ was launched in 1996 in Qatar. From the start, AJ did not shy away from controversial political subjects and guests. It received widespread condemnation from many Arab countries for its coverage of the autocratic nature of many regimes in the region. AJ's stated objective is to provide both sides of the story, and from its inception the channel has explicitly challenged the status quo in Middle Eastern politics. AJ represented the first channel available to Arab audiences that presented a different view from state-controlled television channels.

Al Jazeera was essential to the creation of a new public sphere in Egypt where different ideologies could compete. Through its framing and critical approach to events in the Middle East, AJ managed to explicitly reaffirm a common Arab identity, as well as to overtly bring attention to the authoritarianism pervading the region.[5] "Its talk shows turned an Arab *narrative* into a common Arab *public sphere* through argument."[6] This was no doubt aided by the fact that AJ had become one of the most viewed channels in the Middle East.[7] AJ also represented a conceptualisation of Arab identity that was not subordinate to the hegemonic West. Arab public spheres are saturated with frustration at Euro-American imperialist policies in the Middle East, the Israeli occupation of Palestine and the array of local economic, social and political problems (Lynch 2003, 60).

4.2.   From Satellite Television to Social Media

A useful way of theorising social media is by viewing it as a form of critical media (Fuchs 2010). Critical media is defined as oppositional media that challenges the dominant forms of media. "Such content expresses oppositional standpoints that question all forms of heteronomy and domination" (ibid., 179). In this understanding, critical media gives a voice to groups who have traditionally been marginalised and excluded. Critical media is part of the wider political context, and aims to re-imagine the social order.

In Egypt, social media presented an alternative platform that individuals could use to discuss, debate and transform societal discourses in ways that did not overtly challenge the state's dominance in the public sphere. This had an impact on the relationship between the state and social movements, especially in the years leading up to the uprising, when many movements had a strong online presence.

The number of social media users in Egypt is surprisingly low for a country that has been the centre of attention in debates about social media and social movements. Prior to the January 25 revolution, Facebook users in Egypt were estimated to be four million. By June 2012, this number had jumped to eleven million, the largest in the Arab world.[8] This represents a penetration of 17 per cent. Twitter, on the other hand, has a much lower number of active Egyptian users—less than two hundred thousand. This means that less than 5 per cent of Egyptians use Twitter.

The use of social media to engage in activism has a history that predates the 2011 uprising. Out of the seventy street protests that took place between 2004 and 2011, fifty-four of them involved online activism (Lim 2012, 232). The Kefaya movement in 2004 marks the beginning of activism in Egypt that used social media to organize. During demonstrations, Kefaya would spread information online through websites. Mobile communication in particular allowed the organization to coordinate activities and become less dependent on state-controlled media.

The April 6 youth movement represents another movement that utilised social media to spread its message. In 2008, they created a Facebook page to mobilise support for the Egyptian labour movement. Labour strikes represented one of the most important social and political challenges to the Egyptian state in the years leading up to the revolution. April 6 also made use of Twitter, Flickr, blogs, YouTube, e-mails and text messages. By 2009, the Facebook group had over seventy thousand members—at a time when the total number of Egyptian Facebook users was nine hundred thousand (Lim 2012, 240). This notable online presence did not, however, influence activity on the streets. April 6 demonstrations continued to draw small numbers, largely due to the overly violent responses of the police but also because few movements were able to translate their large online support into concrete street support.

Blogging in particular was an important tool used by Egyptian activists during the last decade of the Mubarak era. By 2006, there were more than 1,800 active Egyptian bloggers who constituted an online sphere of alternative political and social interaction. Blogging provided a space within which free discussions and debates could occur between Egyptian activists. Protesters need to feel that they share the same grievances with many other people (Lim 2012; Lynch 2011). Movements such as Kefaya became intricately reliant on the blogosphere, and this connection managed to create a new form of public engagement that was destabilising to the state (Radsch 2008, 8). The reason blogging was so empowering for activists as well as dangerous for the state was that it created a space where otherwise unconnected individuals with different backgrounds and beliefs could come together and act as an oppositional force (Lim 2012, 237).

The state responded violently to the challenge posed by bloggers. Bloggers were arrested and some began to speak of a "War on Bloggers" (Younis 2007). This intensified after bloggers began to publicise police torture on their blogs, thus directly incriminating the police forces in state coercion and violence. The publicising of police acts such as torture was to be one of the main factors leading to the mass mobilisation during the 2011 uprising.

The Facebook group "We Are all Khaled Said" represents another important online movement in Egypt. The group was created in 2010 after the murder of a young Alexandrian man at the hands of police officers. The twenty-eight-year-old Said was taken from an Internet café and dragged outside, before being beaten to death and left on the side of a nearby street. While some believed that Said's only 'crime' has been refusing to show the police his ID card, others posited that he was targeted because of a video he owned that incriminated police officers in profiting off of drug sales. The official explanation given was that Said had swallowed drugs and died as a result. Soon after his death, images of his severely damaged body and face began to circulate online. The Facebook page was created shortly after.

Large numbers of Egyptians took to the street after the page called for protests against Said's murder. While this page was not the first to tackle the issue of police torture in Egypt, it was the first that had a visible and powerful icon that could mobilise young Egyptians. The graphic images of Khaled Said's face became a symbol with great emotional significance. Moreover, the page's message—that what happened to Said could happen to *any* Egyptian—was an important one. For many, Said represented a normal, middle-class youth who was not politically active, thus allowing them to identify with him. This identification provided a strong incentive for mobilisation. The group Kolena Khaled Said went on to issue the initial call for protests, and many interviewees said they took to the streets because of it: "I found out through an event on Facebook from Kolena Khaled Said and it was being circulated, a lot of jokes about it, a lot of ridicule, how are you going to start a revolution from a Facebook event?"

This brief history shows that social media managed to permeate the existing public sphere and, to some extent, democratise it. According to this view, social media constitutes a means through which different narratives can enter the public sphere and thus compete with those propagated by the elite, in a sense democratising public space. Another way is to see it as having created a counter-public sphere (Fuchs 2010, 184). In this latter view, the counter-public sphere acts as an opposition to the dominance of the (state-controlled) public sphere. The counter public sphere is thus a response to the monopoly of the state in the political sphere. This is especially clear in the build-up to the 2011 uprising.

4.3.   Social Media and Mobilisation

The initial call for protests on January 25 was spread through social media. April 6 and "We Are all Khaled Said" collaborated in order to issue the call for participation online. Posters, banners and videos were shared widely through e-mail, blogs and Facebook. On Twitter, the hashtag #Jan25 was publicised. The "We Are all Khaled Said" page created an event for the January 25 protest, to which more than fifty thousand confirmed their attendance. Most of the respondents had heard about the protests through online media, predominantly the Facebook event.

One respondent, who was in Canada prior to the revolution, also read about it through Facebook:

> I have a Facebook account, and during this time (the days before January 25) I was chatting with friends online and there were a lot of discussions about a revolution, but no one was calling it that at the time. After Tunisia, things sparked on Facebook and I remember chatting with Egyptians who were living abroad about whether it was something worthwhile. Many were considering going back to Egypt.

Social media's role was emphasised, especially in relation to the initial mobilisation. Numerous respondents pointed out that it was very instrumental at the beginning, in order to get people together on the streets.

The links between online and offline communication should not be underemphasised. Efforts towards mobilisation were also being made offline, through the spread of pamphlets, text messages and–most importantly— word of mouth.

> I was talking to people on the street and they knew that the 25th would not be just another protest against Hosni Mubarak or just another strike. From online basically, from social media and from interacting with people on the streets.

Another respondent said,

> There was a lot of word of mouth about the protests, especially the week before the 25th. Everyone was talking about it. They gave fake venues and there were secret venues so the police wouldn't know, my friend told me about these.

The spread of information through word of mouth is a crucial aspect of the revolution that is often ignored. Its importance became especially clear when the government cut off the Internet during the uprising. Despite this, information about protest location and needs still managed to be disseminated widely, largely due to the efficiency of word-of-mouth communication.

More traditional media, including major news channels, relied extensively on social media to cover the uprising. Tweets, Facebook statuses and live videos coming directly from protesters on the ground provided extremely rare and useful footage that was otherwise difficult to obtain.[9] There was also awareness among protesters that pictures, slogans and information from the protests were being broadcast around the world through social media. This touches on the link between social media and emotionality. Scenes and testimonies that are emotional in nature were recorded and spread, before being broadcast to millions around the world (Cottle 2011, 648). One result of this was that both the courage and idealism of Egyptian protesters as well as the brutal force of the state became accessible to people around the world. The link between the protesters on the street and the millions watching at home was often created through social media. Pictures in particular were an important means through which emotions and demands were conveyed. Photographs of the martyrs, for example, were extremely powerful. Moreover, by repeating the demands over social media, protesters managed to express to Egyptians at home what it was that they were fighting for, and the fact that it was for the benefit of all Egyptians. This was a concrete instance of social media directly countering the state narratives that were being spread through national television.

Videos and pictures of police brutality in particular were of major importance in mobilising people against the regime. Khaled Said in particular was a recurrent theme in the interviews:

> I saw the pictures of Khaled Said on the Facebook page, the before and after. Shocking. And there was no investigation, which made people angry. Even though there is no human who can swallow drugs like what the police said. And the public attorney said he swallowed two packets, which is impossible.

The spread of videos and pictures pre-2011 was therefore instrumental to the build-up of anti-Mubarak sentiment, and explains why so much of the focus was on the Ministry of Interior. The spread of Khaled Said's story (as a counter-story to the one presented by the Ministry of Interior) represents a concrete example of how social media can be used to challenge official narratives.

4.4.   Power, the State and the Public Sphere

Coming back to the notion of public sphere, it is instructive to look at the battle over public space. Social media has played a central role in creating new spaces for activism and dissent. By theorising social media in Egypt through the perspective of critical media, it can be shown that social media has given a voice to the voiceless, through transcending the censorship applied by the state to other public spaces (Fuchs 2010, 179). This can be seen clearly in the difference between social media and state-controlled media—the former constitutes a space that allows for a certain level of dissent, while the latter represents a space that is not only tightly controlled by the state but also actively used by the state as a means of controlling societal discourses.

Social media presented Egyptians with new ways of challenging the state *in public space*. New communication technologies allowed for various narratives to compete in the public sphere in new ways, and these narratives contributed directly to the uprising. These spaces are highly contested, and social media has altered the way in which these contestations occur. One concrete example of this is the difference between the narratives put forward by activists on social media outlets as compared to the narrative that emerged from state-controlled media. This is a clear example of the competing narrative present within public space and lends credence to the idea that social media has indeed levelled the playing field to some extent.

Many of the protesters that were interviewed claimed that the uprising could not have happened without the use of new technology and social media, as this allowed activists to organize in a space that was closed to the Egyptian state in general and the Egyptian police and state security in particular. This was confirmed by the older generation of Egyptians that were interviewed. They argued that before social media there was no space within which groups of activists could organize, as state security had thoroughly and violently infiltrated public space:

> Why didn't we do anything (during Nasser and Sadat). We were getting old. We weren't used to the new methods of communication. The people were going out (to protest), like journalist syndicate, medial syndicate, lawyers were going out, labour force. But it was not organized, and *amn el dawla* (state security) quickly infiltrated. The reason the youth succeeded is because they had no leadership; it was through Facebook that everyone said let us meet.

The tight control over mobilising exercised by state security came up in a number of interviews:

> All small demonstrations or even meetings were penetrated. All telephones were tapped. You couldn't organize anything in big numbers. They used to go to factories and syndicates and arrest people. Everyone on television was under control, books and movies were censored. They could stop anything. That's why I think Facebook played such an important role in the revolution, because *amn el dawla* could not control it in the same way.

It thus became clear that the reason social media was seen as particularly important to the uprising was because of the tight control exercised by state security over *concrete* spaces. Congregating in large numbers or organizing meetings or small protests was more often than not shut down by state security before they could turn into movements that could challenge the regime. "We kept trying to organize ourselves into an opposition for twenty years, and the security state was efficient so that whenever we began to make any nucleus for a movement of change we would find security there right away." Facebook changed this in the sense that it represented a reliable source of information, as well as an efficient means through which news and activities could be spread.

Other respondents emphasised the fact that the police and security forces were not expecting mobilisation through social media: "They were expecting a traditional way of communication to start the revolution." Social media was beyond their control, and thus they were unable to control the streams of communication before and during the uprising. Several respondents suggested that *amn el dawla* were not as familiar with social media as was commonly assumed and that it was simply too big and widespread to be controlled. Another respondent stated that the Egyptian government was aware of the danger posed to the regime by social media and that it had already tried to prepare for it:

> I read that Egyptian government sent some specialists to Facebook to try and reach a deal about shutting it down in Egypt, and Facebook refused. The government did that because they were helpless before this new technology. You have two million people who could organize themselves away from your control.

This unfamiliarity with social media links to the argument that the pace with which new technologies are being introduced has had an effect on national responses (Price 2002, 235). Strategies of control must constantly be renewed in order to take into account changes in the way that ideas circulate. The nature of social media means that it is decentralised and thus difficult to control (Bennett in Couldry and Curran 2003, 7).

Social media also became an alternative to state media. Numerous times this binary was brought up in order to highlight the promise of social media as a new source of unbiased information. However, it is important to note that media in and of itself can never be 'unbiased'—social media can be better understood as providing different narratives to state media, rather than 'better' or 'more objective' ones.

The use of social media is never a one-way process, however. "Technology is also allied to force. Technology can be an instrument of force when it allows the state to control the mediation of a legal regime" (Price 2002, 244). Moreover, surveillance and other forms of control have emerged directly from the latest technologies. The Egyptian state has also pushed back and responded to the challenges posed by social media. While social media is usually discussed as a tool that democratises, it is equally being used in a repressive manner (Morozov 2012). New technologies of coercion have added to the already expansive capacities of authoritarian states (Nisbet and Meyers 2010). Surveillance is an obvious example of this. Specific divisions within state security have been created to track online activity (Lynch 2011, 306). Moreover, states have the capacity to cut off Internet and mobile phone connections, as happened during the 2011 uprising. The targeting of journalists, particularly foreign ones, also aimed at preventing the spread of information.[10] Nevertheless, activists often found ways of circumventing censorship—for example, through using landlines or proxies.

While many of the interviewees suggested that the use of social media is a positive development, and this may be explained by the fact that it is often used by activists working for positive change, it is important to note that the Egyptian regime also made use of new technology and social media. Both the government and the military sent out text messages during the revolution and have made announcements on both Facebook and Twitter since then, as has President Morsi. The state also responded strongly to the use of technology by cutting off the Internet as well as mobile phone networks at the start of the uprising. This backfired, however, and actually led to many people taking to the streets to find out what was happening because they could no longer rely on social media to stay informed. "Blocking the Internet infuriated me, and showed me and other people how much the regime could suppress and oppress people. This was a major driving force for people to go to the protests." Moreover, people found ways of ensuring that their tweets reached audiences at home and abroad, either through the use of proxies or by dictating them to people outside of Egypt using landlines.

Activists have challenged the use of social media by the state. Two particular instances have been especially notable. The first followed an incident during an anti-SCAF demonstration, when an Egyptian woman was dragged by military police until her abaya had been stripped off, to reveal her bra underneath.[11] State-controlled media immediately went on the defensive, claiming that the woman had purposively worn nothing underneath her abaya, and that she had insulted the military police. Social media responded on multiple levels: rejecting the sexist accusations about what the woman was/was not wearing, as well as the accusations that she had insulted military police, arguing that even if she had, there was no excuse for what had happened. Additionally, the video and photographs were shared widely. Soon after, graffiti also emerged, critiquing the actions of the military police. The second example is the campaign organized against military trials for civilians, a process that had existed in Egypt since the implementation of Emergency Law in 1958. "No to military trials" became one of the most visible anti-SCAF campaigns, largely due to their presence on social media.

4.5. New Hierarchies of Exclusion: Social Media and Social Class

While the role of social media in creating new spaces for dissent within the public sphere is an important accomplishment, it is necessary to point out the new modes of inclusion and exclusion that this creates, or rather, reproduces. The relationship between social class and social media is one that numerous scholars have discussed. Class and accessibility are especially important to take into account in the Egyptian context. The intensification of neo-liberal capitalist economic policies under Mubarak has led to a deep social crisis in which the gap between the rich and poor has grown tremendously. This is reflected in poverty rates as well as the drastic reduction in social mobility. Class tensions have deepened, and it is unsurprising that one of the major demands of the revolution was social justice.

A group of liberal and westernised young Egyptians was able to influence global opinion through Twitter and Facebook. While there is no doubt that this group was active in the uprising, it is worth nothing that the focus on them has led to a misrepresentation of both Egypt and activists and protesters. Emphasis on this small elite serves to represent Egyptian activists as liberal and 'just like us' in the western media, while ignoring the important fact that this group is not in any way representational.

The issue of social class was a dominant theme in almost all of the interviews. Social class emerged as one of the major stratifying elements of Egyptian society, permeating many of the issues brought up by respondents. The fact that different social classes participated in the uprising was mentioned in almost all of the interviews, which suggests an intense awareness of class. Many spoke of the 'distance' between classes disappearing during the eighteen days, and the connections that were established during that period that managed to override traditional divisions.

The ways in which social class intersects with social media are an important area of research. One respondent pointed out that while social media did not reach many, it did play a role in mobilisation:

> It doesn't reach the whole population. On January 25 protesters weren't in the millions, just a couple thousand, but that got the whole ball rolling. And then people, obviously they're not all on the Internet, and there's like the 6 April movement that hands out flyers and they do a good job of raising awareness. People were ready to protest, they just wanted to see someone take the first step. It broke the barrier of fear.

While there is little doubt that social media remains an exclusive tool within developing countries, it is worth noting that the uprising in Egypt was successful because much of the online content was spread offline, either through the tireless work of activists and groups who distributed flyers and posters, through channels such as Al Jazeera, through graffiti and other forms of public art and music or through word of mouth. It would thus be more useful to see social media as a tool that facilitated the mobilisation of protesters at the start, and that acted as a "watchdog" of state-controlled media (Cottle 2011, 652).

In such a deeply stratified society, access to certain consumer goods (such as smartphones, computers, etc.), as well as to the tools that come along with it, is highly dependent on class. As previously mentioned, the number of Facebook users represents less than 20 per cent of the Egyptian population. While it is true that the majority of Egyptians own a mobile phone, these are unlikely to be of the smartphone variety, which provide access to social media and advanced communication tools. It is clear, therefore, that the upper and middle classes have easier access to social media, and by extension to the narratives and debates being created and spread through social media. Thus it is important to remember that social media is not just a liberalising medium that democratises society; it is equally and simultaneously a medium that creates its own hierarchies of power.

5. CONCLUSION

The use of social media has clearly functioned as a threat to the control of public and private space exercised by the Egyptian regime. As a tool that can publicise regime transgressions, as well as connect activists and allow for organizing, it is one of the most crucial challenges to authoritarian states around the world. However, the limits of social media are important to take into account. Most of the interviews referred to social media as an important tool that helped to *mobilise*. Beyond this, however, it appears that social media has less of an impact that is often assumed. In fact it appears that post-uprising, the state and many institutions have been able to regroup and ensure that pre-uprising patterns of domination have re-emerged. Activists soon realized that challenging this requires activism in multiple spaces, not just online. The battle for narrative as well as justice occurs on multiple fronts. The Internet is one, but factories, workplaces, state institutions and schools are examples of others. While social media may play a role in challenging state narratives, the battle is much bigger than this, and thus the tools needed extend beyond the abilities of social media. In other words, while social media has proven to be extremely effective in mobilising protesters, it has been less effective in grassroots organization and political campaigning—both of which are intrinsic to the act of state building. Thus in the aftermath of the revolution, social media has proven ineffective in building organizations and institutions.[12] Moreover, the nature of social media means that dramatic, sensational news travels faster than more mundane news. While the uprising itself was riveting and followed by millions across the globe, the aftermath and the struggles of rebuilding a new state have not been able to attract the same interest.

A clear example of the limits of social media in terms of creating concrete changes is the first referendum held after the uprising. The referendum was held to vote on specific constitutional amendments. During this referendum, the majority opinion on social media indicated that the result would be an overwhelming no. The end result was that more than 77 per cent voted yes. This led to a period of self-reflection among many activists on Twitter, who realized that what was being discussed online was not necessarily what was being discussed in other spaces. Additionally, while social media has had a subversive effect on the public sphere, it can also be argued that this has negatively affected the traditional public sphere.[13] Another important critique is that the public sphere is not a substitute for democracy, particularly because it does not provide concrete means that can result in institutional changes (Lynch 2003, 67).

It appears that following the initial 2011 uprising, social media has somewhat receded into the background of Egyptian politics, despite continued attention from academics. While many Egyptians continue to be active on social media, the battles have moved on to more concrete levels. The June 30, 2013, uprising represents yet another chapter in Egypt's history, and it seems clear that social media played a more minor role than it did in 2011. Instead, it was a petition—started by a group called *Tamarrod* (Rebel)—that sparked the impetus for the June 30 protests, said to have been larger than the 2011 ones. Thus while social media played an important role in 2011 by opening up public space for dissent, the aftermath has seen different battles being waged. Perhaps it is precisely because public space has become more open that these more concrete and institutional battles are now able to take place.

The overall discussion on social media can benefit from more nuance. Issues of class and accessibility represent a limitation to viewing social media as a democratising tool or as a representative medium. Moreover, social media should not be seen as either positive or negative, but rather as a neutral tool that can be used for revolutionary change *as well as* repression and coercion. Both Egyptian protesters and the Egyptian state made use of social media, for different ends. While the initial success in mobilisation may have been attributable to social media and its impenetrability by state security, the state was also able to use new technologies to exert control over Egypt, with key examples including surveillance, control over state media and the use of social media to address the nation. Thus it is clear that social media can be used by various actors, thus complicating any analysis of its role.

Despite these weaknesses, social media has had a tremendous effect on the nature of the public sphere in Egypt, primarily through challenging the monopoly on information exercised by the state for decades. It remains to be seen, however, whether the power of social media can be absorbed by authoritarian states.

More research is needed to try to understand the specific ways in which specific types of social media affect specific locations and groups of people. The effects of social media are in no way uniform across time and place. Rather, they have very localised consequences. At the same time, social media can also be seen as a global phenomenon that is affecting the ways in which people from different places communicate and view one another. More research is required to show both the local and global effects of social media, especially in light of the uprising in the Middle East and North Africa, the Occupy movement and the movements in Spain, Greece and Portugal against EU austerity measures.

NOTES

1. Although the rhetoric used by Nasser revolved around Arab socialism, in practice the hegemonic economic system of that era is better described as state-led capitalism.
2. Most protesters who were interviewed described these as the main demands they saw during the uprising.
3. Eleven of these were conducted by me and the rest were drawn from a set of interviews conducted by American University in Cairo (AUC) students that were available online for a period of time, as well as some that were published in the AUC journal *Cairo Review* (Spring 2011).
4. This is not to say that social class 'disappeared' during the eighteen days or that divisions were temporarily overcome; there is no doubt that the uprising and its elements were highly stratified by class. However, certain goals did bridge social class.
5. Marc Lynch. Political Science and the New Arab Public Sphere. *Foreign Policy.* http://lynch.foreignpolicy.com/posts/2012/06/12/political_science_and_the_new_arab_public_sphere?wp_login_redirect=0. Published 12 June 2012.
6. Ibid.
7. Al-Jazeera leads Arab news channels. *Your Middle East.* http://www.yourmidd leeast.com/news/aljazeera-leads-arab-news-channels_15263. Published 22 May 2013.
8. Arab Social Media Report: Social Media in the Arab World: Influencing Societal and Cultural Change? Dubai School of Government. http://www.dsg.ae/en/Publication/Pdf_En/826201211212209347849.pdf. Published July 2002.
9. This was especially the case after the government began to target journalists, often violently.
10. It is difficult to censor satellite channels, which explains why journalist or offices are usually physically targeted.
11. Image of unknown woman beaten by Egypt's military echoes around world. Ahdaf Soueif. *The Guardian.* http://www.guardian.co.uk/commentisfree/2011/dec/18/egypt-military-beating-female-protester-tahrir-square. Published December 18, 201.
12. Marc Lynch. Twitter Devolutions: How social media is hurting the Arab Spring. *Foreign Policy.* http://www.foreignpolicy.com/articles/2013/02/07/twitter_devolutions_arab_spring_social_media?page=full&wp_login_redirect=0. Published February 7, 2013.
13. Jürgen Habermas. An Avantgardistic Instinct for Relevances: Intellectuals and their Public. *SSRC.* http://publicsphere.ssrc.org/habermas-intellectuals-and-their-public/, Accessed June 24, 2013.

REFERENCES

Alterman, Jon B. 1998. *New Media, New Politics?* Washington, DC: Washington Institute for Near East Policy.

Cottle, Simon. 2011. Media and the Arab Uprisings of 2011: Research Notes. *Journalism* 12 (5): 647–659.

Couldry, Nick, and James Curran, eds. 2003. *Contesting Media Power: Alternative Media in a Networked World.* Oxford: Rowman & Littlefield.

Downey, John, and Natalie Fenton. 2003. New Media, Counter Publicity and the Public Sphere. *New Media & Society* 5 (2): 185–202.

El-Ghobashy, Mona. 2011. The Praxis of the Egyptian Revolution. *Middle East Research and Information Project* 258. http://www.merip.org/mer/mer258/praxis-egyptian-revolution.

El Shakry, Omnia. 2011. Egypt's Three Revolutions: The Forces of History behind This Popular Uprising. *Jadaliyya*, February 6. http://www.jadaliyya.com/pages/index/569/egypts-three-revolutions_the-force-of-history-behi.

Fuchs, Christian. 2010. Alternative Media as Critical Media. *European Journal of Social Theory* 13 (2): 173–192.

Ghareeb, Edmund. 2000. New Media and the Information Revolution in the Arab World: An Assessment. *Middle East Journal* 54 (3): 395–418.

Habermas, Jürgen, Sara Lennox and Frank Lennox. 1974. The Public Sphere: An Encyclopedia Article (1964). *New German Critique* 3: 49–55.

Hudson, Michael. 2011. Egypt on the Brink: The Arab World at a Tipping Point? *Jadaliyya*, February 1. http://www.jadaliyya.com/pages/index/518/egypt-on-the-brink_the-arab-world-at-a-tipping-poi.

Kazam, Azza. 2011. Reclaiming Dignity: Arab Revolutions of 2011. *Anthropology News* 52 (5): 19.

Khalidi, Rashid. 2011. Preliminary Historical Observations on the Arab Revolutions of 2011. *Middle East Monitor*, March 23. http://www.jadaliyya.com/pages/index/970/preliminary-historical-observations-on-the-arab-re.

Lim, Merlyna. 2012. Clicks, Cabs, and Coffee Houses: Social Media and Oppositional Movements in Egypt, 2004–2011. *Journal of Communication* 62 (2): 231–248.

Lynch, Marc. 2003. Beyond the Arab Street: Iraq and the Arab Public Sphere. *Politics & Society* 31 (1): 55–91.

———. 2011. After Egypt: The Limits and Promise of Online Challenges to the Authoritarian Arab State. *Perspectives on Politics* 9 (2): 301–310.

Morozov, Evgeny. 2012. *The Net Delusion: The Dark Side of Internet Freedom.* New York: PublicAffairs.

Nisbet, Erik C., & Myers, Teresa A. 2010. Challenging the state: Transnational TV and political identity in the middle east. *Political Communication* 27 (4): 347–366.

Price, Monroe. 2002. *Media and Sovereignty: The Global Information Revolution and Its Challenge to State Power.* Cambridge, MA: MIT Press.

Radsch, Courtney. 2008. Core to Commonplace: The Evolution of Egypt's Blogosphere. *Arab Media & Society* 6 (Fall). http://www.arabmediasociety.com/?article=692.

Thomas, Anita Jones, Jason Daniel Hacker and Denada Hoxha. 2011. Gendered Racial Identity of Black Young Women. *Sex Roles* 64 (7): 530–542.

Younis, N. 2007. War on Bloggers Unfolds. May 11. http://norayounis.com/2007/05/11/240.

9 Social Media Activism and State Censorship

Thomas Poell

1. INTRODUCTION

Over the past years, commercial social media such as Twitter, Facebook and Sina Weibo have started to play a central role in protest communication and mobilisation. Particularly striking is the use of these media during recent protests in the Middle East and China, as the regimes in these regions have made elaborate and aggressive efforts to control Internet communication. This chapter investigates how social media activism takes shape in the context of pervasive censorship and state repression.

Examining this topic, the first major protest event that stands out is the Iranian post-election demonstrations of 2009. During these demonstrations over two million tweets pertaining to the protests were sent by several hundred thousand users (Gaffney 2010). Although doubts were later raised as to whether more than a few hundred of these users were actually located in Iran, the massive exchange of tweets did suggest that social media were quickly developing into vital platforms for sharing news about political contention in dictatorial settings, in which it is difficult for international news organizations to operate. The growing importance of social media for activism became even more evident in the Tunisian and Egyptian revolutions of early 2011. During these uprisings, millions of tweets tagged #sidibouzid, #tunisia, #28jan and #egypt were exchanged (Lotan et al. 2011). Moreover, and perhaps more importantly, protesters in Tunisia and Egypt themselves shared a lot of news and information through Facebook (Tufekci and Wilson 2012). Meanwhile, on the other side of the world, the rapidly growing Chinese microblogging website Sina Weibo became the go-to platform for protest communication. While China has, over the last decade, not seen any large-scale protests against the central government, an ongoing stream of political and social critique, as well as calls for local and regional protests, flows through Weibo on a daily basis (Bamman, O'Connor and Smith 2012; Yang 2012).

These instances of social media activism are particularly striking, as the Iranian, Chinese and Tunisian states, and to a lesser extent the Egyptian state, have become infamous for their far-reaching efforts to control Internet communication. Moreover, these instances are remarkable, as the global online environment as a whole is increasingly characterised by surveillance. The recent release of secret documents by Edward Snowden shows that the U.S. has developed several extensive online surveillance programmes, of which PRISM and UPSTREAM are the most well known. Through these programmes, the National Security Agency (NSA), with the collaboration of major telecoms and Internet corporations, keeps systematic track of phone calls and monitors online communication within the U.S., but also internationally (Bamford 2013). Overall, as Deibert et al. (2012, 21) argue, states around the world have "moved rapidly to regulate, shape, intervene, and exercise power in cyberspace across all its spheres." The Chinese, Iranian and Tunisian efforts to control Internet communication are symptomatic of this development, but they also stand out in the willingness of these states to openly use violence and systematically censor communication. Each of these states has, over the past years, jailed dozens of Internet users, especially bloggers, for voicing political critique (Kelly and Cook 2011). Furthermore, these countries have massively blocked national and international websites, including major social media platforms, and filtered Internet communication on the level of keywords, developing highly targeted forms of Internet censorship. Finally, both China and Iran have resorted to offensive online measures, such as denial-of-service attacks against oppositional websites, and hacking of social media accounts of political dissidents (Deibert et al. 2010, 2012).

This chapter critically examines how these aggressive censorship practices shape social media activism. In doing so, it also interrogates how the corporations that manage the major social platforms operate in the face of pervasive Internet censorship. How do the technical and commercial strategies of these corporations affect activist communication and mobilisation in authoritarian settings? And, of course, the investigation looks at the activists themselves. How do they, in the process of challenging dictatorial regimes, tactically navigate the social media landscape, which is simultaneously shaped by the controlling efforts of states and the commercial interests of social media companies?

2.   SOCIAL MEDIA ≠ NEUTRAL TOOLS

In popular scientific discourse, social media are often portrayed as tools used by protesters and blocked by dictatorial regimes. Writer and consultant Clay Shirky (2011) argues, for example, that "social media have become coordinating tools for nearly all of the world's political movements, just as most of the world's authoritarian governments are trying to limit access to it." In a similar vein, Larry Diamond (2010, 70) describes social media as "liberation technology" that "enables citizens to report news, expose wrongdoing, express opinions, mobilize protest, monitor elections, scrutinize government, deepen participation, and expand the horizons of freedom." Simultaneously, he emphasises that "authoritarian states such as China, Belarus, and Iran have acquired (and shared) impressive technical capabilities to filter and control the Internet, and to identify and punish dissenters." This understanding of social media as effective tools for activist mobilisation and communication, which regimes try hard to block and control, also resonates in many of the press reports on the recent protests in the Middle East and China. These reports tell tales of large numbers of protesters rapidly being mobilised through social platforms, as well as of quickly circulating social media reports originating from the streets of Cairo, Tunis, Teheran and Beijing.

While this conceptualisation of social media is highly attractive and easy to comprehend, it leads to a fundamental misunderstanding of how social media activism unfolds in dictatorial settings. It wrongly suggests, as Evgeny Morozov (2011) has pointed out, that freedom and democracy can be promoted by simply increasing the availability of social platforms. As various critical theorists have made clear, social media do not function as tools. Instead these media are entangled in complex sets of socio-economic, political, cultural and technological relations, which very much premeditate and steer *whether* and *how* these media become effective as platforms of activist mobilisation and communication (Aouragh and Alexander 2011; Bennett and Segerberg 2012; Langlois et al. 2009).

When exploring these relations, it is, first, important to see the development of social platforms in the context of what has been labelled 'information capitalism,' 'communicative capitalism' or 'cognitive' capitalism, which can be defined as "a mode of accumulation in which the object of accumulation consists mainly of knowledge, which becomes the basic source of value, as well as the principle location of the process of valorisation" (Moulier-Boutang 2012, 57; see also Dean 2009; Fuchs 2011). Knowledge production, as Fuchs (2011, 280) makes clear, involves not only corporations producing knowledge goods but also everyday mediated activities, including "users of MySpace, YouTube, Facebook and so on who produce informational content." In the case of social platforms, the most valuable informational content is user metadata, which allows corporations such as Facebook and Google to profile users and develop targeted advertising and services (Fuchs 2011; Van Dijck 2013).

These commercial strategies are important because they directly inform the technological architectures and policies of social platforms, which are first and foremost designed and managed to facilitate user profiling. Youmans and York (2012) show that this particular techno-commercial focus can conflict with the interests and needs of activists. Drawing from several case studies, the authors demonstrate that the policies and user agreements of social platforms, including those of Facebook, YouTube and Twitter, have resulted in the banning of anonymous activist users, the removal of activist content and the handing over of sensitive activist user information to governments.

The present investigation will further develop this examination by interrogating how the evolving technological architectures of social platforms affect activism. Work in the tradition of software studies makes clear that these architectures—the customised sets of protocols and algorithmic processes that characterise social platforms—very much steer user activity (Beer 2009; Chun 2011; Langlois et al. 2009). The challenge is to trace how such technological steering affects the character and efficacy of activism.

Second, pursuing this exploration, the chapter examines how social media activism takes shape in the context of the evolving state efforts to control Internet communication. Current research shows that the techniques and practices of Internet censorship have dramatically evolved over the past decade. In its 2012 publication, *Access contested*, the OpenNet Initiative (ONI) makes clear that over the years Internet censorship tactics have become more varied, and more focused on directing online user activity, instead of simply blocking access to particular content. These tactics include "more 'offensive' methods," such as "computer network attacks" and the "projection of ideas favourable to a state's strategic interests." They are "layered on top of the basic filters and blocks established during the previous era," and are combined with the intimidation and arrest of bloggers and online activists (Deibert et al. 2012, 10). While state repression and more offensive methods have been most openly practised by dictatorial regimes, these tactics have very much developed in a global online environment increasingly characterised by surveillance. Both major Internet corporations and states everywhere have made surveillance a central element of their operations. And, as recent evidence and research indicates, these different forms of surveillance are strongly entangled with each other. State-led surveillance is made possible by corporate collaboration: telecoms and social media companies provide access to a wealth of user data, whereas the security industry delivers the necessary surveillance technology (Fuchs 2013; Hayes 2009). The rise of this security-industrial complex is by no means restricted to the U.S., as surveillance technologies are exported globally, and virtually every national state tries to force Internet companies to cooperate with its surveillance programmes.

3.   SOCIAL MEDIA ACTIVISM AND SURVEILLANCE IN THE MENA REGION AND CHINA

The question is how these political and techno-commercial mechanisms take shape in dictatorial settings, and how they steer social media activism. Addressing this question, the various detailed studies on the Egyptian revolution are especially helpful, as they show that both online and offline mobilisation efforts were very much shaped by the Egyptian censorship system and the always-imminent danger of police repression. First, social media were evidently important in this context because the Egyptian state tightly controlled the national television channels and the major newspapers. Social media made it possible to broker connections between previously disconnected groups, and provide platforms for expressing grievances against the dictatorial regime (Gerbaudo 2012, 58–59; Lim, 2012, 244). Second, this is not to say that social media communication was unproblematic. As Gerbaudo (2012, 62) emphasises, a major obstacle in the mobilisation process was the "mutual distrust among Facebook users" and the "fear of police repression." For this reason, along with the fact that the majority of the population was not online, let alone active on social media, offline personal networks and face-to-face communication were especially important (Lim 2012; Rinke and Röder 2011). Third, because the state-controlled mass media essentially functioned as propaganda channels for the Mubarak regime, satellite television, especially Al Jazeera, played a crucial role in spreading information on the uprising to the Egyptian masses (Aouragh and Alexander 2011; Castells 2012; Eltantawy and Wiest 2011). Thus, what the different studies show is that the uprising was articulated through a complex media configuration, which was partly shaped by the protesters themselves, but also for an important part by the Egyptian censorship system. Social media were an essential element in this configuration, but so were the mainstream media and various offline means of communication.

Important insights into how state censorship and repression shape social media activism can also be obtained from research on recent protests in Iran and China. Rahimi (2011, 173) describes how Iranian state-led cyber warfare against the protesters of the 2009 presidential elections had an immediate "sociopsychological" effect. He maintains that in this period "paranoia" over the dangers of using anti-filter software "spread like wildfire," most likely as a result of the attempts of Iran's Revolutionary Guard Corps to monitor oppositional online activities. He depicts a climate of fear and uncertainty concerning online information, as large numbers of websites are filtered and blocked, and misinformation is spread through fake oppositional websites to deceive activists and stifle dissent. This account is confirmed by Freedom House, which maintains in its report on post-election Iran that self-censorship in Iran is currently "very extensive, particularly on political matters. The widespread arrests of reporters and activists after the election, as well as perceptions of pervasive surveillance, have created fear among online journalists and bloggers" (Kelly and Cook 2011, 192).

These observations partly correspond with the research on Chinese Internet censorship. Like Iran, the Chinese state massively blocks websites, filters online content, and in governing Internet communication very much relies on self-censorship on the part of social media users and Internet companies (Qiang 2011; Yang 2009). Yet an important difference is that the Chinese state has, over the past years, started to use online protest in its governing process. Gang and Bandurski (2011, 39) maintain that the Chinese government increasingly considers online communication as the "voice of the public." The Internet allows Chinese politicians to read citizens' views in raw, unfiltered form, allowing them to identify and fix problems before they provoke popular unrest (Shirk 2011, 5, 26). Following this approach, social media protest, especially focused on local and regional issues, has been given a lot of space to develop.

Taken together, current research provides important insights into how social media protest communication in the MENA region and China is simultaneously shaped by the strategic manoeuvring of activists and the controlling efforts of dictatorial states. What is still largely missing, with the exception of Youmans and York's study, is research that examines how social media's techno-commercial mechanisms affect activism in these regions. And, more importantly, missing is research that considers how activist strategies and techno-commercial and political steering become entangled with each other in dictatorial settings.

4. CASE STUDIES

To interrogate these interconnections, the investigation will draw from three case studies on online contention in Tunisia, Iran and China. The first case study examines the role of Twitter in the Tunisian revolution. This study is based on a content analysis, building on digital methods and emergent coding, of a set of +100,000 tweets with the hashtag #sidibouzid, collected between December 18, 2010, and January 15, 2011, when long-term president Ben Ali fled the country (see Poell and Darmoni 2012 for methodology). In addition, ten semi-structured Skype interviews were conducted with Twitter users, central to the #sidibouzid communication. The second case study draws from twenty semi-structured interviews, conducted through Google Talk, with college-educated Iranian bloggers. It investigates how these bloggers have coped with Internet censorship and state repression over the past years. The last case study explores how Sina Weibo was involved in two short episodes of political contention, which generated a lot of traffic on the Chinese Internet in 2011. It draws from collections of the most circulated weibos, the Chinese equivalent of tweets, on the two episodes (Poell, de Kloet and Zeng 2013).

These case studies will be supplemented by the wide variety of current research on social media activism in the Middle East and China. In combination, this material provides insight into how protesters in different parts of the world have used social media in the face of elaborate state efforts to control their communication. In turn, to understand how states have tried to steer social media activism, the inquiry will build on the rich body of research on Internet censorship, which has especially been developed by ONI and Freedom House. Finally, the investigation draws from software studies and political economic research. These approaches help to interrogate how the technology and business models of social platforms direct activist communication and mobilisation. So far, these different research perspectives have largely been developed separately. This investigation will show that it is vital to combine perspectives to understand how social media activism is configured in the context of ubiquitous Internet censorship and state repression.

5. CONTROLLING STATES

Particularly striking is how pervasive censorship forces Internet users to become highly self-conscious with regard to how they use language and present themselves online. To communicate with each other about contentious issues, many users in especially China and Iran adopt symbolic language, misspell potentially forbidden words and hide their identity by adopting a pseudonym.

For example, one of the interviewed Iranian bloggers, who works as an editor for an online magazine, maintains that she had "to change the word 'Dictator' to 'Dic-ta-tor' and the name of the poet Sexton to 'Sekston' to avoid filtering." Another Iranian interviewee recounts that in 2009 she tried to blog about participating in the protests around the presidential election, but was afraid to write about it directly. So she used "codes" to describe the people in the streets, such as "we the people with mineral water bottles at hand" (Anonymous interview, 2011). A similar use of coded language can also be observed in China. Qiang (2011, 210) gives the example of the widely used wordplay on the official Chinese euphemism for censorship, which is carried out under the slogan 'constructing a harmonious society.' "The word 'to harmonize' in Chinese (*hexie*)," he explains, "is a homonym of the word for 'river crab.' In folk language, crab also refers to bullies who exercise power violently." Consequently, the image of the crab has become "a new satirical, politically charged icon," and "photos of a malicious crab travel through the blogosphere as a silent protest."

The use of pseudonyms is another tactic widely employed by Internet users facing censorship and state repression. One of the Iranian interviewees contends that "anonymity gives a sense of liberation, it allowed me to say things that I would otherwise not say" (Anonymous interview 2012). Amir-Ebrahimi (2008, 102) notes that, in Iran, especially "women and youth who write about their personal or private life, as well as those who address political and social issues, do so under a pseudonym." Similar observations can also be made concerning China and other the Middle Eastern countries. Using a pseudonym, however, does not make one invisible for state authorities. Qinglian (2008) stresses, "Those who think that employing online pseudonyms will allow them to safely speak their minds misunderstand the nature of the surveillance systems. The Chinese government's Golden Shield Project allows officials to track any Internet poster's IP address and true identity."

At the same time, the frequent use of symbolic language, pseudonyms and misspelling can also be read as forms of self-censorship. They can be interpreted as the result of states successfully steering Internet users away from directly expressing political critique, and confronting central state authorities. This certainly appears to be the case in China. The Chinese regime has been rather permissive of online parody and critique directed at especially local and regional governors, as these forms of contestation can be used to check and curtail local administrations. Yet, simultaneously, it has aggressively thwarted any attempt to mobilise protests against the central government. Analysing millions of social media posts from nearly 1,400 different social media services all over China, King, Pan and Roberts (2012) discovered that the Chinese censorship system is specifically "aimed at curtailing collective action by silencing comments that represent, reinforce, or spur social mobilization, regardless of content." These authors also found that "posts with negative, even vitriolic, criticism of the state, its leaders, and its policies are not more likely to be censored." Similar observations were made in our case study on contentious communication on Weibo. A lot of jokes and critique aimed at the government remained uncensored. Yet posts that hinted at joined action were deleted. Occasionally, when a scandal or protest has the potential to escalate, the Chinese state has taken further preventive measures. This happened, for example, in February 2011, when Chinese-language websites called for a "Jasmine Revolution" in major Chinese cities. In reaction, the state severely curtailed social media activity: "post forwarding and photo publishing were suspended, and searches for the word *jasmine* were blocked" (Canaves 2011, 77).

From the same critical point of view, it should be noted that not only are pseudonyms, as well anonymous logins, employed by Internet users to veil their identity, but also both the Chinese and Iranian regimes have in different ways exploited online anonymity. Yang (2009, 50–51) points out that the infamous Chinese "internet commentators," which are said to be paid fifty cents for each message they post, tend to sign into popular online forums "with anonymous user IDs, like any other internet user." Under the veil of anonymity, they try to guide the direction of public discussion in accordance with the principles of the state propaganda departments. This resonates with the earlier observations by Rahimi (2011) concerning Iran's Revolutionary Guard Corps, which spreads misinformation through fake oppositional websites to deceive activists.

Whereas the Chinese and Iranian states have, over the past years, succeeded in shaping online communication and steering social media users away from directly confronting central authorities, the Tunisian and Egyptian states have evidently not succeeded in this effort. In the pre-revolutionary years, both states certainly have taken repressive measures against bloggers, and especially Tunisia developed a sophisticated censorship system. However, from the research and press reports on the 2011 revolutions, it also becomes clear that neither state interfered much with Facebook. Under these conditions, the Facebook page "We Are All Khaled Said," created in June 2010 to protest the violent death of Khaled Said at the hands of police officers, could develop into a platform where mostly middle-class Egyptian youth expressed their grievances against the Mubarak regime. It was also from this page that the call was launched and circulated for a mass demonstration on 25 January 2011 (Gerbaudo 2012; Lim 2012). Although this by no means explains why the Egyptian protests were successful, it does indicate that there are vital differences in how dictatorial states steer and control social media activism.

6. COMMERCIAL MECHANISMS AND TECHNOLOGICAL STEERING

Responding to popular claims concerning social platforms as activist tools, the corporations managing these platforms have, albeit cautiously, positioned themselves as protesters' allies. Famously, Facebook's CEO, Mark Zuckerberg, has promoted the platform, when it made its initial public offering (IPO), as an emancipatory and liberating tool. In February 2012, Zuckerberg wrote in a letter to investors, "By giving people the power to share, we are starting to see people make their voices heard on a different scale from what has historically been possible. These voices will increase in number and volume. They cannot be ignored" (Reuters 2012).

Yet, as the research of Youmans and York (2012) indicates, the commercial mechanisms of social media and the needs of activists do not necessarily match. This is not to say, however, that they inevitably clash with each other. On the one hand, social corporations, as they depend on the collection of user metadata to facilitate targeted advertising, have a strong interest in drawing as many users as possible. Consequently, these corporations have tried to develop their platforms in ways that accommodate at least some activist needs. Responding to user feedback and recommendations by security experts, Google has, for example, greatly improved the security on its different services, including Google Plus, Gmail, Docs and Search. By default, users now access these services over HTTPS encryption, which layers the standard HTTP on top of the SSL/TLS cryptographic protocols, making Internet communication more secure (Eckersley 2010; Sullivan 2011). This is obviously particularly important for activists in dictatorial settings.

On the other hand, the same commercial mechanisms that occasionally correspond with the needs of activists also frequently undermine their activities. This is most directly evident in some of the user agreements and policies of social platforms, discussed by Youmans and York (2012, 318–321). Particularly problematic for activist users in dictatorial settings are the 'real name' policies of some of the major social network sites, including Facebook and Google+. The terms of service of these sites require users to provide their real name and information, which is in the corporations' interest as real identities are easier to monetise. This policy has clashed with efforts on the part of some activists to remain anonymous. A striking example of this is the temporary deactivation of the "We Are All Khaled Said" Facebook page. The page was created by former Google executive Wael Ghonim under the pseudonymous account "ElShaheed" (The martyr). In November 2010, just before the Egyptian parliamentary elections, Facebook deactivated the account and more importantly the page, citing that the account violated Facebook's terms of service. Although the page was eventually relaunched, it shows the potential tension between the commercial strategies of social platforms and the needs of activists. In a similar vein, social media corporations have removed activist content. Most social media corporations police their platforms through community mechanisms, allowing users to report each other for terms of service violations, including offensive content and spam. These mechanisms greatly lower the cost of monitoring user-generated material, but they also give state agents and regime supporters the instruments to battle activist social media content, which is what happened during the Arab Spring. While wrongfully removed content can be restored, or circulated through other channels, the content management strategies of social media corporations are clearly prone to abuse.

More difficult to reverse are changes in the architecture of social platforms. Informed by their evolving business models, as well as by aggressive competition, social media corporations constantly tinker with the architectures of their platforms. Such architectural changes can fundamentally affect how activists communicate with each other, and they can undermine the often-vulnerable practices of contentious communication in dictatorial settings. This is precisely what happened in the case of Google Reader, which, for several years, was a vital platform for Iranian and Chinese bloggers to exchange news and opinions. The service could play a pivotal role because it allowed users to share otherwise blocked news items and blog posts, and, most crucially, attach comments to these items. The well-known Iranian blogger Amir (2011a) explains why the service made it possible to circumvent filtering: "Google Reader is not in a separated domain and thanks to its https protocol, it is hard to filter by the government (To filter Google Reader the whole google.com domain should be filtered)." Because many other social platforms, such as Twitter, Facebook, YouTube and Flickr, and many international news websites, such as the BBC and CNN, were often blocked in Iran, Google Reader could serve, according to Amir, as a crucial social platform and news spreading website.

That is until October 2011, when Google scrapped the social functionality of the service, and shifted it to its new social platform, Google+. Alan Green (2011), one of Google's software engineers, announced that "many of Reader's social features will soon be available via Google+, so in a week's time we'll be retiring things like friending, following and shared link blogs inside of Reader." These were precisely the functions that made Google Reader such an important platform for many Iranian Internet users. Google's decision drew a storm of protests in the Iranian blogosphere (Amir 2011b; Visual Vortex 2011). In the hope of changing the corporation's mind, many Iranians, along with many Chinese Internet users, signed a petition started by

Brett Keller (2011) to "save Google Reader." The petition quickly received more than thirteen thousand signatures. But these efforts were to no avail, as Google, engaged in a global competition with Facebook, was set on developing and promoting Google+. Iranian Internet users were certainly not happy with what Google+ had to offer. Amir (2011b) stresses that unlike in Google Reader, users cannot share the full content of a blog post in Google+; one can share only the link. If the linked blog or news site is filtered, which is often the case, it is not possible to access the blocked content. Eventually, in 2013, Google decided to discontinue its reader altogether.

These changes to Google Reader are an example of the kinds of architectural changes that social media corporations, including Facebook and Twitter, implement on a regular basis, reshaping user activity and, consequently, activist practices in correspondence with their global commercial strategies. Activists, like other users, have little control over these technological developments, just as they have little insight into how social media's algorithms and protocols exactly steer their activities and process their data. Commercial social media corporations have a competitive interest in black boxing the back end of their operations. Moreover, they have a strong interest in limited access to the data that is shared and generated on their platforms, as this data allows them to target personalised advertising and services at their users. Consequently, activists have control over neither the social media architectures through which they communicate nor the data they collectively produce through Twitter hashtags, and Facebook pages and groups. Like any other user, they are left to guess what exactly happens with this data, which is evidently particularly problematic for activists facing dictatorial regimes.

7.   ACTIVIST STRATEGIES

Resisting commercial steering and authoritarian state control, activists have developed a range of strategies to tactically manoeuvre in the complex social media landscape. A prominent strategy, discussed earlier, is to veil one's real message and identity by using symbolic language, pseudonyms and misspelling. Although research indicates that these methods are widely used and also allow users facing dictatorial regimes to continue communicating about controversial topics, they are not unproblematic. Not only do such veiling efforts provide users with an unjustified sense of security, as technically sophisticated states have a variety of methods at their disposal to track and identify users, but also they can be interpreted as the result of states successfully steering Internet users away from directly expressing political critique and confronting central state authorities. Additionally, these strategies do not liberate activists from the commercial mechanisms of social platforms.

Another often-employed strategy is the use of Internet filtering circumvention tools to evade censorship, access blocked material and communicate about contentious issues. Research by ONI and Freedom House has demonstrated that a wide variety of tools are used for these purposes, ranging from simple web proxies to HTTP/SOCKS proxies and virtual private network (VPN) services (Callanan et al. 2011; Roberts, Zuckerman and Palfrey 2011). While there is a range of circumvention tools available, these tools do not appear to be widely used to access blocked material. Based on an extensive survey on the global usage of circumvention tools, Roberts et al. (2010, 2) have come to the startling conclusion "that no more than 3% of internet users in countries that engage in substantial filtering use circumvention tools. The actual number is likely considerably less." Moreover, they maintain that users tend to choose the simple web proxies, which are less secure, instead of "more sophisticated tools."

Although the overall use of circumvention tools in dictatorial states seems to be rather low, research on politically more engaged groups of users suggests much higher usage rates. Based on a survey implemented on a set of 244 politically oriented bloggers, some of whom can also be characterised as activists, Roberts et al. (2011, 1) reported that "79% of respondents in heavily filtering countries use circumvention tools at least occasionally." Hence, using circumvention tools appears to be a widely employed activist strategy in the examined regions. Nevertheless, it remains a question whether this tactic liberates activists from political and commercial steering. To reach substantial publics in the current media landscape, activists are still forced to pursue a major part of their communication and online mobilisation through commercial social platforms. Moreover, as most Internet users in filtering countries do not use circumvention tools, activists are required to develop communication strategies within the confines of state censorship.

Perhaps the most sophisticated and effective way in which activists have resisted political and commercial steering is by 'working' the global media ecology as a whole. Our research on Twitter and the Tunisian revolution provides insight in how this strategy is operationalised in the MENA region. One of the interviewees in this research project, Nasser Weddady, the civil rights outreach director for the American Islamic Congress, explains that the use of social media is one component in an integrated approach: "We have been working for years on developing a strategy that includes the complete media machine: understanding media relationships between broadcasted media, printed media, satellite channels, and news agencies." This also entails "identifying, recruiting, and influencing correspondents in strategically chosen places, and building relationships with them." Weddady and the other interviewees emphasise that developing this strategy was very much the work of global diaspora networks, which had been constructed over the course of a decade. Sami Ben Gharbia recounts that the construction process started in 2002 with the first Egyptian bloggers, and picked up speed from 2006 onward because of conferences and workshops organized in Beirut: "These physical meetings helped to create a strong activist diaspora community." In this process, Twitter and various other social media played a vital role. Weddady relates, "We started building an audience all over the world." Recruiting especially focused on "young thinkers, who can be potential future leaders in their countries" (Poell and Darmoni 2012).

During the revolutions in Tunisia and Egypt the key task of the diaspora network was, according to an interview with Ben Gharbia, "information escape, the reproduction and structuring of information." This involved a variety of social platforms: "Our aim was first to get the information out of Facebook because it's a closed platform. Not everybody has access, or knows how and where to find the information on Facebook. In the next step, "we publish it on a blog with a clear structure, pages, archives, where the usability of the information is refined. It can also be re-published on YouTube. Then we tweet the URL to inform, where one can see the information." Using blogs was important, as it allowed activists to increase their control over the curation and circulation of information, making them less dependent on commercial platforms. In the case of the Tunisian revolution, especially the critical independent collective blog Nawaat.org fulfilled this function. Furthermore, by circulating information through Twitter it became "accessible to especially Al Jazeera, which was, like many other television channels, nonstop following our Twitter account." Ben Gharbia emphasised that he and his colleagues could function as important information relays precisely because of the diaspora network, which circulated information and did a lot of translation work across different languages and dialects (ibid.).

By adopting an integrated communication strategy and building a global network, the activists in the MENA region were less dependent on or boxed in by single social platforms. They explicitly focused on circulating information across a variety of platforms. Furthermore, they were able to escape national systems of state censorship. Obviously helped by the significance of the Arab Spring protests, their global network and integrated media strategy gave them the opportunity to plug their message in the global media.

8. CONCLUSIONS AND RECOMMENDATIONS

Instead of celebrating and promoting social media as activist tools in the struggle against dictatorial regimes, this study suggests that it is particularly important to critically examine the complex political, economic and technological relations in which activist social media communication is articulated. This requires research that combines insights from a number of theoretical approaches, and that pays close attention to the particular context in which activist processes of communication and mobilisation take shape.

First, social media activism in dictatorial settings cannot be understood without examining how systems of state censorship shape activist communication. Recent scholarship shows that states have become progressively more sophisticated in controlling online communication through a range of filtering techniques, as well as offensive methods. The presented case studies indicate that these controlling efforts do not necessarily stop activist communication, but rather shape its character. To continue communicating about contentious issues, those within comprehensive systems of state censorship have adopted a range of tactics to veil their identities, as well as the actual content of their message. While these tactics are highly inventive and also partly effective in challenging dictatorial regimes, at the same time they can be interpreted as forms of self-censorship. Especially in China and Iran, state censorship and repression appear to have succeeded in steering people away from directly confronting central state authorities.

Second, instead of constituting neutral or even friendly platforms from which to challenge dictatorial regimes, social media very much shape activist communication, and they do so in contradictory ways. To understand how this works, it is important to see, following political economic research, that the major social platforms are first and foremost commercial operations, focused on generating revenue by systematically collecting and analysing user data to facilitate personalised advertising and a range of services. These commercial objectives inform the user policies and management of social platforms, as well as the frequent changes in their architectures. As social media corporations have a strong interest in maximising user activity, some of these changes and policies cater to the needs of activists. Yet they also often conflict with these needs, especially in circumstances in which there are relatively few platforms available for activist communication.

Third, it remains important to closely examine how activists navigate the contemporary media landscape. Such an examination indicates that it is indeed difficult to emancipate oneself from political and commercial steering. Yet especially the research on the Arab spring protests shows that there are nevertheless ways to tactically mitigate the impact of such steering. These tactics do, however, require substantial organizational efforts. By constructing global activist diaspora networks and by strategically circulating and translating content across different social platforms, activists from the MENA region were able to resist becoming enclosed by particular platforms and systems of censorship.

These observations strongly suggest that it is crucial for policymakers, activists and scholars concerned with social media activism in dictatorial settings to critically interrogate how this type of activism takes shape in complex configurations in which political, commercial and technological mechanisms mutually articulate each other. Such inquiries are important because they show that activist communication and mobilisation especially become vulnerable to political and commercial steering, when these processes are primarily facilitated by a small number of commercial social platforms. Consequently, it is vital to strategically organize activist communication and mobilisation across a range of social platforms, including alternative non-commercial platforms, as well as both offline on the local level and online across national and regional borders. Such a strategy makes activists less vulnerable to political and commercial steering, and it enhances their control over how information circulates and is curated.

This ecology approach, however, requires a major organizational effort. The research presented in this chapter implies that it can be successfully pursued only through networks that connect the protesters on the streets to globally dispersed bloggers and activists. Through such connections the work of circulating, translating and curating information can be shared and organized across different geographical locations. This is where policymakers and NGOs can play a significant role. When developing global activist networks and setting up alternative media platforms in challenging dictatorial regimes, attention is especially needed on the following points. First, particularly important is the security of online communication. Given the increasingly central role played by commercial social media in online activist communication, it is crucial that social media corporations are constantly pressured to enhance the security of their platforms and to take activist interests into account when technologically developing their services and managing their platforms. Second, assistance is also needed in developing alternative online platforms, to allow activists more independence vis-à-vis commercial platforms in curating and circulating their content. Finally, special attention in terms of resources and security should be devoted to the translation of online activism into offline networks of mobilisations and capacity building. The connection between contentious social media communication and offline forms of associations, as the research on the Arab Spring protests showed, is of vital importance, but is also really difficult to establish, as dictatorial regimes are very much focused on repressing such connections.

Whatever aspect of social media activism one is focusing on, it is above all crucial to continuously interrogate how the controlling efforts of dictatorial regimes, the commercial and technological steering of social media corporations and the tactical manoeuvring of activists are mutually entangled with each other. Only by critically examining these interconnections is it possible to arrive at informed assessments of, and interventions in, episodes of social media protest communication and mobilisation.

REFERENCES

Amir. 2011a. Why Google Reader (Gooder) Matters for Us (Iranian)! *Amir*, 22 October. http://www.amirhm.com/2011/10/why-google-reader-gooder-matters-for-us.html.

Amir. 2011b. Why Google Reader Is Important for Us. *Amir*, 29 October. http://www.amirhm.com/2011/10/why-google-reader-is-important-for-us-2.html.

Amir-Ebrahimi, Masserat. 2008. Blogging from Qom, behind Walls and Veils. *Comparative Studies of South Asia, Africa and the Middle East* 28 (2): 235–249.

Anonymous interviews with Iranian blogger. 2012. Niaz Zarrinbakhsh. Google Talk. 26 July.

Anonymous interviews with Iranian bloggers. 2011. Niaz Zarrinbakhsh. Google Talk. 23 and 28 June.

Aouragh, Miriyam, and Anne Alexander. 2011. Sense and Nonsense of Facebook Revolutions. *International Journal of Communication* 5: 1344–1358.

Bamford, James. 2013. They Know Much More Than You Think. *New York Review of Books*, 15 August

Bamman, David, Brendan O'Connor and Noah A. Smith. 2012. Censorship and Deletion Practices in Chinese Social Media. *First Monday* 17 (3). http://www.uic.edu/htbin/cgiwrap/bin/ojs/index.php/fm/article/view/3943/3169.

Beer, David. 2009. Power through the Algorithm? Participatory Web Cultures and the Technological Unconsciousness. *New Media & Society* 11 (6): 985–1002.

Ben Gharbia, Sami. 2012. Interview by Kaouthar Darmoni. The Hague, The Netherlands, 11 February.

Bennett, W. Lance, and Alexandra Segerberg. 2012. The Logic of Connective Action. *Information, Communication & Society* 15 (5): 739–768.

Callanan, Cormac, Hein Dries-Ziekenheiner, Alberto Escudero-Pascual and Robert Guerra. 2011. *Leaping Over the Firewall: A Review of Censorship Circumvention Tools*. Freedom House. http://www.freedomhouse.org/sites/default/files/inline_images/Censorship.pdf.

Canaves, Sky. 2011. China's Social Networking Problem. *Spectrum, IEEE* 48 (6): 74–77.

Castells, Manuel. 2012. *Networks of Outrage and Hope: Social Movements in the Internet Age*. Cambridge, UK: Polity.

Chun, Wendy K. H. 2011. *Programmed Visions: Software and Memory*. Cambridge, MA: MIT Press.

Dean, Jodi. 2009. *Democracy and Other Neoliberal Fantasies: Communicative Capitalism and Left Politics*. Durham, NC: Duke University Press.

Deibert, Ronald J., John G. Palfrey, Rafal Rohozinski and Jonathan Zittrain, eds. 2010. *Access Controlled: The Shaping of Power, Rights, and Rule in Cyberspace*. Cambridge, MA: MIT Press.

———. 2012. *Access Contested: Security, Identity and Resistance in Asian Cyberspace*. Cambridge, MA: MIT Press.

Diamond, Larry. 2010. Liberation Technology. *Journal of Democracy* 21 (3): 69–83.

Eckersley, Peter. 2010. Gmail Takes the Lead on Email Security. Electronic Frontier Foundation. January 13. https://www.eff.org/deeplinks/2010/01/gmail-takes-lead-email-security.

Eltantawy, Nahed, and Julie Wiest. 2011. Social Media in the Egyptian Revolution: Reconsidering Resource Mobilization Theory. *International Journal of Communication* 5: 1207–1224.

Fuchs, Christian. 2011. *Foundations of Critical Media and Information Studies*. New York: Routledge.

———. 2013. Societal and Ideological Impacts of Deep Packet Inspection Internet Surveillance. *Information, Communication & Society* 16 (8): 1328–1359.

Gaffney, Devin. 2010. #iranElection: Quantifying Online Activism. Paper presented at WebSci10: Extending the Frontiers of Society On-Line. Raleigh, North Carolina, 27–26 April.

Gang, Qian, and David Bandurski. 2011. China's Emerging Public Sphere. In *Changing Media, Changing China*, edited by Susan L. Shirk, 38–76. Oxford: Oxford University Press.

Gerbaudo, Paolo. 2012. *Tweets and the Streets: Social Media and Contemporary Activism*. London: Pluto Books.

Green, Alan. 2011. Upcoming Changes to Reader: A New Look, New Google+ Features, and Some Clean-Up. *The Official Google Reader Blog*. 20 October. http://googlereader.blogspot.nl/2011/10/upcoming-changes-to-reader-new-look-new.html.

Hayes, Ben. 2009. *NeoConOpticon: The EU Security-Industrial Complex*. Amsterdam: Transnational Institute/Statewatch.

Keller, Brett. 2011. Save Google Reader. 21 October. www.bdkeller.com/2011/10/save-google-reader/.

Kelly, Sanja, and Sarah Cook, eds. 2011. *Freedom on the Net 2011—a Global Assessment of Internet and Digital Media*. Ifap. http://www.ifap.ru/library/book497.pdf.

King, Gary, Jennifer Pan and Margaret E. Roberts. 2012. How Censorship in China Allows Government Criticism but Silences Collective Expression. Working paper, Institute for Quantitative Social Science, Harvard University. http://gking. harvard.edu/publications/how-censorship-china-allows-government-criticism-silences-collective-expression.

Langlois, Ganaele, Greg Elmer, Fenwick McKelvey and Zachary Devereaux. 2009. Networked Publics: The Double Articulation of Code and Politics on Facebook. *Canadian Journal of Communication* 34 (3): 415–434.

Lim, Merlyna. 2012. Clicks, Cabs, and Coffee Houses: Social Media and Oppositional Movements in Egypt 2004–2011. *Journal of Communication* 62 (2): 231–248.

Lotan, Gilad, Erhardt Graeff, Mike Ananny, Devin Gaffney, Ian Pearce and danah boyd. 2011. The Revolutions Were Tweeted: Information Flows during the 2011 Tunisian and Egyptian Revolutions. *International Journal of Communication* 5: 1375–1405.

Morozov, Evgeny. 2011. *The Net Delusion: How Not to Liberate the World*. London: Allen Lane/Penguin.

Moulier-Boutang, Yann. 2012. *Cognitive Capitalism*. Cambridge, UK: Polity.

Poell, Thomas, and Kaouthar Darmoni. 2012. Twitter as a Multilingual Space: The Articulation of the Tunisian Revolution through #sidibouzid. *NECSUS—European Journal of Media Studies* 1. http://www.necsus-ejms.org/twitter-as-a-multilingual-space-the-articulation-of-the-tunisian-revolution-through-sidibouzid-by-thomas-poell-and-kaouthar-darmoni/.

Poell, Thomas, Jeroen de Kloet and Guohua Zeng. 2013. Will the Real Weibo Please Stand Up? Chinese Online Contention and Actor-Network Theory. *Chinese Journal of Communication* 7 (1): 1–18.

Qiang, Xiao. 2011. The Rise of Online Public Opinion and Its Political Impact. In *Changing Media, Changing China*, edited by Susan L. Shirk, 202–224. Oxford: Oxford University Press.

Qinglian, He. 2008. *The Fog of Censorship*. New York: Human Rights in China.

Rahimi, Babak. 2011. The Agonistic Social Media: Cyberspace in the Formation of Dissent and Consolidation of State Power in Postelection Iran. *Communication Review* 14 (3): 158–178.

Reuters. 2012. Zuckerberg's Letter to Investors. February 1. http://www.reuters. com/article/2012/02/01/us-facebook-letter-idUSTRE8102MT20120201.

Rinke, Eike M., and Maria Röder. 2011. Media Ecologies, Communication Culture, and Temporal-Spatial Unfolding: Three Components in a Communication Model of the Egyptian Regime Change. *International Journal of Communication* 5: 1273–1285.

Roberts, Hal, Ethan Zuckerman and John Palfrey. 2011. *2011 Circumvention Tool Evaluation*. Berkman Center for Internet & Society. http://cyber.law.harvard.edu/ sites/cyber.law.harvard.edu/files/2011_Circumvention_Tool_Evaluation_1.pdf.

Roberts, Hal, Ethan Zuckerman, Jillian York, Robert Faris and John Palfrey. 2010. *2010 Circumvention Tool Usage Report*. Berkman Center for Internet & Society. http://cyber.law.harvard.edu/publications/2010/Circumvention_Tool_Usage.

Roberts, Hal, Ethan Zuckerman, Jillian York, Robert Faris and John Palfrey. 2011. *International Bloggers and Internet Control*. Berkman Center for Internet & Society. http://cyber.law.harvard.edu/publications/2011/International_Bloggers_ Internet_Control.

Shirk, Susan L. 2011. Changing Media, Changing China. In *Changing Media, Changing China*, edited by Susan L. Shirk, 1–37. Oxford: Oxford University Press.

Shirky, Clay. 2011. The Political Power of Social Media Technology, the Public Sphere, and Political Change. *Foreign Affairs*, January/February. http://www.foreignaffairs. com/articles/67038/clay-shirky/the-political-power-of-social-media.

Sullivan, Danny. 2011. Google to Begin Encrypting Searches & Outbound Clicks by Default with SSL Search. Search Engine Land. 18 October. http://searchengineland.com/google-to-begin-encrypting-searches-outbound-clicks-by-default-97435.

Tufekci, Zeynep, and Christopher Wilson. 2012. Social Media and the Decision to Participate in Political Protest: Observations from Tahrir Square. *Journal of Communication* 62: 363–379.

Van Dijck, José. 2013. *The Culture of Connectivity: A Critical History of Social Media*. New York: Oxford University Press.

Visual Vortex. 2011. Gooder Is Gone for Good. 2 November. http://visual-vortex.aminus3.com/image/2011–11–02.html.

Yang, Guobin. 2009. *The Power of the Internet in China: Citizen Activism Online*. New York: Columbia University Press.

———. 2012. A Chinese Internet? History, Practice, and Globalization. *Chinese Journal of Communication* 5 (1): 49–54.

Youmans, William L., and Jillian C. York. 2012. Social Media and the Activist Toolkit: User Agreements, Corporate Interests, and the Information Infrastructure of Modern Social Movements. *Journal of Communication* 62 (2): 315–329.

State Power as Policing and Intelligence

Section Five

State Power as Policing
and Intelligence

10 Vigilantism and Power Users
Police and User-Led Investigations on Social Media

Daniel Trottier

1. INTRODUCTION

This chapter addresses the shifting relation between citizens and state actors as a result of the continued adoption of social media platforms. In particular, it considers the emergence of different kinds of policing on these platforms. This includes individual users performing their own kind of citizen-led surveillance. Such practices are a kind of digital vigilantism, made meaningful through discourses and practices about empowered users. The social software, mobile hardware and telecommunications networks required to perform social media policing often market these products as empowering users by enabling them to coordinate social action. Thus, these practices mark a tendency to bypass existing state branches such as the police—all while maintaining a dependency on corporate social media platforms—in order to perform actions that would otherwise be monopolised by the state. While some commentators focus on positive outcomes associated with user counter-power (Shirky 2008), there is evidence of citizens using social media to harass and persecute fellow citizens.

The proliferation of user-led policing on social media—harmful or otherwise—suggests an increase of citizen counter-power, by virtue of the fact that citizens are able to coordinate on social media platforms. However, state branches such as the police and security agencies are also able to maintain and even further extend state power through their own investment in social media platforms. Furthermore, a range of corporate and state-produced technologies is made available to them in order to obtain a greater visibility over personal information contained on these sites. If citizen-led activity on social media amounts to a kind of empowerment or counter-power, state actors in turn can become power users on social media platforms. Thus, two general sets of policing take place on social media platforms, and both impact the nature of both visibility and sociality on these platforms.

This chapter provides an overview of several assertions of power and policing on social media in order to consider the coexistence of citizen counter-power and state power on these platforms. The following section offers a theoretically informed exploration of relations involving states, police and citizens on social media. Surveillance studies literature, as well as literature on policing and new media, is especially helpful for considering the relations between police and the public. Next, this chapter considers a series of examples that are indicative of state power on social media, citizen-led counter-power, and corporate attempts to enrol and monetise the latter. These examples are substantiated through an analysis of corporate brochures, as well as an analysis of public policing-themed communities on social media groups and websites.

2.   SURVEILLANCE, VISIBILITY, POLICE AND CITIZENS

Social media platforms like Facebook and Twitter allow citizen users to share information with other users, including their own personal details, the details of non-consenting citizens and information about state and corporate actors. Conversely, state and corporate actors have the potential to watch over and intervene on these platforms. As such, it is useful to think about the relations between users, states and corporations from a surveillance studies framework. Here, surveillance refers to the targeted and systematic monitoring of personal information (Lyon 2001). Surveillance is not entirely dissimilar to concepts like visibility, but it maintains a focus on societal consequences of access to and visibility of information, especially as a mode of organization in the context of state-citizen relations (Dandecker 1990). Here, social consequences include loss of privacy, but also categorical discrimination, social sorting and a chilling effect on public speech (Gandy 1993; Bowker and Starr 1999; Lyon 2003).

   Social media surveillance is characterised by the expansive growth of these services. Social media adopt new features and enrol new users, to an extent that challenges scholarly efforts to understand them. This is a challenge for scholars wanting to speak authoritatively about social media. But it is also a challenge that users face in their prolonged engagement with these sites. They invest their time and their identities when creating a presence online, and this investment is tied to assumptions about what the platform is, how it is used, who is using it and which values govern its use. All of these features have changed extensively, leaving users to cope with this volatility. Facebook among others is a public face to a constellation of surveillant agents. In addition to speaking about these separate kinds of monitoring as part of a broader category, we can also see how each of these practices changes as a result of social media. Previous work considers how a convergence of communicative flows leads to a collapse of formerly distinct social spheres (Fuchs and Trottier 2013). This imagery supports a leak-based view of social media. While information leaks were formerly exceptional events, social media's exponential increase of leaks amounts to a kind of convergence of social contexts. Such convergence amounts to a consolidation of visibility (all can be seen on one site), and of watching (all can watch on one site). Surveillance becomes decentralised, yet this convergence also facilitates a centralised kind of watching.

In terms of the way they retain and distribute personal information, social media platforms are a kind of digital enclosure (Andrejevic 2009). This refers to not only the way that information is generated on social media but also how it is retained. Users dwell in a controlled space that yields data from social interactions that occur on these sites. The coexistence of so many surveillance practices contributes to a mutual augmentation of visibility, such that any single act of surveillance has a much greater reach. The convergence of so many populations and institutions on these enclosures means that any single act of surveillance is amplified in its scope (Trottier 2012). One consequence is the extent to which user activity on social media augments police work. This augmentation stems from Andrejevic's study of lateral surveillance (2005), which focuses on how information technologies enhance scrutiny among peers. Social media augment this scrutiny by making these relations visible to police.

Because so many aspects of social life are made visible on platforms like Facebook, police and other investigators can exploit these sites to target suspected criminals and obtain evidence. Social media amplify policing not because of their technological sophistication but rather because of their social saturation. Social media's saturation is a result of their domestication (Silverstone and Haddon 1996)—that is, the extent to which they are embedded in everyday life. Whereas most technologies emerge in other spheres like the military and then spread to the domestic realm, Facebook's origins are firmly entrenched in everyday life. It developed a culture based on making university life visible, and then the consequences of this visibility emerged as Facebook opened up to institutions, including the police. This heightened surveillance of everyday life is noteworthy. Local interactions take place on global telecommunication networks. Mediated everyday activity is more visible to policing and investigations. Using social media technologies, investigators have an enhanced overview of everyday life.

Social media is repurposed for investigative means as a result of 'surveillance creep.' In other words, surveillance technologies deemed appropriate in one context can spread to new contexts and applications (Lyon 2007). Rather than an exceptional development, creeping is Facebook's standard model for growth. In its early days, Facebook restricted access to its information to students from a select range of North American universities. Gradually, Facebook became accessible to virtually anybody over the age of thirteen. And while its users may restrict access to their personal information through privacy settings, a series of advertising schemes and revisions to the interface facilitate information leaks into unexpected contexts. For police and other investigative agencies, this has been an opportunity to access details about individuals (Omand, Bartlett and Miller 2012; Williams et al., 2013). On the basis of these developments, we may consider police adoption of social media as an attempt to make use of an information platform, and integrate it within a broader organizational framework of evidence collection and processing. Social media platforms are sites for new practices, new social struggles and new attempts to assert authority. As social media are saturated in society, they become spaces over which states—and police—may attempt to exert power. Although they are deterritorialised in location (which complicates how they are regulated in terms of taxation, and by data protection laws), states assert their mandate to police these spaces. Insofar as police assert state power, and insofar that citizens are active on social media, police and states extend their mandate onto these platforms.

Social media are distributed technologies, in that dispersed users actively contribute content and coordinate among themselves through these sites. This marks a contrast from more centralised media like broadcast television, and suggests a potential empowerment of civil society in the face of state power. Yet distributed technologies do not preclude asymmetrical power relations. Numerous events show that top-down state power is just as prevalent as ever. In 2011, the Egyptian government shut down its country's telecommunications network, curbing the empowering potential otherwise linked to those technologies (Glanz and Markoff 2011). Likewise, the United Kingdom government allegedly ordered the removal of protest videos from YouTube (Travis 2011). In both cases, technology developers willingly complied with state power. Yet state control of social media goes beyond repression. States and institutions increasingly harness positive control over decentralised technologies, taking advantage of the way they make social life visible. Police and other investigators use it in ways that suggest asymmetrical access and asymmetrical relations of visibility.

As a result of social convergence, social media enables a diffuse kind of visibility for police work. This new visibility is not based on social media's technological sophistication, but simply their broad and enduring saturation in social life. They are diffuse and distributed, yet they are also centrally accessible. Police have relied on other techniques and technologies to watch over social life, but never has so much social life been accessible in a single enclosure. Moreover, the social convergence and mutual augmentation of different surveillance practices on one platform complicate—but ultimately enhance—police scrutiny. Everyday actions and conversations become online content. Archived and searchable, this content can be repurposed as evidence.

Social convergence on platforms like Facebook brings conventional policing closer to the social activity on these platforms. Conversely, this convergence has the consequence that users may also be empowered and compelled to perform policing. As part of social convergence on social media, crime and policing are made more visible and accessible to social media users. Platforms like Facebook are spaces where users can not only view information about crime and policing but also discuss these issues, submit what they believe to be evidence and call for social action beyond these sites.

User-led monitoring of citizens online is a kind of crowdsourced surveillance. Crowdsourcing refers to a process where individuals designated as non-professionals engage in a collaborative project for little to no financial compensation. Large crowds of non-specialised individuals now perform activities that would otherwise be reserved to a skilled few with professional designation. Crowdsourcing as a term emerged in a cultural context that celebrated the social virtues of freely available technologies (Surowiecki 2004; Howe 2008). Crowdsourcing serves as an entry point to conceptualise power and counter-power in a context of ubiquitous devices and shared—but uneven—access to networks. Crowds of empowered users may be considered in the context of citizenship and the manifestation of a kind of public space (Papacharissi 2002). Yet there is also evidence of abusive collective behaviour online in the form of stalking and harassment, but also vigilantism, where citizens police and persecute fellow citizens in a context of criminal justice. Furthermore, this phenomenon can be harnessed by state and corporate power.

The contemporary user is a product of both the entertainment and technology sectors. With crowdsourced CCTV surveillance over the Internet, policing and private security are actively involved in this socio-technical assemblage (cf. Haggerty and Ericson 2000). Galloway and Thacker (2007) consider how decentralised groups of individuals can be regulated through contemporary networking technologies. Crowds of users, or swarms, can operate autonomously within a broader framework that is guided by protocols. Whereas a police officer online is a sole actor, surveillance through crowds relies on a multitude of watchers, and thus more closely resembles a swarm. Human intentionality is thus superseded by the uncanny intentionality of the network as an aggregate and augmented and directed by networked technology. No single entity controls networks, yet networks remain sites of heightened control (ibid., 39). The swarm is a morphology of collective action that is suited for collective action (ibid., 98). Moreover, this collective action can be subsumed as a state or corporate strategy, as "rhizomatics and distribution signal a new management style, a new physics of organization that is as real as pyramidal hierarchy, corporate bureaucracy, representative democracy, sovereign at, or any other principle of social and political control" (ibid., 29). Here, Galloway and Thacker extend from Deleuze's control society framework (1995). The transition from central to decentralised and distributed organization is foregrounded by twentieth-century superpowers being challenged by autonomous insurgent swarms. Following the U.S. military's mandate to adopt distributed tactics, sovereign power can potentially circulate within distributed networks. This is made possible through protocols, which are defined as the broad set of rules that facilitate connectivity within networks (Galloway and Thacker 2007, 28–29). With crowdsourced policing, this includes technological protocols that determine how users submit and access content, but also how their efforts can be integrated into a greater surveillance scheme. Rhizomes, open to autonomous decision making, are thus framed under the domain of sovereign and distributed control at a cellular scale.

The Deleuzian framework lends support to the idea that increasingly open networks and increasingly expansive access do not result in the freedom often imagined in public discourse. Rather, belonging to an open network implies regulation at both a technical and political level. This is most apparently observed in the ongoing shift from broadcast media to two-way 'interactive' communication (ibid., 124). Interactivity suggests an opening-up: a transition towards a decentralised network of information exchange. Yet this also marks an exponential increase in visibility, surveillance and control. Protocols exist as taken-for-granted routines for organizing information, ensuring that categories and control can emerge from complexity. The formerly passive user is continuously encouraged to speak up. At best this information is simply exploited through monetisation strategies; at worst it is used to determine citizens' life-chances.

The kinds of surveillance made possible by crowdsourced efforts mark an "exponential multiplication of visibility" (Haggerty and Ericson 2000, 605), as formerly discrete surveillance practices (citizens watching citizens) are assembled into decentralised schemas. This presents two risks: on the one hand, distributed actors lack professional training, and can further discriminatory profiling and other concerns that have already been identified with professional surveillant agents (Norris and Armstrong 1999). Yet distributed networks also augment the possibility for centralised coercion and force. Thus, citizen counter-power does not always exist in direct opposition to state power, but instead can be a distributed manifestation of state power.

3. SOCIAL MEDIA POLICING: TOOLS FOR STATE POWER

Social media activity is typically framed in terms of user activity and, by extension, user empowerment (Shirky 2008). However, new technologies and legal protocols transform police and other agencies into power users. Investigative agencies benefit from an augmented visibility of social media content—and by extension the visibility of social life on these platforms. Social media were originally framed as part of the 'dark web,' which existing online surveillance techniques could not access. However, this is changing as a result of new ambitions envisioned by law enforcement (Gallagher 2013), proposed revisions to existing laws (Nazer 2012) and new social media surveillance technologies. This section considers the latter in some detail. We may think of police surveillance on social media as one single process, yet there are several categories of technologies available to agencies. Moreover, these technologies search social media content through different access points. As a result, they produce differing relations between state branches like the police, social media users and corporations that own and manage these platforms. What follows is a tentative set of social media surveillance technologies that have the potential of becoming tools of state power. This is not meant to be an exhaustive account of state-led social media surveillance, as both social media platforms and the monitoring technologies that accompany them are still in a formative stage. Moreover, we may assume that technologies and practices exist which may be knowable only through revelations similar to those by Edward Snowden in 2013.

First, police can perform manual searching on social media platforms. This technique refers to when an investigator takes advantage of content on sites like Facebook and Twitter as would a conventional user. This process is the most manual of all technologies described, as the investigator manually navigates the site's interface. This most typically involves publicly accessible data. In order to obtain private data on a social networking site, an investigator may submit a friend request to a targeted individual, or request to join a private group. Manual searching can be employed to target either a specific individual or a group of individuals. In the latter case, the investigator can either target a series of individual profiles or investigate a group, fan page or event page. Social media emerged as a possible investigative tool when individuals affiliated with security and intelligence organizations discovered that they could search these sites for information, as they would in an interpersonal context. Thus, it was a ground-level realization, rather than a top-down mandate, that introduced social media as an investigative tool (Trottier 2011).

Second, law enforcement agencies can contact social media companies directly and request specific content about a suspect. This is also a manual process, as investigators have to determine what content they want to obtain. However, the process of collecting the data is offloaded onto the social networking site company themselves. The data involved can be publicly accessible, but private data can also be retrieved. One can presume that this method is employed primarily to obtain private data, as public data can simply be obtained from the website directly.

Third, investigators can perform searches of 'open-source intelligence' (OSINT). This refers to the use of non-private online data for intelligence and investigations (Omand, Bartlett and Miller 2012). This includes social networking site data that is not protected by privacy settings. This approach is a mix of manual and automated searching. While the investigator has to manually specify the search criteria and range, the tool will then automatically retrieve this data. Such tools can be used to target groups of individuals, whereas it would be unconventional to use them to target a single individual. As social media platforms develop a greater presence in social life, their users will continue to submit information, much of which is publicly accessible. As a result, these publicly accessible bodies of information provide unique insight into past, ongoing and future criminal events.

Fourth, lawful interception involves directly intercepting the communication flow and obtaining information that is sent or received by a suspect. Lawful interception allows investigators to obtain information that is both private and public according to a social networking service's privacy setting. However, it is also private in the sense that it is intercepting a secure information flow. Lawful interception refers to "the process of secretly intercepting within a network communications between parties of interest to Law Enforcement Agencies" (Branch 2003, 1). This process is commonly referred to as 'wire-tapping,' and has been used historically to intercept telephone networks. As communications increasingly take place over the Internet, including social media, there is a push among law enforcement agencies and private security technology manufacturers to facilitate lawful interception online. Lawful interception targets an individual connection, yet this connection can either belong to a group or contain information pertaining to a group of individuals. Once the data has been intercepted, Deep Packet Inspection (DPI) is the process by which the flow of online content is rendered legible. By monitoring the message content, DPI allows for real-time surveillance, and can be integrated into other equipment, "thus creating the possibility for major economies of scope in implementation" (Bendrath and Mueller 2011, 1144).

Fifth, investigators can obtain social media information by installing software on the targeted individual's computer. This is typically done with a Trojan, which is software that masks its true functions by appearing to perform a separate—and more benign—function. Once the Trojan has been installed, it automatically intercepts data generated on the target's computer. It also automatically distinguishes between different kinds of data, and can specifically target data from a social media service. This is arguably the most private kind of surveillance, as it collects data directly from the targeted end user's computer. Not only can information obscured by privacy settings be obtained, but also user names and passwords to social media accounts can be sought. This approach targets an individual's computer, but the targeted computer may be employed by several individuals—for instance, a criminal enterprise or political group. This technology has been publicly associated with state surveillance in Germany (DW.de 2011), among other countries. Due to its ability to access the entirety of a targeted citizen's computer, it allows for a comparatively totalising optic over citizen communication.

Sixth, social media data that has been captured can then serve as the basis for subsequent kinds of analysis. Various applications can accept social media input in order to provide some kind of social mapping. These systems do not distinguish between private and public data, but rather function with whatever data has been previously collected. Four categories of analysis are considered ahead.

First, event reconstruction services can provide a reconstruction of an event by sorting out and mapping social media data in a temporal and spatial manner, using time- and location-based data and metadata. The London Metropolitan Police purchased such software (Gallagher and Syal 2011), which provides an aggregated account of future riots and other activity through the collection and processing of citizen communicative data.

Second, sentiment analysis services claim to be able to assess the emotions and opinions of a group of people, based on words used in social media communications. Sentiment analysis has a number of practical applications. In the domain of market research, it provides insight into how a targeted market segment feels about a particular product, brand or public relation concerns. In the domain of security and law enforcement, sentiment analysis purportedly can assist in identifying violent extremists—but also peaceful activists—as a result of the textual content that they upload. Thus, state-led sentiment analysis can amount to a kind of polling of citizen opinion, albeit without citizen awareness or consent. Third, images and names obtained on social media platforms can be assessed using facial recognition software. This is a feature that social media companies have integrated into their platforms—for instance, with Facebook's introduction of Tag Suggestions in 2011. Tag Suggestions works by requesting that the user identify faces that appear in photographs. Once names are associated with faces, the Tag Suggestion features purports to then automatically identify those users in subsequent photographs. Following the 2011 riots in Vancouver, the Insurance Corporation of British Columbia (ICBC) provided the Vancouver Police with their driver's licence database, and also offered their facial recognition software (CBC 2011) in order to identify the faces of suspected rioters in social media content provided by citizens. Fourth, social media profiles contain relational data. This includes not only an individual's friends, subscribers, etc. but also data that measures the extent to which one individual communicates with these associates. Mapping out social relations is relevant in its own right, as communication patterns online can serve as intelligence in an investigation, especially when this information also contains locational and temporal metadata. In addition, recent scholarship on social networking sites provides support for the idea that we can predict attributes about people on the basis of the company they keep.[1]

The foregoing constitutes a range of techniques and technologies that exploit social media data, as well as social media platforms. These six methods each target specific points in the communication process on social networking sites. Manual search on a platform involves creating a profile on the social networking platform, and accessing either public information from public sections of profiles or private information from profiles with which the investigator has a connection. In the case of legal compliance by social networking sites, police will contact the platform operator directly, who will then provide both public and private content from the site. In the case of open source intelligence, an external service is used to access public content from the platform. With lawful interception, data is accessed at the communication stage. This is typically performed at the level of the service provider, but interception can occur at other stages—for instance, on a telephone line. Targeted interception, such as Trojans, retrieves data directly from the target's computer. Finally, once social networking data has been collected, investigators can then perform further types of analysis, including sentiment analysis and facial recognition. As such, virtually any point in the communication process between citizens can be repurposed as intelligence or evidence. A broad range of technologies—including hardware, software, techniques and assemblages of the foregoing—make up a robust set of systems from which social media content is accessible to police and other investigators. Given the novelty of these technologies, coupled with a general lack of awareness of how they function, several concerns are apparent.

For the public, relations with the police and awareness of current and potential police practices are compromised by a general opacity surrounding social network analysis by investigators. This opacity is twofold: not only are the public unaware of when the systems just described are put to use, but also they are often unaware that these systems are used in their jurisdiction. The lack of public knowledge surrounding these systems, their affordances and their social consequences is striking when public interest in social media platforms is so high. Moreover, this asymmetry of visibility between the public and the police can harm civil society. Thus, any discussion of citizen counter-power and social media communication must consider the multifaceted possibility that this communication is intercepted and repurposed by branches of state power.

4.   VIGILANTISM AND THE FULL SPECTRUM OF USER/CITIZEN POWER

The previous section considered the expansion of police powers through new investigative techniques and technologies on social media platforms. In contrast, this section considers bottom-up (that is, user-led) crowdsourced policing. Users are able to direct visibility and scrutiny against instances of police misconduct (Goldsmith 2010; chapter 11, this volume). Yet there is a broader spectrum of user activity of relevance to notions of state activity, politics and power. Citizens may use social and mobile media to target and persecute fellow citizens in what can be considered digital vigilantism, a form of crowdsourced policing. Digital vigilantism is a process where citizens are collectively offended by other citizen activity, and respond through coordinated retaliation on digital media platforms, including mobile devices and social media platforms. The offending acts range from mild breaches of social protocol to terrorist acts and participation in riots. These offensive acts are not meant as a provocation in the context in which the vigilantism is situated. Therefore, the targets of digital vigilantism are typically unaware of the conflict in which they have been enrolled.

This vigilantism includes but is not limited to a 'naming and shaming' style visibility. This typically involves sharing the targeted individual's personal details by publishing/distributing them on a public site ('doxing'), including highly sensitive details like the target's home address, work details and financial/medical information. This is done with the intention of supporting conventional criminal justice procedures by making the target visible to police and other agencies, but also through unconventional forms of justice such as harassment. The visibility produced through digital vigilantism is unwanted (the target is typically not soliciting publicity), intense (content like blog posts, photos and video evidence can circulate to hundreds of thousands or even millions of users within a few days) and enduring (the vigilantism campaign may be the first item to appear when searching the individual's name online, and may become a cultural reference in its own right).

These practices rely extensively on contemporary digital media culture. Social media platforms, including social news platforms like Reddit, serve as locations where citizen users can easily converge to discuss and coordinate a response. These are also locations where the target's personal details are published. In addition, mobile devices such as smartphones, tablets and digital cameras enable real-time recording and transmission of an offending act onto social media platforms, and thus to other citizen-users. As an example of digital vigilantism, consider the response to the 2011 Vancouver riot, where Facebook users identified and shamed suspected criminals. Users took advantage of ubiquitous mobile cameras, an element that was missing from previous hockey riots. These riots are not a novelty in Canada, but they have always had a degree of anonymity; they were never this visible. Yet in 2011 they yielded an unprecedented amount of social media content. Riot-themed groups grew on Facebook, and one entitled "Vancouver Riot Pics: Post Your Photos" garnered over one hundred thousand users, over five million views, and countless photographs in under five days. The group marks a shift towards greater citizen-led policing of social life through social media and mobile technology. Users directly contributed photographs, names and descriptions of incidents. When suspected rioters are made visible online, 'naming and shaming' becomes a distinct kind of punishment. Following the Vancouver riot, the first charges were not issued for six months (VPD 2011), yet the visibility and persecution found on the Facebook group had an immediate impact on the lives of suspected rioters (*Globe and Mail* 2011). Other instances of such digital vigilantism can be found on social media. Following the Boston Marathon Bombing, Reddit wrongly identified Sunil Tripathi as one of the suspects, resulting in an intense visibility and persecution that pushed him to commit suicide. Other sites allow users to post identifying information about petty thieves[2] and bad drivers.[3]

Prior to social media, vigilantism was typically framed as a kind of private violence (Culberson 1990) whereby citizens would take criminal justice matters into their own hands. Whereas the state is said to hold a monopoly on violent activity, vigilantism refers to instances where citizens deny this state monopoly, in an attempt to legitimate their own violent acts. In the case of digital media, claims of legitimated violence are more explicit, as these conversations are posted to these platforms. Related to this is the fact that vigilantism is typically related to the nation: vigilantism is a national problem manifest within national borders (ibid.). This can be seen in the use of nationalist and xenophobic rhetoric in vigilantism. However, the coupling of digital media and vigilantism complicates the relation to any single nation. While there is evidence that digital vigilantism retains some nationalist sentiment, it is in no way contained to any single border. The backlash to the 2011 Vancouver riot made a clear distinction between a local 'us' and an outsider 'them' (Schneider and Trottier 2013). Yet even criminal acts such as uttering death threats and harassment can occur in any jurisdiction. As a result, the relation between vigilantism, citizenship and nationalism needs to be reconsidered in the digital age.

Digital vigilantism is taking place in a context where citizens are coming to terms with the relation between online activity and offline consequences. While the 'early web' was characterised by a distinction between online and offline, the emergence of social, geolocated, ubiquitous media has led to a dissolution to any such barrier, to the extent that digital media activity can have lasting consequences in both a local and global context. Thus, digital vigilantism participants may not be aware of the actual impact of their actions. It is also important to note that digital vigilantism is as much a communicative and mediated act as it is a collective social act. In other words, vigilantism on digital media can be framed in the context of online communication: the sharing of personal details, photos and videos, adding commentary, discussion, debate and calls for grounded/situated action. However, all of these actions amount to coordinated mass persecution of a targeted citizen. Researchers, but also courts, educators and policymakers need to consider the full ramifications of this activity.

There are a series of social problems linked with digital vigilantism. First, it constitutes a severe violation of privacy and data protection rights of the targeted individual, as his or her personal details are publicly transmitted without their consent. Beyond this, targets may be selected on the basis of visible identifiers, such as ethnicity and religion, which can further discrimination. Digital vigilantism also mounts to a kind of parallel policing, or a kind of criminal justice response that is performed by untrained nonprofessionals (Trottier 2013). This policing is typically manifest as a series of crimes, including harassment, stalking and death threats.

Digital vigilantism is indicative of a complicated relationship between citizen counter-power and state power. While citizens are bypassing police to perform their own kind of policing—and violating state laws in the process— they are often guided by a loosely interpreted form of law-and-order politics that may in fact support state power. Subsequent research will need to consider this potential in further detail. Yet it is clear that police are developing ways to exploit digital vigilantism with strategies that simultaneously bypass and enrol users. While the police still rely on social media users to submit this content, it is only their content that matters. The increased scrutiny of sites like Facebook suggests that while users can be active agents through self-expression and social coordination, so too are they visible and accessible to institutions and governments, reduced to searchable and contextually relevant content. They may choose to actively contribute to police work and social scrutiny more generally, but they are always involved through their digital presence. Individuals and police are collaborating, but this is often an unwilling partnership. The developments described ahead suggest that users are made all the more visible as a result of the personal information that they and their peers upload on social media. They are also decoupled from that evidence when it comes to investigative practices. In effect, social media content speaks on users' behalf.

5. CROWDSOURCING USER EMPOWERMENT AS CORPORATE STRATEGY

Digital vigilantism is a phenomenon where policing is performed by a self-organizing crowd of users. Yet many examples of such crowdsourcing have a top-down organizational structure. In the context of crowdsourced surveillance, business models harness user activity in order to supplement existing top-down policing and surveillance, but also to yield a profit. Thus, state power and corporate power intersect in exploiting user activity on digital media platforms. While these initiatives are not exclusively located on social media, they represent an increased presence of crowdsourced surveillance on digital media that are regulated by institutions. An early example of such criminal justice crowdsourcing is Blueservo. This project was first proposed in 2006 with the intention of crowdsourcing the policing of the Texas region of the U.S.-Mexico border. It is "designed to empower the public to proactively participate in fighting border crime."[4] Its creators also emphasise the fact that this is a free service for users. Likewise, this crowdsourcing intersects with the media culture of crime-based reality shows like *Crimewatch* and *America's Most Wanted*, which made appeals to their audiences for personal information about suspects (Fishman and Cavender 1998).

Following BlueServo, other initiatives attempted to regulate the crowd-sourced surveillance of social life online. Internet Eyes[5] acted as an intermediary between businesses that require personnel to sort through their CCTV footage and individuals who want to do this work. Businesses paid seventy-five pounds per month to have a crowd of individuals watch over their shop via CCTV footage that is live-streamed over the Internet. Individuals included anyone from EU/EEA countries, as well any countries with a data sharing agreement with the EU. For legal reasons they also paid a membership fee of up to £1.99 per month. CCTV feeds were transferred from the store's cameras to the site's servers, at which point it was encrypted and then accessed by the user. Feeds from all clients were combined, randomised and anonymised, in order to prevent users from determining the location of a camera. Users accessed four feeds at once, which they could refresh at any point to obtain new feeds. Otherwise, new feeds were automatically selected after twenty minutes. As an element of gamification (Whitson 2013), users were awarded points if they alerted the business to a crime, and they lost points if the business suspected they provided a false or malicious alert. Internet Eyes offered a monthly £1,000 reward to the user with the highest score, as well as hourly payments well below the minimum wage.

Although Internet Eyes had many supporters between its user base and the media, it also elicited controversy and sanctions. The UK Information Commissioner's Office (ICO) ordered the company to take better measures when footage from their site was leaked onto YouTube (Brewster 2011). James Welch, legal director of the civil liberties organization Liberty, questioned the professionalism of crowdsourced operators: "If we're going to have so many CCTV cameras in this country, then we need to be reassured that they're being operated professionally" (Price 2010). With Internet Eyes, a kind of corporate power called upon untrained citizens to act as surrogates of state power. Internet Eyes has also received the attention of civil liberties group Big Brother Watch. This group also expressed concerns over privacy, describing Internet Eyes as "a rather, well, creepy project which allows voyeurs sitting in their living room to watch CCTV networks and report people suspected of committing crimes for cash rewards" (Big Brother Watch 2011). They also raised concerns that users outside of the UK would not be bound by national data protection laws. In effect, these watchers were "outside of the law" (ibid.). This calls into question notions of state sovereignty, as citizens of one state may be enrolled to watch over citizens of another state.

In September 2013, the Internet Eyes Facebook page reported that they have "ceased trading with immediate effect,"[6] citing a series of financial and organizational obstacles. This suggests that novel attempts to couple state power, corporate power and citizen counter-power may be fledgling, and felled not by citizen protest or policy recommendations, but simply through their own insolvency. Yet corporate and state power continues to intersect in their respective management of citizen-led activity on social media, as the other chapters in this volume attest. Other corporate efforts will emerge in the coming years in order to revisit this potential exploitation of crowdsourced policing. As Internet Eyes' Facebook page also reports, "Hold fast our friends, for patience gives us new dawn, new light, a new horizon of united possibilities, what mirth awaits our eyes this morn."[7]

6. CONCLUSION

Social media platforms are repurposed not only for conventional policing online but also for user-led vigilantism and corporately managed crowdsourced policing. Ground-up and top-down forms of policing do not exist independently. Rather, they interact with and influence one another. In some instances bottom-up policing can counter conventional police work (e.g., through initiatives like CopWatch),[8] or interfere with it (through acts of digital vigilantism). Yet in other circumstances it reinforces police work, regardless of whether this is the intention. The foregoing examples suggest that although digital media can potentially empower users, so too does it enable a ground-up manifestation of state power in the form of law-and-order politics, including profiling and discrimination. User-led activity is not necessarily socially progressive, as it can potentially be a reproduction of discriminatory and other harmful police practices. At the same time, while all of the foregoing may be a kind of general counter-power by the mere fact that users themselves are performing a kind of policing, actual police activity on social media suggests that conventional state power prevails. Users and members of the public may be willing participants in police work, but also unwilling participants when their personal information is repurposed as evidence. Thus, the relationship between citizens, states and corporations is not revolutionised by social media platforms. While the communicative and other technological affordances of these platforms may impact state power, corporate power and citizen counter-power, these too will in turn influence what is possible and what is probable on Facebook, Twitter and others.

Both individual users and the state have embraced social media, and seemingly they have also embraced the policing of these platforms. With emerging techniques and privileged access, police can effectively bypass privacy barriers and other attempts to maintain secrecy. Social media policing is indicative of a new paradigm of visibility. Social media users produce staggering quantities of information on social media and other domestic technologies that are currently not fully visible to conventional watchers. A number of new police technologies and practices ensure a heightened surveillance of social media. A mix of domestic, decentralised technologies like social media and ubiquitous mobile devices, coupled with centralised databases and mandates, amounts to an exponential increase in visibility (Haggerty and Ericson 2000). All are made more visible, but these developments also augment the possibility for profiling, as well as anticipatory policing. Another risk is that the foregoing techniques become standard and reproduced in other branches of social media sociality. Not only does social media visibility creep into policing, but also social media policing may creep into the rest of social media sociality. This risk is especially viable when users come to criminalise their content and connections, and begin policing their own interpersonal networks.

Subsequent research requires multiple sites of focus. To be sure, investigative agencies ought to be under greater scrutiny. Agencies that are able to know so much about social life should in turn remain visible to scholarly research. In addition, research should focus on how these technologies and practices reshape relations between suspects and peers. As social media policing shifts from exceptional to default, criminal suspects will undoubtedly rethink their relations with peers. The continued saturation of social media platforms in social life, including state surveillance and policing, as well as the revelation of high-powered methods to aggregate and sort out social media data, amounts to a perpetual 'beginning' in this domain. Police users in particular report that their activity on sites like Facebook is both formative and tentative. Along new social, technological and legal developments, scholars in critical digital media studies as well as public figures should maintain a focus on the growth of social media policing, in order to maintain public awareness of how social media data renders social life visible to police and other investigators.

NOTES

1. For an example of determining sexual orientation based on social networks, see Jernigan and Mistree (2009).
2. Robbed in Barcelona, http://www.Robbedinbarcelona.com. Accessed 15 April, 2014.
3. Bad Parking, Tumblr, http://www.Bad-parking.tumblr.com. Accessed 15 April, 2014.
4. Blueservo. http://www.blueservo.net/. Accessed 21 September, 2013 [Note: this site has been shut down.]
5. InternetEyes EP[10] http://interneteyes.co.uk/. Accessed 15 April, 2014.
6. InternetEyes, Facebook. https://www.facebook.com/InternetEyes/posts/101516 49235249072?stream_ref=10. Accessed 21 September 2013 [Note: this posting has been removed.]
7. Ibid.
8. Welcome to Copwatch.com, Copwatch. http://www.copwatch.org/. Accessed 15 April, 2014.

REFERENCES

Andrejevic, Mark. 2005. The Work of Watching One Another: Lateral Surveillance, Risk, and Governance. *Surveillance & Society* 2 (4): 479–497.
———. 2009. Privacy, Exploitation, and the Digital Enclosure. *Amsterdam Law Forum* 1 (4): 47–62.
Bendrath, Ralf, and Milton Mueller. 2011. The End of the Net as We Know It? Deep Packet Inspection and Internet Governance. *New Media & Society* 13 (7): 1142–1160.
Big Brother Watch. 2011. New Privacy Concerns about Internet Eyes. http://www.big brotherwatch.org.uk/home/2011/03/new-privacy-concerns-about-internet-eyes. html.
Bowker, Geoffrey C., and Susan Leigh Starr. 1999. Sorting Thing Out: Classification and Its Consequences. Cambridge, MA: MIT Press.
Branch, Philip. A. 2003. *Lawful Interception of the Internet*. CAIA Technical Report 030606A.
Brewster, Tom. 2011. CCTV Service Internet Eyes Forced into Privacy Changes. *IT Pro*. 14 June. http://www.itpro.co.uk/634201/cctv-service-internet-eyes-forced-into-privacy-changes.
CBC. 2011. Insurance Corporation Offers to Help ID Rioters. CBC.ca. 18 June. http://www.cbc.ca/news/canada/british-columbia/insurance-corporation-offers-to-help-id-rioters-1.1050024.
Culberson, William. 1990. *Vigilantism: Political History of Private Power in America*. Westport, CT: Greenwood Press.

Dandecker, Christopher. 1990. *Surveillance, Power and Modernity: Bureaucracy and Discipline from 1700 to the Present Day.* Cambridge, UK: Polity.

Deleuze, Gilles. 1995. Postscript on Societies of Control. *October* 59 (Winter): 3–7.

Dw.de. 2011. Several German States Admit to Use of Controversial Spy Software. 11 October. http://www.dw.de/several-german-states-admit-to-use-of-controversial-spy-software/a-15449054-1.

Fishman, Mark, and Gray Cavender, eds. 1998. *Entertaining Crime: Television Reality Programs.* New York: Aldine De Gruyter.

Gallagher, Ryan. 2013. FBI Pursuing Real-Time Gmail Spying Powers as "Top Priority" for 2013. Slate.com. 26 March. http://www.slate.com/blogs/future_tense/2013/03/26/andrew_weissmann_fbi_wants_real_time_gmail_dropbox_spying_power.html.

Gallagher, Ryan, and Rajeev Syal. 2011. Police Buy Software to Map Suspects' Digital Movements. *Guardian*, 11 May. http://www.theguardian.com/uk/2011/may/11/police-software-maps-digital-movements.

Galloway, Alexander, and Eugene Thacker. 2007. *The Exploit: A Theory of Networks.* Minneapolis: University of Minnesota Press.

Gandy, Oscar. 1993. *The Panoptic Sort: A Political Economy of Personal Information.* Boulder, CO: Westview.

Goldsmith, Andrew J. 2010. Policing's New Visibility. *British Journal of Criminology* 50 (5): 914–934.

Glanz, James, and John Markoff. 2011. Egypt Leaders Found "Off" Switch for Internet. *New York Times*, 15 February, A1.

Globe and Mail. 2011. Water Polo Player Suspended over Alleged Involvement in Canucks Riot. 19 June. http://www.theglobeandmail.com/sports/hockey/water-polo-player-suspended-over-alleged-involvement-in-canucks-riot/article583671/.

Haggerty, Kevin D., and Richard V. Ericson. 2000. The Surveillant Assemblage. *British Journal of Sociology* 51 (4): 605–622.

Howe, Jeff. 2008. *Crowdsourcing: Why the Power of the Crowd Is Driving the Future of Business.* New York: Three Rivers Press.

Jernigan, Carter, and Behram F.T. Mistree. 2009. Gaydar: Facebook Friendships Expose Sexual Orientation. *First Monday* 10 (5). http://firstmonday.org/htbin/cgiwrap/bin/ojs/index.php/fm/article/view/2611/2302.

Lyon, David. 2001. *Surveillance Society: Monitoring Everyday Life.* Buckingham: Open University Press.

———. 2003. *Surveillance after September 11.* Cambridge, UK: Polity.

———. 2007. *Surveillance Studies: An Overview.* Cambridge, UK: Polity.

Nazer, Daniel. 2012. Australia Moves to Massively Expand Internet Surveillance. Center for Internet and Society Blog. 28 August. http://cyberlaw.stanford.edu/blog/2012/08/australia-moves-massively-expand-internet-surveillance.

Norris, Clive, and Gary Armstrong. 1999. *The Maximum Surveillance Society: The Rise of CCTV.* New York: Berg.

Omand, Sir David, Jamie Bartlett and Carl Miller. 2012. Introducing Social Media Intelligence (SOCMINT). *Intelligence and National Security* 27 (6): 801–823.

Papacharissi, Zizi. 2002. The Virtual Sphere: The Internet as a Public Sphere. *New Media and Society* 4 (1): 9–27.

Price, Peter. 2010. Who Is Watching You on CCTV? BBC News. 27 November. http://news.bbc.co.uk/2/hi/programmes/click_online/9232158.stm.

Schneider, Christopher J., and Daniel Trottier. 2013. Social Media and the 2011 Vancouver Riot. *Studies in Symbolic Interaction* 40: 335–362.

Shirky, Clay. 2008. *Here Comes Everybody: The Power of Organizing without Organizations.* New York: The Penguin Press.

Silverstone, Roger, and Leslie Haddon. 1996. Design and the Domestication of Information and Communication Technologies: Technical Change and Everyday Life. In *Communication by Design: The Politics of Information and Communication*

Technologies, edited by Roger Silverstone and Robin Mansell, 44–74. Oxford: Oxford University Press.

Surowiecki, James. 2004. *The Wisdom of Crowds*. New York: Anchor Books.

Travis, Hannibal. 2011. YouTube from Afghanistan to Zimbabwe: Tyrannize Locally, Censor Globally. Florida International University Legal Studies Research Paper No. 11–10. http://ssrn.com/abstract=1809952.

Trottier, Daniel. 2011. Mutual Transparency or Mundane Transgressions? Institutional Creeping on Facebook. *Surveillance & Society* 9 (1–2): 17–30.

———. 2012. *Social Media as Surveillance: Rethinking Visibility in a Converging World*. Farnham: Ashgate.

———. 2013. Crowdsourcing CCTV Surveillance on the Internet. *Information, Communication & Society*. doi:10.1080/1369118X.2013.808359

VPD. 2011. Crown Counsel Approves First Wave of Riot Charges. Vancouver Police Department. 30 November. http://mediareleases.vpd.ca/2011/11/30/crown-counsel-approves-first-wave-of-riot-charges/.

Whitson, Jennifer. 2013. Gaming the Quantified Self. *Surveillance & Society* 11 (1–2): 163–176.

Williams, Matthew L., Adam Edwards, William Housley, Peter Burnap, Omer Rana, Nick Avais, Jeffrey Morgan and Luke Sloan. 2013. Policing Cyber-neighbourhoods: Tension Monitoring and Social Media Networks. *Policing and Society: An International Journal of Research and Policy* 23 (4): 461–481.

11 Police 'Image Work' in an Era of Social Media

YouTube and the 2007 Montebello Summit Protest

Christopher J. Schneider

1. INTRODUCTION

The Sûreté du Québec (SQ, the provincial police force of Quebec, Canada) and the Royal Canadian Mounted Police (RCMP, Canada's national police force) were each tasked with overseeing security at the 2007 Montebello summit held August 20–21 at the Château resort in western Quebec. Clandestine police tactics at the summit that might have otherwise gone unnoticed were brought to the attention of the public by a citizen-recorded video posted to popular social media site YouTube.

The summit is noteworthy because the short 5:23 minute video led to the eventual police admission of the use of undercover officers disguised as protesters at the summit. Critics charged that the officers were *agents provocateurs* sent to disrupt the protest by inciting violence. After a short period of denials, the SQ admitted planting undercover officers, but maintained (through official statements located in news media reports, as detailed ahead) that the officers were not acting as *provocateurs* and had no intention of inciting violence. This circumstance is unique because it was among the very first occurrences in Canada where user-generated footage uploaded to video-sharing site YouTube elicited an official police response *offered in defence* of police tactics.

This chapter examines police 'image work,' or how police maintain control over their public perception via the media as *the* legitimate authority (Ericson 1982, 10). The importance of amending Ericson's ideas on image work is relevant to our greater understandings of the expansion of police 'legitimation work' (Ericson 1982, 1): it now includes social media. Examining this process following the 2007 Montebello summit provides insight into contemporary developments of police social power in response to the circulation of discrediting materials online.

A basic argument advanced herein is that police social power—by way of controlling the definition of the situation—is *reinforced* by social media users who cite news media reports that feature official police statements as affirmation of police planting undercover agents at the 2007 Montebello summit protest. This finding underscores a tension between police power and citizen counter-power that is not addressed in the research literature on the Montebello summit.

Altheide (1995, xi) tells us, "Social power is about controlling and enforcing the definition of a situation." Social power is closely connected with social control, or the process in which situations are understood *and* defined; however, "those who are in the situation ordinarily do not *create* this definition" (Goffman 1974, 1 emphasis in original). Situations are more ordinarily defined by powerful state-sanctioned social control agencies, such as police. Police are a unique group with special powers that include the authorised use of deadly force. Power "involves the probability that one party in an encounter can effect a course of action and outcome he desires in spite of the contrary wishes and/or actions of the other parties" (Ericson 1982, 12). This process[1] now includes growing numbers of people online who collectively challenge police authority (i.e., definitional claims).

Social media offer widely accessible public platforms that allow citizen challenges to definitional claims to emerge and sometimes quickly gain momentum. Police authority has been directly challenged in the past in the form of public protests and demonstrations; however, a key contemporary difference concerns the manner in which social media platforms allow users to mobilise en masse much more quickly, and often around some form of publicly accessible empirical evidence (e.g., videos of police brutality).

Social media consist of a hybrid between media and social interaction. A key feature of these media involves user-generated content, which can include, for instance, the recording, uploading and online circulation of amateur videos. The presence and widespread availability of this content online have ushered in a new era of citizen-led challenges to police control and authority. Police respond to these affronts as contests over their social power, thus providing perspective into the legitimation of police authority as a broadly constituted meaning-making process.

According to Manning, the "legitimation of the police in terms of legal authority flows from the power of the state and citizens' deference" (1997, 49). Police accomplish this control over citizens through "impression management" (Manning 1978). This includes bringing selected information "into play" (e.g., demonstrating competence and trustworthiness to an intended audience) which helps to define a situation (Goffman 1959).

Police 'presentational strategies' are largely symbolic (Manning 1978, 1997) and usually require explicit promotion in both news media (Fishman 1980) and, more recently, in social media (Schneider forthcoming a). These strategies are conveyed through rhetoric (Klockars 1988; Manning 1978) that includes claims of professional and bureaucratic competency that demonstrate organizational effectiveness (Skolnick 1966) as the primary controllers and definers of crime-related matters (Doyle 2003; Ericson 1982, 1995; Tuchman 1978).

Because of the use of violence in policing, police work is subject to citizen complaints, complicating police 'professionalism' (Manning 1997). For this reason, police conceal this information from the public whenever possible: police misconduct has gone almost entirely unmonitored by members of the public (ibid.). Recent developments in social media have changed this process, lending increased importance to police 'image work'—an important strategy that police employ "to support the view that the police are struggling to keep the lid on massive amounts of deviance in the community" (Ericson 1982, 10). Increasingly, this includes police deviance (Kappeler, Sluder and Alpert 1998).

The proliferation of social media has exacerbated the increased necessity for police image work in two discernible ways. First, police may choose to respond to public demands only when crimes are brought to their attention. The production of user-generated materials on social media can lead to increased pressure on police agencies to appear efficient in dealing with, and responding to, public concerns of crime. Second, police are increasingly less able to control information that might cast officers or the institution in an unfavourable light (e.g., citizen accusations and user-generated videos of misconduct, brutality and other forms of police deviance).

Police image work has become increasingly visible to the public through social media. These changing conditions allow a few basic questions to emerge: How do police maintain control over their public image and legitimate authority in an era of social media? And what insight might this provide to our understandings of social power? To address these questions, I consider police image work in response to a video posted on YouTube of a protest at the 2007 Montebello summit (Quebec, Canada). The importance of the event rests less with the summit itself and more with the YouTube revelation and subsequent police admission of the use of undercover police at the protest.

2. POLICE AND YOUTUBE

YouTube launched (to the public) on December 15, 2005 (Ratliff 2006), as a video sharing site when sharing videos online was still a relatively novel idea. In February 2006, the site attracted unwanted attention from corporate television giant NBC for copyright infringement, and over the ensuing months, the site exploded in popularity. Acquired later in the year by Google Inc., YouTube is now one of the most popular search engines in the world. Each day the site streams billions of videos and users upload dozens of hours of video by the minute (Oreskovic 2012). The popularity of the site is driven, in large part, by the uploading of user-generated amateur videos.

Due to the integration of mobile phones with recording technologies (camera and video), amateur-produced content can now include surreptitious recordings of people engaged in deviant acts or, worse, conduct run afoul of the law, including actions of police misconduct and brutality. The first reported video documentation of police abuse posted to YouTube appears to have occurred late in 2006.

In November of that year, a citizen-recorded mobile phone video of an arrest made by two officers of the Los Angeles Police Department (LAPD) in California sparked relative controversy when it was posted by 'Cop Watch LA' to YouTube (a few months following the August arrest). An investigation of the incident had begun immediately following the arrest (prior to the posting of the video on YouTube), as this is reportedly standard LAPD protocol regarding all allegations of police abuse. The video, denounced by groups like the American Civil Liberties Union (ACLU), was instead used as evidence *against* the arrestee for resisting arrest. According to a report published in the *New York Times*,

> At a hearing in September, a court commissioner found [after reviewing the video that was provided to lawyers] that [arrestee] Mr. Cardenas used force to resist arrest and that the officers' response was "more than reasonable."(*New York Times* 2006, A20)

By the end of 2006, sometimes referred to as "the year of online video," reports of various YouTube facilitated arrests begin to surface more regularly. For instance, a December *Globe and Mail* (Canada's national newspaper of record) story with the headline "YouTube clips led to racers' arrest" profiles the arrest of two street drag car racers. In the article, it is also noted that,

> in what is believed to be a Canadian first, police in Hamilton [Ontario] are using the website [YouTube] to find people. Earlier this month, a police officer posted a surveillance video clip in an effort to identify persons of interest in a homicide case. (Mahoney 2006, A15)

Similar news articles in Canada follow in 2007, increasing in frequency, and with shorter duration between reports, as the popularity of YouTube expands into the realm of law enforcement. At this time, reports typically highlight how police are using the site either as a surveillance tool or for the explicit purpose of aiding police investigations. Reports with headlines like "Police turn to YouTube in search of teens" (*Toronto Star* 2007) or "Police probe video on how to disrupt trains" (*Globe and Mail* 2007) illustrate the point. It is not until August that a seemingly innocuous video posted to YouTube put police on the defensive, and while this may not have been the first video to profile police in a negative manner, it seems to be among the very first examples in Canada where a police agency offered an official response *because* of a YouTube video discrediting police.

A 5:23 minute video recorded the afternoon of August 20, 2007, by filmmaker Paul Manly and posted to YouTube later that same evening led to the police admission of the use of undercover agents at the Montebello summit protest. Critics charged that the agents were planted to disrupt the protest and demanded an explanation. At the time, something was awry, which prompted Manly to post the video. Later that year, in an interview with the *Globe and Mail*, he recalled,

> Putting the video on YouTube made me nervous [. . .] I didn't know who these guys [undercover agents disguised as protesters] were. CIA? [Central Intelligence Agency, United States] CSIS? [Canadian Security Intelligence Service] Blackwater (security firm) agents? [a private U.S. security agency]. (Hawthorn 2007, S3)

The posting of the video, and subsequent police response, appears to be the first documented case in Canada of an official police acknowledgement (in the defensive) provided *directly* in reaction to public criticism garnered over police work depicted in a YouTube video.

3. METHODOLOGY

Police use news media to manage and maintain control over situations (Ericson 1982), including their public image (Manning 1978). The results of these relations produce media documents. The use of document analysis is a well-suited technique for understanding how police define situations (Altheide and Schneider 2013). The expansion of social media has created a new media domain in need of control and management for police. In the case of the 2007 Montebello summit, we might first consider *how* police actually responded to the YouTube video in an effort to maintain control over their public perception of authority as legitimate (Ericson 1982). It makes sense to begin on YouTube—where users, possibly police, are able to post comments in response to uploaded videos.

These data (YouTube comments) can be collected and systemically analysed to determine: (1) if any official police responses were made directly to YouTube, and if so, what was said; (2) the evolution of the online reaction in response to the video; and (3) how users made sense of the video in light of the police admission of the use of undercover agents. How users interpret the admission provides insight into the public perception of the police as *the* legitimate authority (social power).

The original[2] Montebello video was posted to YouTube on August 20, 2007. The original video received 2,866 comments[3] over a period of five years, four months and twenty-six days. During this time, the video was viewed more than 657,190 times in Canada, the U.S. and the United Kingdom (the three top viewing locations by order of views). The video received 2,800 thumbs up or 'likes' (often consistent with an endorsement) and 73 thumbs down or 'I dislike this.' User comments were accessed by clicking on "show more" at the bottom of the page until all posts were viewable. The posts were then downloaded and saved collectively as a 204-page PDF document.

After an initial review of these data, various terms were then entered into the search function. Searches began with the word 'police,' which appeared 964 times across the document. This search netted forty-one pages of aggregated data. Additional search terms emerged upon further review of these aggregated data; these included 'admit' (and derivations such as 'admitted' and 'admission'), 'agent,' 'provocateurs,' 'Quebec,' 'Sûreté du Québec,' 'RCMP' and 'official.' These terms were re-entered into the original 204-page dataset for further review. These searches were conducted to enable a complete range of user posts for examination.

A careful examination of the dataset indicates that there was no evidence to suggest any type of official (sanctioned) or unofficial (unsanctioned) police response offered in the form of posts made to the examined YouTube comments. At the time the Montebello video was posted, neither police agency involved in the incident (SQ or RCMP) had official YouTube accounts—each later set up an account on February 3, 2010, and June 8, 2011, respectively. Noting their official absence, however, is not meant to suggest that police were not monitoring user activity. Because such surveillance tactics are often secretive, this can never be known with certainty. Nevertheless, some users openly accused other users of serving as police officers or doing police work.

One user, for instance, wrote the following: "I read your post and it sounds like you are a policeman doing damage/psych-out control," which prompted the reply, "I'm a history student in Montreal not a cop." The closet form of any admission as a state agent (assuming the statement was true) was one user who noted that they were "ex military"—only to immediately follow with "Many cops have no sense of honor or true commitment to duty."

A large number of YouTube posts (and discussions between users) of the incident (and police admission) relied nearly exclusively on news media reports as the official evidence of confirmation of the police admission of planting undercover agents. These news reports, referenced by YouTube users, cited official police statements featured in news media. Through media police continue to remain *the* 'authorized knowers' of the situation (Tuchman 1978), a finding consistent with previous research on this issue (Doyle 2003; Ericson 1995; Fishman 1980).

Further, the YouTube data suggest that police continue to provide official accounts strictly to news media. Official police accounts are still 'fed' to news media through press officers in the form of scripted statements (Fishman 1978, 1980, cited in Ericson 1982, 8). This indicates that police continue to favour news media contacts to control and frame events. The lack of these data (police accounts) on YouTube prompted me to redirect my attention to an empirical assessment of news media documents, such as those featuring official police statements.

News media documents were retrieved from the online searchable database LexisNexis. Reports from the following four news publications were selected: the *Globe and Mail*, the *National Post*, the *Toronto Star* and the

Montreal Gazette. The first two represent the only two national English language newspaper publications in Canada. The *Toronto Star* was selected because it is the largest circulated newspaper in the country, and is circulated in the most populated province (Ontario). The *Montreal Gazette* was selected for regional significance and for English language consistency. The *Gazette* is published in Montreal (the city's official language is French), the most populated city in Quebec.

I began searches of the LexisNexis database using the same aforementioned search terms, with one addition—'YouTube.' Several search results returned reports that featured official police accounts (e.g., admission of undercover agents), which were offered in response to the Montebello protest provided by police spokespersons.

The names of specific police spokespersons that emerged from these searches were re-entered into the search engine—for example, RCMP members Corporal Sylvain L'Heureux and Constable Kane Kramer, and SQ members Constable Melanie Larouche and Inspector Marcel Savard. These names were also entered into Internet search engine Google, along with keywords like 'Montebello' and 'agents provocateurs' (a phrase that appears in the official SQ police admission news release) to ensure that the complete range of responses was collected for analysis. These include quotations from multiple news sources as different publications featured variations of direct quotes from police spokespersons (mostly those offered by Inspector Savard).

These searches produced additional data from various other news media outlets[4]—for example, Canadian Broadcast Corporation (CBC) news (links to some of these stories also appear in the YouTube comments). This process was repeated until no new data emerged. These data were then reviewed and coded for further analysis to better understand how police maintain control over their public image in response to social media. This process provides insight into our understandings of social power in relation to the maintenance of the legitimisation of police authority. I now turn to previous research of the summit protest in order to highlight how little has been said about the police response, and, more importantly, for our purposes here, to set up and contextualise the ensuing discussion concerning the official police (re)action to the YouTube revelation of SQ officers disguised as protesters at the summit.

4. THE 2007 MONTEBELLO SUMMIT, QUEBEC, CANADA

4.1. Previous Research: The Security and Prosperity Partnership (SPP)

Activists organized in Montebello to protest the secret "non-transparent and exclusionary character of the SPP negotiations" held there in 2007 (Ayres 2011, 83; see also Anderson and Perez-Rocha 2008). The reported secretive nature of the Montebello meetings was also publicised ahead of the summit in news media. The meetings consisted of North American leaders engaging in trilateral discussions over the (now defunct)[5] SPP.

Launched in 2005, the stated purpose of the SSP was to "improve the quality of life" for citizens. (Government of Canada 2009). This was reportedly accomplished through collaborative dialogue between Canada, the U.S. and Mexico on shared concerns about security and prosperity, including border security, food and product safety, and environmental issues.

The meetings in Montebello were met with the ire of protest groups for various reasons: the "SPP was unpopular and without legislative support in Canada and the United States" (Moens 2011, 53). Protests were first organized in the Canadian capital city of Ottawa, Ontario, ahead of the summit. It was reported that activists were concerned about the potential to relax worker and food safety standards in Canada in an effort to appease the interests of the U.S. and Mexico. Other reported issues of concern for activists groups included climate change and the U.S.-sponsored wars in Iraq and Afghanistan.

Previous research that has discussed the summit has nearly altogether ignored the police admission of the use of undercover agents and has almost exclusively focused on the political and economic stipulations (and secrecy) of the SPP negotiations. For this reason this research tells us very little about police power or citizen counter-power.

A policy paper published by the Hudson Institute, for instance, referred to these stipulations as the "negotiation of North America" (Anderson and Sands 2007). This report (like others: Foster 2007; Healy 2007) does not adequately discuss the aftermath of the protest following the YouTube revelation of the police use of undercover agents. Other policy reports either ignore or underscore the role of the police to allegedly disrupt the protest. In regard to the latter, for instance, a forty-one-page report written by a labour analyst for the Canadian Labour Congress states,

> The news spread like wildfire and after a couple of days of unrelenting pressure, the Sûreté du Québec had to admit the three masked men with duct tape on their police boots and carrying rocks were, indeed, undercover cops. (Healy 2007, 30)

This tells us nothing about how the news actually spread nor does it explain the police strategies used to control the definition of the situation following the news. In addition to the inaccuracy of the foregoing statement (only one officer was carrying a single rock—discussed in more detail ahead), there is also no discussion of police statements offered in response to the incident. Other research provides only fleeting references to the response following the YouTube revelation and police admission.

In "Stifling Dissent through Creative Use of the Criminal Law: The Charge of Wearing a Mask with Intent," the police use of undercover officers at the Montebello summit is only footnoted (in passing reference): "confirmed[6] use of *agents provocateurs* by Canadian police is a reality, not a paranoid fantasy" (Hachey 2009, 130). Despite the significance of the YouTube elicited admission, the issue is fleetingly referenced elsewhere (also as a footnote!). For instance, Salter (2011, 226), an assistant professor in peace studies at McMaster University in Ontario, notes,

> The use of Agents [sic] provocateur is not without precedent in Canada [. . .] This incident received mainstream press coverage as it was captured on video and uploaded to the internet [sic], forcing a formal admission by Quebec Police.

While the Internet is mentioned (it remains absent elsewhere in the aforementioned research on the 2007 Montebello summit) nothing more is said. Other research that has, albeit, only briefly, broached the Montebello summit has usually done so in relation to the examination of the mobilisation of activism, on the one hand, and, somewhat limited discussions of protest policing, on the other hand.

Regarding activism, Ayres (2011, 76), for instance, contends that the growth of North American networks has done very little to challenge "deeper neoliberal policy underpinnings of continental integration." While the Montebello summit is mentioned, nothing is said in relation to the police response to the event, or the YouTube video, or the even Internet for the matter.

Other research explores the issue of space and protest policing, but does not directly examine Montebello, other than to suggest "that there remains a willingness on the part of state officials to utilize highly repressive forms of protest policing" (Zajko and Beland 2008, 732). The aforementioned article "stresses the growing impact of the mass media [. . .] on contemporary protest policing" (ibid., 720), but does not include the relevance of social media (YouTube) or how these media contribute to changes in policing, such as how the police definition of the situation is now managed and enforced in response to user-generated content.

Indeed, while the 2007 Montebello summit is referenced elsewhere as a precursor to protest policing, particularly in relation to the G8 and G20 meetings (Monaghan and Walby 2012), nothing more is discussed in specific relation to the accusations stemming from the YouTube video of the allegations surrounding the police use of *agents provocateurs* to purportedly disrupt the Montebello summit.

While some research has addressed the emergence and use of protest policing in relation to various meetings held in Canada (ibid.; Zajko and Beland 2008), no research has addressed the role of YouTube in relation to the police admission following the summit. The importance here should not be understated. It is worth repeating that this was the first instance in Canada where social media played an active and direct role in contributing to changes in police social power—that is, placing police image work on the defensive in order to control and define the situation.

4.2.   News Media and Police Control before the Summit

The question noted by Williams (2007, 177) is not whether police should control political protest but how to do so (see also Donner 1990). This becomes increasingly evident in an era of social media, where police can quickly lose control over public perceptions of a given situation on sites like Facebook (Schneider, forthcoming b; Schneider and Trottier 2012; Schneider and Trottier 2013). Mass media coverage of previous international summits held in Canada contributed to unfavourable public perception of police. The most pertinent example of this was the aftermath for police following the 1997 Asian-Pacific Economic Cooperation (APEC) summit held in Vancouver, British Columbia: it was at the time "the largest and most complex security operation undertaken by the RCMP" (Holmes and Hasan 2010, 6–7; see also Doyle 2003; Pue 2000; Zajko and Beland 2008).

It was evident that the police were very clearly aware of reported plans to protest the 2007 Montebello summit, and according to various news reports, police were prepared for the protesters. Consider the following that was reported in a *Toronto Star* article published on August 17, 2007, in advance of the summit:

> A broad coalition of labour activists, environmentalists, anti-war groups and human rights advocates *served notice at a press conference in Montreal that the closed-door talks will be fiercely opposed.* (Campion-Smith 2007, A13, emphasis added)

The report, like others, makes explicit note of the aftermath following the 1997 APEC summit (mentioned earlier) that involved the police use of "indiscriminate pepper spray" against student protesters (and news media), including, most famously, a television cameraman (Leblanc 2007). The footage, taken by a CBC cameraman, of the "unusually strong police response" was broadcast nationally and "shocked Canadians" (Pue 2000). This is an implicit reminder to police of their vulnerability when policing large crowds in the presence of news media cameras (Doyle 2003).

These concerns surely added increased pressure upon the SQ and RCMP to appear to effectively manage and control the *expected* dissent, all the while ensuring not to repeat previous actions taken at APEC. Indeed, not repeating these past actions, seen as unfavourable to police 'professionalism,' was a basic theme of news media reports preceding the 2007 Montebello summit.

These actions led to fifty-two formal complaints against the RCMP, which collectively became the subject of a public inquiry that produced the *APEC Commission Interim Report*. In the report, retired judge Ted Hughes indicated that protesters have the right to "see and be seen" by "visiting leaders" in an area, described in the report as the "line of sight" assembling place for demonstrators (Commission for Public Complaints Against the RCMP 2001).

From the conclusion of the four-year inquiry emerged the use of "protest TV" (Leblanc 2007), and it was determined by Montebello summit organizers, not police (CanWest News 2007), that broadcasting a video feed of the protesters inside the Château resort in Montebello was in accordance with the recognised legal rights of protesters. According to one senior government official, the video feed inside the resort would ensure that the "protest will be visible to those participating in the summit" (Campion-Smith 2007) because "people have the legitimate right to protest" (Leblanc 2007). Alan Borovoy, an affiliate of the Canadian Civil Liberties Association, noted in an article published in the *National Post* on August 17,

> The RCMP is in charge of security, providing two protest zones, each holding up to 2,000 people, outside the perimeters of the grounds of a resort in Montebello, Que., where the summit is taking place. The fence around the grounds of the Montebello will be reinforced and a forest of trees will obscure any protests from the participants. Summit organizers will firm [sic] footage of the protesters to pipe into the lodge where the prime minister, presidents and their delegations will meet Monday and Tuesday. (CanWest News 2007, A5)

In a *Globe and Mail* report published the same day, well-known protester and self-proclaimed 'anti-colonial anarchist'[7] Jaggi Singh indicated his intention to disrupt the summit meetings, noting that "we believe we should be able to directly confront these three leaders, and not virtually" (Leblanc 2007). Following these comments, RCMP Corporal Sylvain L'Heureux is quoted as saying, "Our actions will be dictated by the actions of the demonstrators," and that any attempts to gain access to the Château resort will "not be tolerated" (Leblanc 2007). This statement represents an explicit *pre-emptive* (even before the meetings) threat of the use of the *escalated force* in lieu of softer policing approaches (e.g., *negotiated management strategy*), when policing organized gatherings (della Porta and Reiter 1998; McPhail, Schweingruber and McCarthy 1998). One might surmise that the Canadian government, given the decision to broadcast video feed of the protests, usurped the police use of the negotiated management strategy in advance of the summit protest.[8]

Further evidence of the police *planned* use of escalated force is supported by published media reports preceding the summit that indicated that residents and business owners were told by police to "barricade everything" in advance of the summit (CBC 2007). A few days later, A *National Post* article published on August 20, headlined "Protesters get jump on three-nation meeting," warned of the reportedly destructive presence of "anarchists":

> OTTAWA—A loud, but peaceful, crowd gathered yesterday on Parliament Hill to oppose talks on continental integration *while anarchists claimed responsibility for weekend vandalism against Ottawa*

> businesses connected to the Security and Prosperity Partnership.
> (Thomson 2007, A6, emphasis added)

Framed largely in favour of police and police control, news media reports preceding the Montebello summit set the stage for the public *expectation* of confrontation, ensuring a "desirable course of action and outcome" (Ericson 1982, 12) for police, *a process that lends tacit support to protester assertions that the police in fact sought to incite violence*. What the police were not expecting was the subsequent challenge to their authority, which was revealed by their clandestine use of undercover agents and the public response that materialised on YouTube and spread to news media.

4.3.   YouTube Video and Police Response

> We sent Paul Manly to film at Montebello because we're producing—
> the Council of Canadians Nanaimo—a documentary called "Trading
> Democracy for Corporate Profit." We were, unfortunately, fortunate to
> have the 'authorities' add to our message in this documentary by their
> covert actions. (post made to YouTube by CanadiansNanaimo)

The YouTube video, posted by CanadiansNanaimo, shows three men with bandanas covering their faces approaching a riot line made up of the SQ. One of the men is in possession of a large rock, and refused to put it down at the strong vocal insistence of union leader and reported anti-SPP protester David Coles.

Coles can be heard on the recording telling the three men that "this is our [riot] line, bugger off [. . .] get out of here." Coles and a small group of others are shown standing in front of the riot line to prevent the escalation of violence (by providing a barrier to thwart any advancement upon the riot line by protesters). Coles then proceeds to angrily demand that the man with the rock "take [his] mask off" and that he "put the rock down." A nearby protester, who is also wearing a mask and did not appear to be affiliated with the three men (undercover officers), then points at the man with the rock and begins to chant "*Policier*"—the French word for police officer—drawing the increased attention of others, who proceed to surround the three men.

One of the three undercover men is then shown speaking to a riot officer *behind* his riot shield, which had been lowered, an observation noted by several users on YouTube prior to the official police admission. One user noted that the three men "certainly seemed pretty cozy with the cops." Shortly after, the three men (officers) are brought behind the riot line and are 'arrested' (but never charged)—one of the men is even shown rolling himself over to be placed in plastic handcuffs. The 'staged' arrest was a recurring topic of discussion on YouTube, and was representative of citizen-directed social power (i.e., defining the situation). Another user wrote in response to the incident, "That is the FAKEST staged arrest I've ever seen."

The 'fake' arrest suggests that the SQ did not have complete control over the arrests of the undercover officers, and, in this way, is in stark contrast to the four reported 'real' arrests of protesters at the summit, who were, according to Coles, "roughed up pretty good, and dragged away" (Bryden 2007). Additionally, news reports indicated that the four people that were really arrested were later charged with obstruction and resisting arrest, two common *post facto* accounts recognised as legally defensible in order to justify police action in response to those who fail to meet police expectations in a given situation (e.g., a protest) (Van Maanen 1978).

The SQ denied the use of "*agents provocateurs*" to incite violence at the protest, but did not explicitly deny the use of undercover officers, as evidenced in the official SQ statement on the matter,[9] lending creditably to undercover police work. The legitimacy of undercover police work is further reinforced when Inspector Savard noted of the circumstance, "If there are methods or procedures that need to be changed or adjusted, you can be reassured, that will be done" (Clark, Peritz and Bailey 2007). Nevertheless, according to early news reports, the SQ and RCMP each refused to even offer specific comment on the incident, despite the existence of the YouTube video. This fact became a focal point of user discussions on YouTube as challenges to police claims mounted as a form of citizen counter-power. One user wrote (prior to the police admission),

> Check the news reports now. The police said they arrested 4 people—two women and two men. They did not mention the 3 guys in this video and refused to comment on them. If these guys were real protesters, why weren't they on the arrest records and why won't the police comment on them?

When pressured to responded to allegations similar to the one earlier made on YouTube, the RCMP, the federal police with jurisdictional authority (in absolute charge of security), stated on August 21, through their spokesman, Constable Kane Kramer, "I cannot answer your question because I don't have the information" (Canadian Press 2007). Two days following this deflection, SQ Constable Melanie Larouche noted in a *Globe and Mail* report, "I confirm [to] you that there are no agents provocateurs in the Sûreté du Québec" (Bryden 2007).

The ensuing political pressure even prompted the Office of the Prime Minister to issue a statement denying any role in the incident. Stockwell Day (then public safety minister) deflected criticism away from his office by reportedly referring all questions to the RCMP (ibid.), who had already acknowledged not having any information. The deflection of responsibility by the public safety minister's office—also tasked with overseeing summit security (alongside the RCMP)—added increased pressure upon the police, in this case the SQ, to formally respond to the incident.

Later in the evening of August 23, after a period of days of deflections and denials, the SQ, in an official statement, finally admitted involvement, but strongly denied that the undercover officers were attempting to instigate violence or acting as "criminals." According to the statement, the cover of the officers was "discovered" when they *refused* to throw the rock.[10] Stockwell Day reaffirmed this sentiment, despite that "reporters at the scene said they did not see extensive rock-throwing" (Clark, Peritz and Bailey 2007), and earlier published reports that rocks had in fact been removed from the area in advance of the summit *at the insistence of police* (CBC 2007).

Excerpts of the original police statement in French (notes 9–10), translated into English and reported in the *Globe and Mail*, further maintained that "their mandate was to seek out and identify non-peaceful demonstrators to avoid having things boil over," and "at no point did Sûreté du Québec policemen act as agents provocateurs or criminals" (Gandhi 2007). Additionally, Inspector Savard, a senior officer with the SQ, further asserted that the YouTube video was in fact not a complete depiction of the incident. According to a report in the *Toronto Star*, "Savard suggested the video had been edited to cast the officers in an unflattering light" (Gordon 2007), a statement intended to discredit citizen counter-power to define the situation.

Elsewhere Savard was directly quoted as saying, "Of course we wish it hadn't happened" (Harrold 2007). The ambiguity of this and other similar official police statements on the matter leaves one wondering if this was said in reference to the exposure of the SQ engaging in secretive tactics, or if this was in reference to the claims of the incomplete depiction of the event in question. Reports seem to support the latter, which helps to control and enforce the definition of the situation by further deflecting criticism away from police.

For instance, the *Globe and Mail* reported that the YouTube clip showed "only a portion of the events" (Clark, Peritz and Bailey 2007). At 2:41 of the Manly (2007) YouTube video, an SQ officer can very clearly be seen holding a video camera, suggesting that the SQ were also recording. It is unclear why the SQ never released its video to provide the public with a 'complete' depiction of the incident. Perhaps this video may have contradicted the 'official' police version of the summit. It is worth noting that this never-released video is also apparently what allowed the SQ to identify the undercover agents despite the 'fake' arrest, which suggests that the SQ in fact knew that the men were officers at the time of the arrest.

> The police said after viewing a video clip from YouTube.com *and video shot by police officers*, they were able to confirm the three were Quebec provincial police officers. Earlier, both Quebec police and the RCMP denied any of their officers were involved. (Lambert and Banerjee 2007, A19, emphasis added)

It was fervently maintained that the undercover officer with the rock had been given the rock earlier from a separate group of 'extremists' and, as

Inspector Savard put it, maintained possession of the rock only because "he was still hoping that his cover was good [. . .] [but] he never had the intention of using that rock" (Clark, Peritz and Bailey 2007). "He was asked by extremists to throw the rock at the police" who "did not know that they were undercover officers" (Harrold 2007). The police did not offer empirical evidence (e.g., video) to support these statements.

The rhetorical shift away from the pre-emptive use of force to the *suggested* use of the rock (as a weapon against uniformed riot police) effectively dismisses the allegations of the undercover use of force. Such force would allow undercover officers disguised as protesters to gain advancement upon uniformed police to facilitate the riot police taking control (by force) of the protesters with the use of escalated force. News reports prior to the summit protest warning of dangerous protesters ("anarchists"), coupled with the explicit police threat of the pre-emptive use of force, set the stage for the expectation of confrontation. This lends support to assertions that police did in fact intend to incite violence at the protest, contrary to their claims otherwise. Police power (social power) was maintained through official statements made following the summit that were published in news media. Citizen counter-power was diminished when users cited police statements on YouTube as official affirmation that police used undercover agents at the summit. This process illustrates how police were able to control and enforce the definition of the situation through news media following the summit.

5. CONCLUSION

Police image work now includes responses to user-generated materials, including videos posted on YouTube. How police respond to user-generated content and what this tells us about social power remain a developing area of inquiry. While videos, such as the one from the 2007 Montebello summit, can offer user-driven challenges to police authority, police in this circumstance continue to remain the authorised definers of the situation. In other words, as advanced herein, social power—by way of controlling the definition of the situation—remains unchanged. In fact, this process *continues* through news media and is *reinforced* by social media users who cite news media reports as official affirmation of the definition of the situation (information provided by police and published in news media).

While social media sites like YouTube offer spaces to contest and criticise police actions, such challenges did little in the case examined herein to thwart or subvert police authority, even in response to the questionable police use of undercover agents. Indeed, even user comments posted to the YouTube page cited the police admission as itself "proof" of the use of undercover police agents. Prior to the admission some users were reluctant to accept this version of events. Users also relied on official police arrest records as evidence that the arrest of the undercover agents was not real—that is, police evidence was said to reveal that they were officers.

What remains less clear is why police admitted to the use of agents at the 2007 Montebello summit, why the SQ did not release their video of the event, and how recordings such as the YouTube summit video gain viral momentum on social media. Likely this is because police are increasingly unable to conceal what was once secret information from the public. YouTube (and other social media sites) increasingly subject police work to immediate public monitoring, spotlighting brutality, misconduct and the use of questionable tactics, things that would have otherwise gone entirely unnoticed prior to the last decade. Future research might explore the impact that public monitoring continues to have upon police image work, especially in terms of how police proactively and reactively now manage this process through visible public relations (news media) and less visible monitoring of social media.

This chapter: (1) provides empirical evidence to demonstrate the process by which police agencies continue to maintain control over their public authority through traditional mainstream media channels; (2) amends some of the research literature on police image work to include user-generated content circulated on social media; and (3) contributes to the developing research on police image work in response to unfavourable user-generated content circulated online. Recommendations for future research might include further exploration of how police use sites like YouTube to promote image work or might build on developing scholarship that examines police accounts offered through social media platforms like Twitter (Schneider forthcoming a) to better understand what proactive police responses on social media suggest about social power.

ACKNOWLEDGEMENTS

I would like to acknowledge my colleague Ariane Hanemaayer for her very helpful suggestions. I also wish to acknowledge Dan Trottier for his helpful feedback.

NOTES

1. Process here refers to Ericson's (1982) aforementioned definition of power—a paraphrasing of Weber's (1978, 53) definitive statement on the issue in *Economy and society.*
2. Original is used in reference to the first video posted by filmmaker Paul Manly. Other versions were posted to YouTube, including a 9:20 minute clip with slow motion stills and audio commentary.

3. These data were retrieved from YouTube on January 15, 2013, at 3:19 PM.
4. According to SQ spokesman Sergeant Gregory Gomez del Prado, as noted in a July 2013 *Montreal Gazette* report, the "SQ has only had a social media presence for about a year" (Beeston 2013). Following the 2007 Montebello summit it was noted that a press release was issued in French to news media. It is important to acknowledge that police websites are spaces to make official statements; however, at the time following the summit such statements made by police were largely reproduced in news media.
5. By 2010, the SPP website had been turned into an archive (Ayres 2011). In the documentary *You, me and the SPP* (2009), the "leaders of civil society organizations congratulated themselves for having defeated the SPP" (Ayres 2011, 84).
6. This statement is not technically accurate as the police officially "confirmed" the use of undercover officers disguised as protesters but strongly denied that they were acting as "*agents provocateurs.*"
7. Jaggie Singh (JaggiMontreal) on Twitter (https://twitter.com/JaggiMontreal) Accessed 16 April 2014.
8. Conveniently this also helps to maintain the appearance of the police as an apolitical organization.
9. An excerpt of the official admission statement in French read, "En aucun temps, les policiers de la Sûreté du Québec ont agi comme agents provocateurs ou commis des actes criminels."
10. An excerpt of the official admission statement in French read, "Les policiers ont été repérés par les manifestants au moment où ils ont refusé de lancer des projectiles."

REFERENCES

Altheide, David L. 1995. *An Ecology of Communication.* Hawthorne, NY: Aldine de Gruyter.

Altheide, David L., and Christopher J. Schneider. 2013. *Qualitative Media Analysis.* 2nd ed. London: SAGE.

Anderson, Greg, and Christopher Sands. 2007. *Negotiating North America: The Security and Prosperity Partnership.* Hudson Institute. http://hudson.org/files/pdf_upload/hudsonnegotiatingnorthamericaadvanceproof2.pdf.

Anderson, Sarah, and Manuel Perez-Rocha. 2008. Three Amigos Summit. Institute for Policy Studies. http://www.ips-dc.org/articles/324.

Ayres, Jeffrey. 2011. The Limits of Power and Protest: Civil Society Mobilization against North American Integration. In *Power and Transnational Activism (Rethinking Globalizations)*, edited by Thomas Olesen, 75–90. London: Routledge.

Beeston, Laura. 2013. Social Media Plays Key Role in Modern Crisis Situations. *Montreal Gazette*, 19 July.

Best, Joel. 2008. *Social Problems.* New York: W.W. Norton.

Bryden, Joan. 2007. Police Planted Provocateurs, Protestors Say. *Globe and Mail*, 23 August.

Campion-Smith, Bruce. 2007. Closed-Door Talks Rile Protesters; Summit Leaders Will See Demonstrators Only if They Watch Television. *Toronto Star*, 17 August.

CanWest News. 2007. Protesters to Be Kept Away from Summit and Seen by Participants Only on Video. *National Post*, 17 August.

Canadian Press. 2007. Police Accused of Using Provocateurs at Summit. *Toronto Star*, August 21. http://www.thestar.com/news/article/248608-policeaccused-of-using-provocateurs-at-summit.

Canadian Broadcast Corporation (CBC) News. 2007. Quebec Community Erects Fences before PM's Trilateral Summit. *CBC News*, 16 August. http://www.cbc.ca/news/canada/montreal/story/2007/08/16/otmontebello-070816.html.

Clark, Clark, Ingrid Peritz and Ian Bailey. 2007. Sûreté du Québec to Review Practices; Police Say Undercover Officers Were Not at Protest to Incite Violence; Union Leader to File Charges. *Globe and Mail*, 25 August.

Commission for Public Complaints Against the RCMP, APEC—Commission Interim Report. 2001. Commissioner: Ted Hughes, Q.C. 31 July. http://www.cpc-cpp.gc.ca/prr/rep/phr/apec/apec-31-eng.aspx.

Courvette, Phil. 2007. Sûreté Spent $7 Million on Montebello Summit; Just One of Police Forces Guarding Leaders. *Montreal Gazette*, 6 November.

della Porta, Donatella, and Herbert Reiter, eds. 1998. *Policing Protest: The Control of Mass Demonstrations in Western Democracies*. Minneapolis: University of Minneapolis Press.

Donner, Frank. 1990. *Protectors of Privilege: Red Squads and Police Repression in America*. Berkeley: University of California Press.

Doyle, Aaron. 2003. *Arresting Images*. Toronto: University of Toronto Press.

Ericson, Richard V. 1982. *Reproducing Order: A Study of Police Patrol Work*. Toronto: University of Toronto Press.

———. 1995. News Media and Account Ability in Criminal Justice. In *Accountability for Criminal Justice: Selected Essays*, edited by Phillip C. Stenning, 135–161. Toronto: University of Toronto Press.

Ericson, Richard V., Patricia M. Barnek and Janet B. L. Chan. 1991. *Representing Order: Crime, Law, and Justice in the News Media*. Buckingham: Open University Press.

Fishman, Mark. 1978. Crime Waves as Ideology. *Social Problems* 25: 531–543.

———. 1980. *Manufacturing the News*. Austin: University of Texas Press.

Foster, John W. 2007. Beyond NAFTA: The Security and Prosperity Partnership. *Europa World Online*. www.europaworld.com.

Gandhi, Unnati. 2007. Police Admit Planting Officers at Protest; Critics Demand Full RCMP Review. *Globe and Mail*, 24 August.

Goffman, Erving. 1959. *The Presentation of Self in Everyday Life*. New York: Doubleday Press.

———. 1974. *Frame Analysis*. New York: Harper and Row.

Gordon, Sean. 2007. Police to Review Tactics Used at Leaders' Summit; Demands Grow for Inquiry on Role of Undercover Agents. *Toronto Star*, 25 August.

Government of Canada. 2009. Security and prosperity partnership of North America. 13 May. http://www.spp-psp.gc.ca/eic/site/spp-psp.nsf/eng/h_00003.html.

Hachey, Jean-Pierre. 2009. Stifling Dissent through Creative Use of the Criminal Law: The Charge of Wearing a Mask with Intent. *Criminal Law Quarterly* 55 (1–2): 120–134.

Harrold, Max. 2007. Undercover Cops Never Incited Violence: SQ; At Summit Demo Infiltrating Protests "Standard Procedure." *Montreal Gazette*, 25 August.

Hawthorn, Tom. 2007. The Man Who Filmed the Montebello Provocateurs. *Globe and Mail*, 5 December.

Healy, Teresa. 2007. North American Competitiveness Council and the SPP: Les Agents Provocateurs at the Montebello Leaders' Summit. Research Paper 44, Social and Economic Policy, Canadian Labour Congress. http://www.canadianlabour.ca/sites/default/files/pdfs/NACC_SPP_MontebelloSummit-RP44.pdf.

Holmes, Robert and Hasan Junaid. 2010. Freedom of expression and international events: From APEC to 2010. May 7. http://www.cba.org/cba/cle/PDF/INTL10_Holmes_paper2.pdf.

Kappeler, Victor E., Richard D. Sluder and Geoffrey P. Alpert. 1998. *Force of Deviance: Understanding the Dark Side of Policing*. 2nd ed. Prospect Heights, IL: Waveland Press.

Klockars, Carl B. 1988. The Rhetoric of Community Policing. In *Community Policing: Rhetoric or Reality*, edited by Jack R. Greene and Stephen D. Mastrofski, 239–258. New York: Praeger.

Lambert, Steve, and Sidhartha Banerjee. 2007. Quebec Police Admit Agents Posted as Protestors; But Deny Role of Undercover Officers Was to Provoke Violence at Summit of North American Leaders. *Toronto Star*, 24 August.

Leblanc, Daniel. 2007. Coming to a Summit Near You: Protest TV. *Globe and Mail*, 17 August.

Mahoney, Jill. 2006. YouTube Clips Led to Racers' Arrest. *Globe and Mail*, 14 December.

Manly, Paul. 2007. Police provocateurs stopped by union leader at anti SPP protest. YouTube video, 5:23 posted by "CanadiansNanaimo," 20 August. http://www.youtube.com/watch?v=St1-WTc1kow

Manning, Peter. K. 1978. The Police: Mandate, Strategies and Appearances. In *Policing: A View from the Street*, edited by Peter K. Manning and John Van Maanen, 97–125. Santa Monica, CA: Goodyear.

———. 1997. *Police Work: The Social Organization of Policing*. 2nd ed. Prospect Heights, IL: Waveland Press.

McPhail, Clark, David Schweingruber and John McCarthy. 1998. Policing Protest in the United States: 1960–1995. In *Policing: A View from the Street*, edited by Donatella della Porta and Herbert Reiter, 49–69. Santa Monica, CA: Goodyear.

Moens, Alexander. 2011. "Lessons Learned" from the Security and Prosperity Partnership for Canadian-American Relations. *American Review of Canadian Studies* 41 (1): 53–64.

Monaghan, Jeffrey, and Kevin Walby. 2012. "They Attacked the City": Security Intelligence, the Sociology of Protest Policing and the Anarchist Threat at the 2010 Toronto G20 Summit. *Current Sociology* 60 (5): 653–671.

New York Times. 2006. Latest Video Brings More Controversy to Los Angeles Police. 15 November.

Oreskovic, Alexei. 2012. YouTube Hits 4 Billion Daily Views. *Reuters*, 23 January

Pue, Wes. 2000. *Pepper in Our Eyes: The APEC Affair*. Vancouver: University of British Columbia Press.

Ratliff, Ben. 2006. A New Trove of Music Video in the Webs' Wild World. *New York Times*, 3 February.

Salter, Colin. 2011. Activism as Terrorism: The Green Scare, Radical Environmentalism and Governmentality. *Anarchist Developments in Cultural Studies* (1): 211–238.

Schneider, Christopher J. (forthcoming a). Police Presentational Strategies on Twitter in Canada. *Policing & Society: An International Journal of Research and Policy*.

———. (forthcoming b). Meaning making online: Vancouver's 2011 Stanley Cup riot. In Kleine Geheimnisse: Alltagssoziologische Einsichten (trans: Little Secrets: Everyday Sociological Insights) edited by Michael Dellwing, Scott Grills, and Heinz Bude. Springer Germany.

Schneider, Christopher J. and Daniel Trottier. 2012. The 2011 Vancouver Riot and the Role of Facebook in Crowd-Sourced Policing. *BC Studies* 175: 57–72.

———. 2013. Social Media and the 2011 Vancouver Riot. *Studies in Symbolic Interaction* 40: 335–362.

Skolnick, Jerome. H. 1966. *Justice without Trial: Law Enforcement in Democratic Society*. New York: Wiley.

———. 1994. *Justice without Trial: Law Enforcement in Democratic Society*. 3rd ed. New York: Wiley.

Thomson, Andrew. 2007. Protesters Get Jump on Three-Nation Meeting. *National Post*, 20 August.

Tuchman, Gaye. 1978. *Making News: A Study in the Construction of Reality.* New York: Free Press.

Van Maanen, John. 1978. The Asshole. In *Policing: A View from the Street*, edited by Peter K. Manning and John Van Maanen, 302–328. Santa Monica, CA: Goodyear.

Weber, Max. 1978. *Economy and Society: An Outline of Interpretive Sociology.* Berkeley: University of California Press.

Williams, Kristian. 2007. *Our Enemies in Blue: Police and Power in America.* 2nd ed. Cambridge, MA: South End Press.

Zajko, Mike, and Daniel Beland. 2008. Space and Protest Policing at International Summits. *Environment and Planning: Space and Society* 26 (4): 719–735.

Contributors

Jonathan Cable—Cardiff University

Jonathan Cable completed his PhD in journalism studies at Cardiff University in July 2012. His thesis examined the impact of the media and protest tactics of three different protest groups, and the effect these tactics had on their ability to publicise their key messages. It used the concept of political opportunity structures to explore the external influences on protest groups which guide the relative success and failure of these protest groups to reach their aims and goals. Since then he continued to work at Cardiff University as a researcher on a variety of projects, from a BBC Trust–funded project at Cardiff University investigating BBC impartiality across various forms of programming to an AHRC-funded project focusing on public engagement activities in the arts and humanities. This project developed an online resource aimed at the academic community, which helps with the design, delivery and evaluation of public engagement activities.

Donatella della Porta—European University Institute

Donatella Della Porta is professor of sociology in the Department of Political and Social Sciences at the European University Institute, where she directs the centre on Social Movement Studies (Cosmos), and a professor of political science at the Instituto Italiano di Scienze Umane (on leave of absence). She directed the Demos project, devoted to the analysis of conceptions and practices of democracy in social movements in six European countries. She is now working at a major ERC project, Mobilizing for Democracy, on civil society participation in democratisation processes in Europe, the Middle East, Asia and Latin America. She is co-editor of the European Political Science Reviews (ECPR/Cambridge University Press). In 2011, she was the recipient of the Mattei Dogan Prize for distinguished achievements in the field of political sociology. Her main fields of research are social movements, the policing of public order, participatory democracy and political corruption.

Christian Fuchs—University of Westminster

Christian Fuchs is a professor of social media at the University of Westminster. His fields of expertise are social media, Internet and society, political economy of media and communication, information society theory, social theory and critical theory. He is author of numerous publications in these fields, including the books *Internet and Society: Social Theory in the Information Age* (Routledge 2008), *Foundations of Critical Media and Information Studies* (Routledge 2011), *Digital Labour and Karl Marx* (Routledge 2014), *Social Media: A Critical Introduction* (SAGE 2014) and *OccupyMedia! The Occupy Movement and Social Media in Crisis Capitalism* (Zero Books 2014). He has co-edited the collected volumes *Internet and Surveillance: The Challenges of Web 2.0 and Social Media* (Routledge 2012) and *Critique, Social Media and the Information Society* (Routledge 2014). He is editor of *tripleC: Communication, Capitalism & Critique: Open Access Journal for a Global Sustainable Information Society* (http://www.triple-c.at), chair of the European Sociological Association's Research Network 18—Sociology of Communications and Media Research, co-founder of the ICTs and Society network and vice chair of the European Union COST Action 'Dynamics of Virtual Work.'

Paolo Gerbaudo—King's College London

Paolo Gerbaudo is a lecturer in digital culture and society at King's College London. He has worked as a reporter for the Italian Left newspaper *Il manifesto* and has been involved in anti-corporate, global justice and ecologist campaigns. His current research focuses on the use of new media and social media by social movements and emerging digital parties. He is the author of *Tweets and the Streets* (2012), a book analysing social media activism in the popular protest wave of 2011, from the Arab Spring to the Indignados and Occupy Wall Street. He has a PhD from Goldsmiths College, where he worked under the supervision of Professor Nick Couldry. He has previously taught at Middlesex University and the American University in Cairo. He is currently the convenor of the Digital Culture and Political Protest module at King's College.

Panos Kompatsiaris—University of Edinburgh

Panos Kompatsiaris is a PhD candidate in visual and cultural studies at the School of Art, University of Edinburgh, with a background in economics, visual culture and art theory. His thesis employs ethnographic methods to look at the ways that institutions of contemporary art responded to the recent European crisis. He has published academic papers and reviews on creative industries, visual ethnographies, artistic labour and the political turn in contemporary art.

Alice Mattoni—European University Institute

Alice Mattoni is a research fellow in the Centre on Social Movement Studies (COSMOS) at the European University Institute, where she works for the Anticorrp research project, developing a study on social movement and civil society actors in fighting corruption. Before joining COSMOS, she was a postdoctoral associate fellow in the Department of Sociology at the University of Pittsburgh. She obtained her master of research and PhD in political and social sciences at the European University Institute. She is a co-convener of the standing group Participation and Mobilization of the European Consortium of Political Research (ECPR) and co-editor of *Interface: A Journal for and about Social Movements*.

Yiannis Mylonas—Lund University

Yiannis Mylonas is an external lecturer at the Film, Media, Cognition and Communication Department at the University of Copenhagen in Denmark and a researcher affiliated with the Department of Media and Communication at the University of Lund in Sweden. He has published studies on discourse analysis of war representations, political subjectivity and civic cultures and on the political economy of copyrights.

Thomas Poell—University of Amsterdam

Thomas Poell is an assistant professor of new media and digital culture at the Department of Media Studies (Faculty of Humanities), University of Amsterdam (UvA). He studied political science at the University of Amsterdam and the New School for Social Research. In 2007, he defended his dissertation at Utrecht University on the democratisation and central-isation of the Dutch state during the revolutionary period around 1800. Currently, his research focuses on social media and public communication. Together with professor José van Dijck, he leads the KNAW 'Over Grenzen' research program on 'Social Media and the Transformation of Public Space' (June 2013 until August 2015). He has published on, among other topics, social media as platforms of alternative journalism (*Journalism*), Twitter as a multilingual space (*NECSUS*), social media and the transformation of activist communication (*Information, Communication & Society*), Weibo and Chinese online contention (*Chinese Journal of Communication*) and social media logic (*Media and Communication*).

Sara Salem—Erasmus University

Sara Salem is a PhD researcher at the Institute of Social Studies in the Netherlands. Her work focuses on historical and institutional perspectives on political economy, and centres specifically on the recent wave of uprisings across the Middle East and North Africa. Her interests include decolonial theory, third world feminism, critical political economy and theories of post-development. She has lived in Zambia, Egypt and the Netherlands, and is especially interested in southern Africa and the Middle East. She has worked at numerous NGOs in Cairo, mainly on issues of political participation and gender. She completed her BA in sociology at the American University in Cairo and went on to complete an MA in Middle East studies and an MA in international development in the Netherlands.

Christopher J. Schneider—University of British Columbia

Christopher J. Schneider is an assistant professor of sociology at the University of British Columbia, Okanagan (UBCO), Canada. Dr Schneider is co-author/co-editor of three books. His research and publications investigate crime, deviance and information technologies in daily life. Dr Schneider received the 2013 Distinguished Academics Early in Career Award from the Confederation of University Faculty Associations of British Columbia (CUFA BC). He was the recipient of the UBCO 2010/2011 Award for Teaching Excellence and Innovation—Junior Faculty, and the 2009/2010 Provost's Public Education through Media Award. He has given hundreds of interviews with news media across North America, including the *New York Times*.

Elise Danielle Thorburn—University of Western Ontario

Elise Danielle Thorburn is a PhD candidate at the University of Western Ontario, and a Fulbright fellow at the University of North Carolina–Chapel Hill. Her research investigates the convergences of digital media, technology, feminism and activism in the directly democratic structure of the assembly. Her research aims to understand the techno-scientific, Deleuzian 'assemblage' as a mode of class recomposition, and the political usage of the general assembly as its specific form. She is also mother to Olive Josephine, a co-founder of the Feminist Action Committee and an editorial collective member of the Canadian political theory and action journal *Upping the Anti*.

Daniel Trottier—University of Westminster

Daniel is a postdoctoral fellow in social and digital media at CAMRI, which he joined in 2013. Prior to this appointment, he was a postdoctoral fellow in the Department of Informatics and Media at Uppsala University Sweden, and the Department of Sociology at the University of Alberta, Canada. His current research considers the use of social media by police and intelligence agencies, as well as other forms of policing that occur on these platforms. As part of this research, he is participating in two European Union FP7 projects on security, privacy and digital media. He has authored several articles in peer-reviewed journals on this and other topics, as well as *Social Media as Surveillance* (Ashgate 2012) and *Identity Problems in the Facebook Era* (Routledge 2013).

#0169 - 270317 - C0 - 229/152/14 - PB - 9781138798243